FOOTBALL IMMORTALS

FOOTBALL IMMORTALS

◆ ◆
◆

ALEXANDER M. WEYAND

Foreword by Earl "Red" Blaik

THE MACMILLAN COMPANY   New York

MACMILLAN NEW YORK London

To MY MOTHER
Aged ninety-two
"An Immortal Fan"

FOREWORD

Football Immortals is a fascinating book of short biographies of football greats written most interestingly by Colonel Weyand, an authority on American football. His intimate knowledge of the game over the past fifty years has given him the unusual opportunity to judge past and present greats of football. *Football Immortals* is a blue book of the Football Hall of Fame.

EARL "RED" BLAIK

PREFACE

Because the author numbers among his friends many truly great football players, in order to avoid any appearance of bias he has chosen as subjects of these sketches men who have appeared on any of the following All-Time All-America teams: Walter Camp, *Century*, 1910; Fielding H. Yost, *Collier's*, 1920; George Trevor, *New York Sun*, 1927; "Gulf Football Manual" consensus (John W. Heisman, Big Bill Edwards, Philip King, and Parke H. Davis), 1933; Clark Shaughnessy, *Esquire*, 1943; Associated Press, 1951; Grantland Rice, in *The Tumult and The Shouting*, 1954; Alexander M. Weyand, in *The Saga of American Football*, 1955; and Helms Athletic Foundation, which keeps its selection up to date. Shorter sketches of a few additional men have been included for reasons stated in each case.

Added at the end of each chapter are the names of men who have been awarded one or more of the trophies established in memory of John W. Heisman (Player of the Year), New York Downtown Athletic Club; Robert W. Maxwell (Player of the Year), Maxwell Football Club of Philadelphia; Walter Camp (Back of the Year) or Knute K. Rockne (Lineman of the Year), Washington Touchdown Club; or John B. Outland (Best Guard or Tackle of the Year), Football Writers Association.

All-Time All-Professional selections considered are those of

Sporting Life, 1942; Roger Treat, *The Encyclopedia of Football: The Official Encyclopedia of the National Football League*, 1952; Stephen Owen, in *My Kind of Football*, 1952; and Helms Athletic Foundation, to date.

Now for acknowledgments: Particularly deserving of my gratitude are Colonel Red Blaik, Tim Cohane, Earl Ruby, and Professor Lacy Lockert, who read and criticized the manuscript. In the field of original research, I have been privileged to consult with such pre-World War I heroes as Heffelfinger, Hare, Daly, De-Witt, Heston, Fish, Thorpe, Mahan, and Oliphant, and I have corresponded or talked with other "Immortals" of later vintage. Mrs. Emilie V. Schulz very kindly sent me the files of her late husband, the famous "Germany."

Unfortunately, I was unable to obtain the names of all the people who assisted me. I am indebted to them and to the following: James E. Armstrong, Larry H. Bankart, Everett D. Barnes, John H. Barnhill, Edgar O. Barrett, Clair F. Bee, Charles M. Bellatti, Frank S. Bergin, William H. Britton, James Brock, Philip J. Burke, Joseph M. Cahill, Charles M. Callahan, G. H. Carlock, Agnes M. Clarey, Gloria Clark, A. K. Collingwood, Josh Cody, Walter R. Collins, Carroll H. Cook, Hector E. Cowan, Walter G. Cowan, Logan Cunningham, Rudolf P. Custer, Quinn Decker, James F. Dickinson, Leonard C. Dill, Otis J. Dypwick, Les Etter, Amos F. Eves, Ray L. Fisher, Dick Fry, Edgar W. Garbisch, Finus C. Gaston, John Gould, Wiles Hallock, Harry S. Hammond, Donald Grant Herring, Carl E. Higgins, Florence S. Kimball, Don E. Liebendorfer, Charles Loftus, Jean MacIver, Gus Manning, Charles C. Mather, Robert Matson, Roscoe P. McClave, Mary McQuay, Tom Miller, John H. Minds, William G. Mokray, E. S. Molloy, Arthur Monke, Carol J. Montgomery, Ralph Morgan, George W. Neumann, D. R. Nugent, Paul B. Parker, E. G. Patterson, Walter Paulison, Baaron B. Pittenger, Edward J. Powers, Harry C. Price, Kenneth W. Rapp, Juan J. Reid, Claude Rich, Ridge Riley, Stan Saplin, William R. Schroeder, Sarah J. Sillcocks, Mitchell Gray Simon, Ted Smits, Walter D. Splain, John S. Steckbeck, Louis Stewart, William C. Stryker, James T. Tarman, Walter H. Trumbull, Glenn C. Urban, William J. Van Cleve, B. G. Waters, III, Morris W. Watkins, W. Daniel Wefler, Sanford B. White, J. A. Widder, Arlo Wilson, and Robert C. Woodworth, as well as to the abler and more authoritative authors than myself whose works I have had occasion to refer to in the text.

In addition to the above, I am appreciative of the help afforded me by the staffs at the Congressional Library, New York Public Library, West Point Library, and other libraries I visited during my travels in various parts of the country.

ALEXANDER M. WEYAND

PRESIDENTS

& FOOTBALL

Theodore Roosevelt

while President, inaugurated a reform movement in 1905 that saved football.

Woodrow Wilson

was Secretary of the Board of Coaches at Princeton in 1878 and 1879 and again in 1890, and Faculty Adviser at Wesleyan in 1888 and 1889.

Calvin Coolidge

was informal counselor at Amherst in 1894, according to the coach, Parke H. Davis.

Herbert Hoover

assisted in organizing football at Stanford in 1891; he was Financial Manager of the team in 1891, 1892, 1893, and 1894.

Franklin D. Roosevelt

was end and halfback on the second team at Groton School in 1899, after having played tackle and fullback on the third team in previous years. At Harvard, he was elected captain of a freshman scrub team in 1900.

Dwight D. Eisenhower
was varsity halfback at West Point in 1912; he was also head coach at St. Louis College (now St. Mary's University), San Antonio, Texas, in 1916, and of the Third Army Corps All-Stars, Fort Meade, Maryland, in 1921.

John F. Kennedy
was an end at Harvard: of the freshman team in 1936 and of the junior varsity in 1937.

CONTENTS

1

ENDS

CAMP, 1910	Hinkey, *Yale*	Shevlin, *Yale*
YOST, 1920	Hardwick, *Harvard*	Shevlin, *Yale*
TREVOR, 1927	Hinkey, *Yale*	Hardwick, *Harvard*
GULF, 1933	Hinkey, *Yale*	Hardwick, *Harvard*
SHAUGHNESSY, 1943	Hutson, *Alabama*	Muller, *California*
A.P., 1951	Hutson, *Alabama*	Oosterbaan, *Michigan*
RICE, 1954	Hutson, *Alabama*	Oosterbaan, *Michigan*
WEYAND, 1955	Hutson, *Alabama*	Muller, *California*
HELMS, TO DATE	Hinkey, *Yale*	Muller, *California*
ADDITIONAL	Campbell, *Harvard*	Fesler, *Ohio State*

FRANK AUGUSTUS HINKEY

(5:09; 157)

It would seem almost unbelievable that a scrawny little consumptive like Frank Hinkey was the greatest football player of all time. Yet there are those who hold to that belief. True, the players of his generation were not so huge as those who now grace our gridirons, but they were not so small either, and among them Hinkey was king. What the knowing ones thought of the little man may be judged from the opinion of Mike Murphy, veteran Yale trainer. Ten years after Hinkey's heyday, Tom Shevlin, a bruising 195-pound end, was the toast of the football world. Asked how he compared with Hinkey, the "Old Mike" squelched the questioner by saying that if the two were played in the same game, no one would know that Shevlin was on the field. When Caspar Whitney, the foremost sportswriter of that age, first saw Hinkey, as a freshman in 1891, he wrote, "One never would suspect that cadaverous-looking fellow of any athletic aspirations." Hinkey was deceptive in appearance. Although slim and sickly, he had the muscular development and coordination, the nervous energy and combative instincts of a leopard. Walter Camp told Grantland Rice, in 1920, that he believed Hinkey had more explosive energy in his system that any athlete he ever saw. Pop Warner admired him chiefly for his "determination and fighting spirit."

A case in point! Harvard had an 185-pound All-America guard named Bertram Waters who was reputed to be able to start faster than any sprinter on the track team. In 1893, when he was captain, he moved himself into the backfield. The basic idea seemed to be for him to take the ball and run at Hinkey in an effort to throttle the little pest. It was not until the second half was well under way that he was helped off the field to play no more that season. Hinkey, of course, went the full ninety minutes, then constituting a game. Charley Daly, in analyzing such deadly tackling, said that Hinkey seized the ballcarrier at the knees and turned with him in midair so that the latter was pitched headlong to the ground by his own weight and momentum, sometimes facing in the direction from which he had come. Yale men like to say that no one gained an inch around Hinkey's end, but that is a slight exaggeration. He *was* human, even though some of his opponents might have entertained serious doubts. But the gains were so few as to be almost negligible.

One wonders if Waters might not have accomplished more in the role of a blocker, but blockers never meant much to Hinkey. Herbert Reed, another noted sportswriter, pictured him as crouching motionless and then with a "sudden sinuous glide" weaving through the interference. Walter Camp said that "he drifted through the interference like a disembodied spirit." Hinkey was a bit more substantial than a spirit. He played very low and brushed aside would-be blockers with his muscular arms. He had great driving power in his legs. In 1893 he got through George Woodruff's terrible "flying interference" and saved the day for Yale. Pennsylvania started four men before the ball was snapped. They clasped hands and were traveling at top speed when they struck the end. Even Hinkey was smothered the first time, but no human agency could consistently block him out of a play. Just before the wave of blockers reached him, he dropped to the ground, came up under it, and attacked the ballcarrier. John C. Greenway, at the other end, followed Hinkey's example, and Yale was able to overcome Penn's early lead and win, 14–6.

Hinkey was an enigma, possibly the strangest figure ever to appear in the sports arena. He avoided people, shunned publicity, never laughed in public, and seldom spoke, even to return a "Good morning." Through the years writers have tried to find words to describe his peculiar personality. The adjectives employed are suggestive: mysterious, odd, queer, shy, sensitive, misunderstood, saturnine, morose, taciturn, moody, introspective, hated, brutal, murderous, merciless. The names they gave Hinkey are also suggestive. He was called the "Living Flame," the

"Shadowy End"; and Senator Chauncey Depew once hailed him as the "Silent Man of Destiny." He made few friends, but those that he did, men who had proved their worth on the athletic field, worshiped him and remained firm in their devotion until his death. Donald Grant Herring, former Princeton player and coach, was one who got close to Hinkey. He considered Frank "an excellent companion, considerate, hospitable and appreciative of the other fellow's point of view."

Early in life, Hinkey learned that he had lung trouble. Doctors warned him not to engage in strenuous sports. Disregarding this advice, he played all four years while at Yale, and each year Caspar Whitney, the designer of All-America teams, placed him on his first team. At that time, medical science had not advanced far in providing means to arrest and cure tuberculosis. The knowledge of his hopeless fight against the disease seemed to have embittered Hinkey and made him enjoy hurting people. When he snarled and frothed at the mouth and a murderous glare appeared in his eyes, sunk deep in a face of deathly pallor, even his own teammates feared him, according to the recollection of Heffelfinger. Hinkey captained the Elis in 1893 and 1894. Billy Rhodes, the field coach of both teams, said that the players stood in such awe of him that they obeyed his every order, down to the most minute detail. In those days the captain was supreme —he even appointed the coaches!

Whitney wrote that any team captained by Hinkey could be expected to play without regard for flesh and blood. After a rough game in 1893, Yale and Pennsylvania severed athletic relations, and in the following year Yale and Harvard came to a parting of the ways. Curiously, Princeton had no complaint concerning Yale's rough play, and Sheppard Homans, a Tiger two-time All-America fullback, went out of his way to state that, although Hinkey played like a fiend, he played clean. That statement must have startled Harvard, because it was against the Crimson that Hinkey behaved like "a raving maniac," to use the words of his one-time teammate, George Foster Sanford. His depredations against Harvard at Hampden Park, Springfield, were memorable.

In 1892 he just about wrecked the left side of Harvard's line. That was the year that Lorin Deland introduced the "flying wedge." In a play from scrimmage, called the "horse's neck," a wedge was formed and was in motion before the ball was snapped. On such a play, while Hinkey was fighting to break through the side of the wedge, Bob Emmons, an end, hit him from behind and pinned him to the mass while Joshua Upton, a tackle who had not committed himself in the wedge, received the ball on a delayed pass and made a nice gain on Hinkey's side. Frank was beside himself with rage and humiliation. According to newspaper accounts, at the first opportunity he jumped on Upton feet first while the latter was prone on the ground, and soon afterward he kneed Emmons in the epigastric region. Both men had to leave the game, and it was through their substitutes that Yale pounded out the winning touchdown.

The *Boston Globe* called the 1894 meeting of the Crimson and Blue "a most atrociously brutal game throughout," while the *New York Post* announced that "no father or mother worthy the name would permit a son to associate with the set of Yale brutes on Hinkey's football team." When Yale punted, the ends, Frank and his brother Louis, covered the kick. On one such play Louis downed Madison Gonterman, who had caught the ball. Perry Trafford, a Harvard coach who was sitting beside a writer for the *New York Herald*, grabbed the reporter's arm, and shouted, "Watch Frankie!" Hinkey, running at top speed, broad-jumped at the prostrate Harvard man. Louis held fast, but Gonterman managed to wiggle out of the way. Later, under somewhat similar but not so obvious circumstances, Edgar Wrightington sustained a broken collarbone, and Harvard insisted that Frank Hinkey was the culprit.

While that snarling savage was breaking bones and jumping on people's epigastric regions, what were the other fellows doing? That is what makes one wonder if Hinkey could not have held his own in present-day company. Of course, the opponents ganged up on him. He was the key man of the Yale team, and even called signals the years he was captain. In every way, opponents tried to put him out of action. Heffelfinger remembered that, in the Harvard-Yale game of 1891, a Johnny uppercut Hinkey hard enough to have floored an ordinary man, but Hinkey merely sneered and told him he might break his hand if he tried it again. The only protection that he wore was light padding in his pants, but only once was he hurt sufficiently to cause his removal. In 1893 he had a head-on collision with Jim Blake of Princeton and had to be helped off the field in a dazed condition. Significantly, that was the only game that Yale lost during Frank's four years on the team. During that period, the Elis won 52 games and scored 1,738 points and yielded 25.

Hinkey's champion 1894 team won 16 games and allowed only 13 points. In addition to Hinkey, Whitney selected William Hickok, guard; Phillip Stillman, center; George Adee, quarterback; and Frank Butterworth, fullback, for the first All-America team, with Anson Beard, tackle, and S. Brinckerhoff Thorne, halfback, in reserve. The next year Thorne and Fred Murphy, tackle, made the first team.

Frank Hinkey was born at Tonawanda, New York, on December 23, 1871. His father was a partner in a hardware business, and Frank was able to attend Phillips Academy at Andover prior to matriculating at Yale. He was a good but not brilliant student. Following his graduation from Yale, he engaged in industrial work in Iowa and frequently returned to New Haven to help with the coaching, although his nervous temperament was such that he usually became ill after watching a game. In 1914 he was appointed head coach at Yale. He adopted the lateral-pass attack from Canadian Rugby, and was the first coach to use motion pictures to study plays. In those and other aspects he was ahead of his time, but he neglected fundamentals. In 1914 Yale won seven games, and lost to Harvard and Washington and Jefferson. Among those beaten were Princeton and Notre Dame. The following year Yale fared so poorly that, to all practical purposes, Hinkey was supplanted by Tom Shevlin prior to the game with Princeton.

Hinkey returned to the Midwest and settled in Morrisonville, Illinois. For a time he was interested in zinc mining in the Ozarks. But his health worsened and he entered a sanitarium at Southern Pines, North Carolina. For three years he fought for his life. As the end approached he was visited by two old football associates, Frank Butterworth and George Adee. When the time came to say goodbye, tears broke through his hard exterior while he gamely cursed the dope in the medicine for making his eyes water. Ironically, as he lay dying, the combined instrumental and glee clubs of his old enemy, Harvard, were performing in nearby Pinehurst. The "flame" went out during the early hours of December 30, 1925. One of his last acts had been to dispatch a telegram to George Adee. It read, "Charon is at the crossing."

THOMAS LEONARD SHEVLIN

(5:10½; 195)

It would be difficult to find a more contrasting pair than the most famous of Yale's ends. Shevlin was a big, powerfully built man, verbose and vain, ready to admit that he was the greatest football player in the world and a really remarkable all-around man. He generally made good his boasts, and there seemed to be no limit to his capacity. In a poll conducted in 1926, Fred Dawson, noted coach and a Princeton man, felt that Shevlin was the outstanding player of all time, while Wilmer Crowell, a leading official of the time, ranked him second only to Jim Thorpe.

Tom was born in Muskegon, Michigan, on March 1, 1883, and was raised in Minneapolis where his father was a lumber tycoon. The old gentleman and his two daughters did everything they could to spoil the only son, and met with some success. At Yale, Tom had almost unlimited spending money; his wardrobe was extensive and expensive; he frequently spent weekends at the Waldorf-Astoria in New York City, and he liked racing through the countryside at the wheel of his 60-horsepower Mercedes. He cut quite a figure on Fifth Avenue, in his fashionable suit with a black derby perched jauntily over one eye while he nonchalantly puffed at a big black cigar and twirled a gold-headed cane.

It is believed that, even while a student, he gave generously to charity, but if he did he kept the philanthropic side of his nature under cover, and most people knew him as a self-indulgent swashbuckler. His conceit was so colossal it made him amusing. When he heard that John DeWitt, the Princeton strong boy, had shoulders in inch wider than his own, he arranged with his tailor to remedy the matter, at least to all external appearances. At a hotel, he had himself paged so that the other guests would know that the great man was in residence. Although he was the finest athlete and most widely known member of his class, he was not popular. He was not tapped for any of the senior honorary societies, and he narrowly missed losing the football captaincy, winning by a single vote. Jim Hogan, the outgoing captain, walked out of the room without congratulating him.

At Hill School, where Tom was coached by Mike Sweeney, holder of the world high-jump record for seventeen years, he showed promise in both athletics and studies. Upon his arrival at New Haven, in the fall of 1902, the coaches did not know where to use him. End, tackle, halfback, fullback—he seemed a "natural" for each position. He was extremely muscular, quick on his feet, and well coordinated—he came to be second only to DeWitt among college hammer throwers. He was fast and a sure tackler and he diagnosed plays so well and possessed such natural football instinct that it was almost impossible to fool him. A keen student of the game who thought things out and was willing to take a chance, despite his cockiness he was a hard worker and a team player.

Those were the days of the tackle-back tandem, and Tom played at tackle for the first eight games of the 1902 season. By that time it became apparent that, in addition to Shevlin and Hogan, there were other tackle candidates who showed All-America potential. Because Yale was having trouble with the ends, for the game with Army, Tom, with only a few days of preparation, was placed at right end. The sportswriters reported Yale's ends as weak against the cadets. If so, at least one of them did not remain weak. At the end of the season—his freshman year—Tom was generally considered the best wingman in the entire nation. Many critics felt that he deserved that distinction for all four years, as Hinkey had, but Walter Camp demoted him to the second All-America team in 1903.

But Tom was cockier than ever the next season (1904), and insisted upon playing fullback. He was at that position for the first six games, and again it was on the eve of the game with a tough Army team that he was shifted back to end—on the left side that time. He was back on the right side his last year. During Shevlin's four years Yale won 42 games, lost 2, and tied 1. Princeton took the championship game in 1903, while Army tied the Elis in 1902 and beat them in 1904. Tom's 1905 team went all the way—10 straight victories; 222 points against 4, a field goal by Princeton.

As may be guessed, Tom did not play in a silent rage as did Hinkey. He shouted and quipped and found joy in combat. In 1905 Jim Cooney, All-American and captain although only a junior, was considered to be the strongest man in the Princeton line. With Cooney at left tackle, Tom hailed the arrangement as an opportunity to settle the issue in personal combat between the two captains. He ordered his quarterback to run the first five plays at Cooney, with him, mighty Shevlin, doing the blocking. Yale rolled for an average of three yards a crack, remarkable for those five-yards-in-three-downs days. Tom was jubliant and, throughout the game, frequently ordered the same play. He shelved his famous end-around play and devoted his energies to blocking Cooney as Yale won, 23–4. In justice to Cooney, it should be said that he played with an injured leg in a brace.

Shevlin was also a strong ballcarrier. By the time he was a sophomore (in 1903) his end-around play was gaining fame. He also ran back kickoffs. Against Princeton or Harvard he never got back for much over 30 yards, but in a game with Columbia in 1903 he went 95 yards to a touchdown, and in the following year an 85-yard runback set up a score against Brown. The same year he got away for a 50-yard run against Penn State.

An example of Shevlin's quick thinking and logical reasoning in the heat of battle occurred in the 1905 game with Harvard. The incident does not reveal good sportsmanship, but Tom never gave or expected quarter. Francis "Hooks" Burr of Harvard signaled for a fair catch not far from a sideline. Shevlin, followed by Jim Quill, the fullback, piled into Burr. Shevlin later explained that he took a chance that the umpire might not recognize the signal for a fair catch, but if he did, and penalized Yale 15 yards, it would create an extremely difficult angle for kicking a goal. Tom guessed correctly. The umpire, Paul J. Dashiell, ignored the signal. Near the end of the game, Shevlin scooped up a fumble and carried it to the 31-yard line, from where his team scored in six smashes at the line. Yale won, 6–0.

There was an aftermath of the roughhousing of Burr. Shevlin had tackled him low, and Quill, in hitting him high, broke his nose. To Harvard's anger and disgust, not only did Mr. Dashiell ignore the signal for a fair catch; he failed to penalize Yale because he was not certain that Quill's act constituted intentional unnecessary roughness. It so happened that Mr. Dashiell was a chemistry instructor at the United States Naval Academy at Annapolis whose life ambition was to become a professor. When his appointment went to Washington, the President of the United States, Theodore Roosevelt, Harvard, '80, saw to it that Mr.

Dashiell sweated it out for approximately six months before favorable action was taken.

At Queen's Club Athletic Ground in London during the summer of 1904, Shevlin broke the Harvard-Yale versus Oxford-Cambridge dual meet hammer-throw record with a toss of 152 feet 8 inches. He played on the Yale baseball team in 1903.

After graduation, Tom went to work for his father and, during the fall, found recreation in assisting another old Blue, Dr. Henry L. Williams, to coach the University of Minnesota team. In 1910 he helped Dr. Williams fashion a system of plays based on what came to be known as the "Minnesota shift," the first of the two-part shifts later improved by John Heisman and Knute Rockne. Tom wrote to Yale about the new system, but Ted Coy, who coached the Blues, was not interested. After Yale was beaten by Army and Brown and tied by Vanderbilt, with undefeated Princeton and Harvard still to be faced, Fred Daly, the captain, requested Walter Camp to obtain the assistance of Shevlin. In a week of secret practice, Tom installed the shift—and his own fighting spirit. Princeton ruled a 4–1 favorite, but Yale won 5–3. At Harvard, Percy Haughton had a week in which to prepare a defense against the shift, and as a result the game ended in a scoreless tie. John Reed Kilpatrick, later head of Madison Square Garden, played so brilliantly against both Princeton and Harvard that he was hailed as one of the greatest ends in history. Tom's comment: "He should be good; I coached him." Shevlin's father always made a point of coming east in his private car to see Tom's important games and wagering a few thousand dollars on the outcome. In 1910 he refused to take advantage of the prevailing odds because, as he told Walter Camp, it might look as though he lacked confidence in his son.

In 1912 the elder Shevlin died, and Tom became executive head of a vast lumber empire. He was not yet thirty, and there was concern that he might fail to measure up to his responsibility. But Tom plunged into his work with the same dynamic energy he had displayed on the gridiron. It was not long before it was prophesied that he would soon be one of the most influential men in the West. His life was insured for $1,500,000, and he paid out about $30,000 each year on premiums alone.

In the fall of 1915, Tom was unusually busy, but Yale then had another sad season. Virginia, Washington and Jefferson, Colgate, and Brown downed the Elis, and mighty Princeton and Harvard were still to be played. Tom was again invited to New Haven. This time he had no new system to offer. His friends, even old Mike Sweeney from Hill School, begged him not to sacrifice himself, but when Yale called, Tom felt he must obey. He strengthened Yale in certain neglected fundamentals and instilled the team with his own will to win. When Yale unexpectedly downed heavily favored Princeton, critics revived memories of the twin miracles of 1910, but, as Tom was to say, "You can't make two lemonades out of one lemon." Yale had spent itself in its supreme effort against the Tigers, and Haughton's Harvard team, captained by peerless Eddie Mahan, triumphed.

During his concentrated drive to put fire into the team, Tom had contracted a severe cold. Never the one to spare himself, he neglected it. Weak and disappointed, he tried to recuperate in the sunshine of California. Before he could shake off the cold, he had to return to his business in wintery Minneapolis. The day after his arrival, he developed pneumonia. Four physicians were at his bedside, and a specialist was brought from Chicago by special train, but it was too late. On December 29, 1915, Tom Shevlin died.

Shevlin was dead, but his spirit was to help Yale to another important victory. Tad Jones was coach in 1916. Before the game with Harvard, he told his players that he felt certain that Tom Shevlin was pacing up and down in the hereafter, smoking his big black cigar and askings the boys to win again for "Papa." Probably it was not so dramatic an appeal as Rockne's "one for the Gipper" of later date, but it accomplished the same results. "Cupie" Black's fired-up team defeated Harvard 6–3 and brought the "Big Three" championship to Yale for the first time in seven years.

HUNTINGTON REED HARDWICK

(6:00; 174)

"Tack" Hardwick was a blue-blooded aristocrat, well fixed financially and socially, but he was generally regarded as a "regular fellow," friendly and unassuming, with a fondness for rough sports, such as football and boxing. The rougher the play, the better he liked it. He handed out punishment with a lavish hand, and could absorb a great deal of it himself. In one Yale game, he played through an entire half with a broken collarbone. He was a halfback at prep school, and during his early years at Harvard. Leo Leary, the end coach, wanted badly to shift him, probably reasoning that such exquisite combativeness could be better used in the line, "where the game is played," as Knute Rockne said, but it was not until the latter part of 1913 that Percy Haughton was able to spare him from the backfield.

Hardwick was born at Quincy, Massachusetts, on October 15, 1892, and attended Groton School. There is a by now old adage, "When Grotons are tough, they are tough." Either that expression was coined for Hardwick or he became the most noted exponent of it. His competitive spirit was unexcelled. Essentially a team player, he was one of the best blockers and tacklers of all time. He was also a powerful, fast, and shifty ballcarrier, a skilled place-kicker, passer and pass receiver, and a good though not exceptional punter.

In 1912 Haughton called Hardwick "the most valuable player who ever played football at Harvard," and his 1914 captain, Charlie Brickley, a star in his own right, said he was "the most finished player in all-around play" he had ever seen. Other impartial observers were equally laudatory. Bill Langford, the referee, pronounced him "the finest player of all time"; Walter Camp said "he could star in any position"; Grantland Rice called him "the top man in the matter of flaming spirit"; and Herbert Reed claimed that he could carry out blocking assignments that were usually assigned to two men.

Hardwick entered Harvard in the fall of 1911 with the famous athletic class of 1915 that was to play such a prominent part in elevating the Crimson to the top of the football world. The freshman team included a number of future All-Americans, and Hardwick, who in time would outshine all of them, played right halfback. Despite such talent, the team was held to a scoreless tie by the Yale cubs. The varsity was also tied by the Elis, as it had been the previous year, but that was the farthest Yale got for several seasons. Hardwick and his talented classmates not only participated in three straight victories over the Blue varsity; they were unbeaten in three years.

Hardwick stepped up to the left halfback post on the varsity in 1912, one of the four sophomores to make the grade. While his forte was blocking and line smashing, in a game with Amherst he broke loose for a 60-yard touchdown run. Being a 10.2-second man, he was especially dangerous when he got in the clear. His work marked the victories over Princeton and Yale. Going into the last quarter of the Princeton game, Harvard led, 9–6. The Tigers used the forward pass with considerable success. They had scored their touchdown through a pass and were still dangerous until Hardwick intercepted a pass on Princeton's 25-yard line and ran it back seven yards. He hit the line and, to quote the *New York Times*, "bored through the Jerseymen like a drill goes through rock." That put the ball on the five-yard line, from where other backs advanced it to the one. Then he blasted through for a touchdown and kicked the extra point to make the score 16–6, and seal the victory.

In the game won from Yale by 20–0, Hardwick forced the break early. Covering one of Sam Felton's booming left-footed punts, Hardwick tackled the Eli receiver so savagely that the ball was fumbled. Bob Storer, a tackle, grabbed it and ran to a touchdown—Harvard's first against Yale in eleven long years. The Crimson, victorious in all its nine games, was given first place in the unofficial national ratings. Hardwick's spectacular classmate, Charlie Brickley, and the captain, Percy Wendell, came in for most of the acclaim, but at least two discerning critics, W. B. Hanna of the *New York Sun* and L. R. Murdock of the *Boston American*, placed Tack on their all-star teams.

With Felton graduated, Hardwick did much of the punting in 1913. Bob Storer captained the team, which again won all games to retain its place as Number One in the nation. Harvard defeated Yale 15–5 and Princeton 3–0, with Brickley's educated toe accounting for all Harvard points in both games. That year Hardwick developed into a pass receiver and caught touchdown passes in the important games with Cornell and Brown. Against Brown, and also against Yale, he played right end. From that position he made vital gains on an end-around play. He was considered All-American by various observers, but Camp, to Haughton's disgust, gave Hardwick second-team rating.

The Harvard team of 1914, after crushing Princeton 20–0 and Yale 36–0, was hailed as "the perfect machine" and "Harvard's greatest eleven." But the early season proved most difficult. On the eve of the game with Washington and Jefferson, a team that later defeated Yale, Brickley, the captain, underwent an appendectomy, and Mahan was incapacitated. Hardwick was shifted into the backfield and proved his versatility by scoring all of Harvard's points. He kicked a 27-yard placement field goal and ran around end to a touchdown. With the score tied, he kicked the goal to give the Crimson the game, 10–9. The backfield was unchanged for the Michigan game. When the Wolverines halted the Harvard running attack, Hardwick whipped a 12-yard pass to Henry Smith, who took the ball to the eight-yard line. A few plays later, Hardwick himself plunged to a touchdown and then kicked the goal to make the count 7–0.

Against Princeton, Hardwick also scored a touchdown and booted two conversions. He was back at right end for that game and finished the season at that position. Against Yale, he caught two touchdown passes and contributed two conversion points. That season the *Spalding Guide* listed 20 All-America selections and 27 All-Eastern, and Tack Hardwick appeared on every one, the only unanimous choice. Camp was so impressed by that Harvard team that he named five members to his All-America lineup: Hardwick, end; Eddie Mahan and Frederick Bradlee, backs; Stanley Pennock, guard; and Acting Captain Walter Trumbull, tackle. Jeff Coolidge, an end who ran 96 yards against Yale after recovering a fumble; Mal Logan, the quarterback; and Donald Wallace, the center, received recognition from other sources.

Hardwick was fortunate in his coach. Percy Haughton was another tough Groton man, a stern disciplinarian and relentless taskmaster who demanded and got rough, rugged, aggressive, bruising football—the only kind that Tack thought worthwhile. He liked to tell a story to illustrate the blind confidence that the players had in their coach, although possibly all of them were not so worshipful as he thought they were and as he himself was. He said that if Haughton had ordered the Harvard squad to jump off a cliff 100 feet high and promised to catch them as they came down, every man would have jumped without hesitation. And, he added soberly, "Haughton would have caught us."

Football was not Hardwick's only major sport. For three seasons he played on the baseball team at third base and in the outfield. In those days college baseball was at its highest level. In 1915 Yale defeated the New York Giants, of blessed memory, while in the following year Harvard downed the world-champion Boston Red Sox. The Crimson teams, coached by Dr. Frank J. Sexton, were uniformly successful. The record against Princeton was clean, but Harvard lost one series, in 1914, to Yale. Hardwick fought hard to save that one. He collected four hits in five times at bat in the decisive game, but his mates failed to help. In his sophomore year, after the Elis had won 17 consecutive games, he won the second game of the series, in the 14th inning, with a home run with a man on base. He captained the team in 1915. It was one of Harvard's greatest, winning 23 and losing but 6. He led the team in batting with a lusty .357 average. That was the first season for which Edward B. Moss selected an All-Eastern team for the Spalding publications. He named Hardwick as his left fielder.

Tack was the strongest man at Harvard, winning Dr. Dudley A. Sargent's strength test with a record 1,381 points. He also was a brilliant tennis player, a skilled oarsman, and did some shot putting and broad jumping for the track team when it did not interfere with baseball. Next to football, he liked boxing best, and Grantland Rice felt that he might have been a champion had he tried the professional ring. He certainly possessed one of the most lethal straight-arms in football history. It is claimed that he once bowled over a bull. Dan Daniel of the *New York Telegram* felt that because of his speed, strength, and scrappiness, Hardwick would have made an ideal All-Time All-America tackle. That opinion was expressed in 1928 after Henry, Hubbard, and other king-sized tackles had already appeared.

After his graduation, Tack helped coach the Naval Academy football team for one season, 1915. He joined Hayden Stone and Company, bankers and brokers specializing in investments, but with the coming of World War I, he left to take the officers' training course at Plattsburg, New York, and was commissioned a second lieutenant in the Regular Army. He went overseas in September, 1917, helped organize the American Trench Mortar School at Fort de la Bonnelle in France, and later commanded a trench-mortar company of the 30th Division in combat. When he resigned in January, 1919, he was a captain. He rejoined Hayden Stone and Company, but in 1933 he transferred to the advertising firm of Doremus and Company, as account executive. He also served as director of three different companies and was highly regarded in the business world. Tack was one of the founders of the Boston Garden, was president of the Boston Madison Square Garden Club, a private organization of 300 members and, for a time, was vice president of the Boys' Club of Boston.

His love of sports did not lessen during his busy years in finance. Frequently he assisted with the coaching at Harvard, and he still enjoyed the scrimmage. All his life he was an ardent deep-sea fisherman. On one occasion he harpooned a whale and towed it forty miles. He also organized a shark-fishing expedition to the Galápagos. The nickname "Tack," which he received long before he went to Harvard, came from his fondness for sailor's hardtack, which he liked to munch when out at sea. He was also fond of hunting, and spent months at a time in the Maine woods.

Grantland Rice, who was a close personal friend of Hardwick from the time they served together as artillery officers in France, wrote an interesting story in the *Boston Globe* that illustrates Hardwick's inclination to get the most out of life while it lasted. "Granny" warned him that he was driving himself too hard, especially in the pursuit of his strenuous hobbies, and that his heart couldn't take it. According to Rice, Hardwick replied: "It can for a few years. After that—who cares?"

His heart failed him on June 26, 1949, not in the boxing ring or on the football field, in the forest or on the high seas, and not even in his office, but while he was engaged in the prosaic task of looking for clams in the shallow water near his summer home at Cuttyhunk, Massachusetts. The "Spirit of Football," Rice called him.

HAROLD POWERS MULLER

(6:03; 194)

Albert, King of the Belgians, descended from the royal box at the Olympic Stadium at Antwerp and made his way out on the field to congratulate the winners of the running high jump— tall, skinny, yellow-haired, bespectacled Dick Landon of Yale, Brick Muller of California, and Bo Eklund of Sweden. Landon had just broken the Olympic record with a leap of 6 feet 4⅕ inches. The other two had tied for second place at 6 feet 2¾ inches, but in a jump-off Muller had earned the silver medal. It was remarkable jumping, considering that they took off from a soggy turf. That event occurred on August 17, 1920. Muller, who had completed his freshman year at California the previous June, was now an internationally known figure in track sports. Within five months he would become one of the most widely discussed players in football.

Muller, called "Brick" because of his flaming hair, was a natural athlete. There was none of the fanaticism of Hinkey, the insolence of Shevlin, or the intensity of Hardwick about him. He played football for the sheer fun of it. He was a jovial youngster with a ready smile who moved gracefully despite his bulk, full of animal energy but calm in a crisis. In three varsity years he never played in a losing game. His enormous hands, which enabled him to handle a football almost as though it were a baseball, made him the best passer and receiver in the game. Against Stanford in his sophomore year (1920) he leaped high in the air and speared the ball with one hand. One-handed catches were not unusual for him, and those were the days of the blimp-shaped ball. His speed and sheer power enabled him to box a tackle without assistance and contributed to his success in carrying the ball on end-around plays. He was used to running back kickoffs as had Shevlin in bygone days. Aggressive on defense, and a deadly tackler, he was also very clever at sifting through interference to get at the ballcarrier.

The play that focused the spotlight on him took place at the Tournament of Roses (now Rose Bowl) game on New Year's Day, 1921, at the end of his first year of varsity competition. Andy Smith, onetime Pennsylvania All-America fullback, was the California coach, and had been since 1916, the year after California returned to American football after having played British Rugby for nine years. One of his associates was Clarence M. "Nibs" Price, who later became head coach and was even more famous as a basketball mentor. Price had coached at San Diego High School, one of the few schools in California that did not follow the lead of the colleges in abandoning the American style of football. When his alma mater returned to the game, Price encouraged his players to go to California, and they followed him to Berkeley after he joined Andy Smith's staff. One was Brick Muller, born in Dunsmuir, California on June 12, 1901, who had also attended Oakland Tech, for a short time, prior to entering the university.

Smith and Price slowly restored the prestige of the Golden Bears. The freshman team of the season of 1919, with Muller at end, gave great promise for the future when it easily trounced the traditional rivals Stanford, 47–0, and Southern California, 20–12. With Muller and his classmates available for 1920, Smith was ready with his first "Wonder Team," as it was called by Clinton R. Morse of the *San Francisco Chronicle*. After California had chopped down St. Mary's, 127–0; Nevada, 79–7; Utah, 63–0; Oregon State, 17–7; Washington State, 49–0; and Stanford, 38–0, it was considered to be the strongest aggregation yet to appear on the Golden Coast, but that meant nothing to the arbiters in the East. They couldn't see anything on the coast; the Rocky Mountains intervened. It seemed absurd to consider California in the same category with Ohio State and Notre Dame in the Midwest or Princeton and Harvard on the Atlantic Coast.

In this one game California was to enhance the prestige of Pacific Coast football to such an extent that it would be rated on a par with that of any other section of the United States. The Tournament of Roses game had been revived at Pasadena in 1916. Since then, Washington State had beaten Brown and Oregon had won over Pennsylvania. Service teams performed during the two war years while Harvard nosed out Oregon 7–6, in 1920. Now, for the 1921 edition of the classic, unbeaten Ohio State, monarch of the Western Conference, was invited to oppose California. The Buckeyes, coached by Dr. John W. Wilce, ruled an 8–5 favorite. They came west with a half-dozen men who had been named for All-America laurels by Walter Camp or other critics. Approximately 100,000 people sought tickets for only 42,000 seats.

The dramatic play that will always be associated with Muller occurred early in the second quarter. California, leading 7–0, was in possession of the ball on Ohio State's 37-yard line. Archie Nisbet, the fullback, stood near the ball talking to one of the players while six other Californians strung along the line. Suddenly, Nisbet stooped and flipped the ball back to Albert "Pesky" Sprott. The latter faked a run but then passed to Muller, who stood 15 yards in the rear of his normal position—Nisbet having taken his place as the seventh man on the line of scrimmage. Muller then fired the ball to Howard "Brodie" Stephens, an end, who had sprinted downfield. Stephens caught it and dived over the goal line. It was the turning point of the game.

California scored two more touchdowns before the afternoon was over to bring the score to 28–0 and its season total to 510 points against 14 in 9 games. California had as good a claim as any to the mythical national championship.

But the question everyone asked after the game was How long was *the* pass? Parke H. Davis, the noted statistician, listed it as 70 yards, and that figure was, and still is, widely quoted. The late Bob Ripley, who claimed he could prove any statement he made, called it 70 yards in his "Believe It or Not" series. Maxwell Stiles, a Los Angeles sportswriter, after comprehensive research, established the pass as 53 yards. Whatever the exact distance, the prodigious heave made Muller famous. But he did other things equally important in that decisive game. He recovered three key fumbles (one on California's eight-yard line in the first quarter), completed three forward passes, caught five, intercepted two, and on several occasions tackled a punt receiver before the latter could take a step. In fact, he got downfield so fast that Ohio State began to make fair catches. Elmer Henderson, the Southern California coach, called him "the best player I ever saw in a football suit," while Dr. Wilce classed him as "about" the greatest he had ever seen. Bill Roper, Princeton coach, said he was "the peer of any end the game has produced."

Walter Camp's face must have been red when he realized that, for 1920, he had relegated the best end in the country to his third All-America team. At the time of the selection, he probably felt that he was doing the handsome thing for the Westerners, especially since he had placed Dan McMillan, a Bear tackle, on his second team. Cort Majors, captain and guard, received All-America rating from various other sources. Camp erred no more concerning Muller. For his two remaining years of college competition, the big readhead was a first-team choice, even though he was not quite up to par in 1921. McMillan and Stephens rated third-team berths that year, and Duke Morrison, who led the nation in scoring with 131 points, was on the second team in 1922. Sprott, Nisbet, and Toomey, backs; Lee Cranmer, guard, and Stanley N. Barnes, tackle, who became a federal circuit judge, were mentioned favorably by other critics during those years. George "Fat" Latham, center, was captain in 1921, and Charley Erb, 143-pound quarterback, in 1922. Those were the brightest stars of the three "Wonder Teams" of the Muller era.

Despite his All-America rating, 1921 was not a happy one for Brick. He suffered from a leg infection and missed quite a bit of play, but the Bears kept on rolling and went through the regular season all-victorious. In the Southern California game, with the score tied at 7–7, Muller was injected for just one play. From the fullback position, he tossed a 28-yard pass to Erb to place the ball in scoring position. After that the Bears caught fire and ran up a 38–7 score. Stanford was overwhelmed 42–7, but the Tournament of Roses game, with underdog Washington and Jefferson, resulted in a scoreless tie. Muller played in both games as a substitute. He did well but in no way distinguished himself.

Washington and Jefferson's talented coach, A. Earl "Greasy" Neale, had played baseball for eight years with the St. Louis "Gas House Gang," and was thoroughly versed in "old pro" tactics. He is understood to have signaled every play from the bench. His players were adept at "riding" the opposition. On a wet day, on a swampy field, the Presidents had the better of the heavily favored Bears. Muller did not go in until near the end of the first half. He took an awful razzing from the Easterners, who crowded around him and wiped their muddy hands on his clean jersey. Against the weather and the fierce-charging visitors, Muller was not able to complete a pass.

The third of Andy Smith's "Wonder Teams," that of 1922, was rated by many Coast critics as his best. The tremendous victory, 45–7, over powerful Washington, is rated the finest game played by any of his teams. For the fifth straight year, Stanford was beaten; this time 28–0, with Muller scoring the opening touchdown on a 30-yard pass from Don Nichols. California was invited to play in the Rose Bowl, which was dedicated in 1923, the year when the name was changed to "Rose Bowl Game," but declined. Southern California, beaten by California 12–0, represented the Pacific Coast, and downed Penn State 14–3.

Although California did not play at Pasadena, Muller was not denied the privilege of participating in a high-caliber post-season game. He played with the Western Stars against the Eastern Suns in a game for charity at Columbus, Ohio, on December 2nd. As the Associated Press reported, "Due chiefly to the individual prowess of Brick Muller, the West triumphed, 6–0." The Easterners had worked their way into a scoring position, and Red Roberts, Centre College All-American, attempted a goal from placement. Muller blocked the kick, picked up the loose ball, and galloped seventy yards to the only score of the game. The Associated Press went on to state, "Muller stood head and shoulders above the galaxy of three score stars who participated." And what stars they were, the pick of contemporary All-Americans! The burly Californian had ended his college playing career in the proverbial blaze of glory.

Muller was a capable baseball player who played on state interscholastic champion nines at both San Diego High School and Oakland Tech, but at college he preferred to concentrate on track and field sports. In the Eastern Intercollegiates in his sophomore year, following the Olympics, he tied with Dick Landon for the high-jump championship, and in the same meet he placed fourth in the broad jump. The next year, when California captured the National Collegiate title, he placed second in the broad jump, third in the high jump, and fourth in the discus throw, while at the Intercollegiates he tied for second place in the high jump and finished second in the discus throw. In his last year he again aided the Bears to the National Collegiate championship through a third place in the high jump and fourth in the broad jump.

Following his graduation, he coached the ends at his alma mater in 1923, 1924, and 1925, played professionally with Los Angeles in 1926, and was back at California for the next three seasons. In 1928 he produced Irvine Phillips, the second Bear to make the All-America team. In the meantime he earned an M.D. degree. During World War II he served in the Army Medical Corps for four and a half years, becoming a lieutenant colonel. He was in charge of an orthopedic team that traveled extensively in England and, later, on the Continent. In 1956 he served as head team physician for the United States Olympic team at Melbourne. A prominent figure in the medical profession, he practiced at Berkeley—the home of his alma mater. He was stricken suddenly while on a house call and died later in the hospital on May 17, 1962.

BENJAMIN GAYLORD OOSTERBAAN

(6:00; 190)

Big-league baseball and football clubs were hot on the trail of the Big Dutchman when he terminated his college career. Had professional basketball been of its present stature he would have received bids from that source too. He turned down all of them in order to remain at Michigan, and he is still there after more than thirty-five years of service. For a score of those years he toiled in comparative obscurity as an assistant coach, developing great ends and assisting in the molding of championship teams. It was not until 1948 that he was chosen as head coach of the Maize and Blue. In his first season he hit the "jackpot" and was named Coach of the Year in a nationwide poll of football coaches conducted by the *New York World-Telegram*.

Oosterbaan was born in Muskegon, Michigan, on February 4, 1906. He came naturally by his habit of persevering on the job; his father was postmaster of Muskegon for sixteen years. At the local high school, Bennie was all-state at football and the state interscholastic champion discus thrower, but it was at basketball that he achieved national recognition. An All-America interscholastic team was selected after a national championship tournament at Chicago, and he was a member of it. And basketball came close to being his Number One sport at Michigan. Early in the fall of 1925, he had so failed to impress one of the assistant coaches that he was advised to turn in his football uniform and concentrate on basketball. But Fielding H. Yost, the head coach, did not obtain his great reputation by chance. He had already spotted the big fellow as a likely prospect. When he learned what action had been taken, he quickly saw to it that Oosterbaan was back in uniform.

It is hard to believe that Oosterbaan so narrowly missed playing varsity football. He not only made the team at left end as a sophomore; he also became one of the great players of the year. Walter Camp had died during the previous March, but many leading critics attempted to take his place. Of 26 All-America teams selected in 1925, Oosterbaan was on 20 of them. Yost called the Michigan team of that year the greatest he had ever seen in action. It won seven, and lost only to Northwestern in a rain-and-wind storm on a field of mud and water. Captain Tim Lowry of Northwestern gave Michigan an intentional safety so that his team could take the ball out of danger, and the Purple won by a baseball score of 3–2. However, Michigan won the conference title. Another Bennie, Friedman, the quarterback whose field goal defeated Red Grange's Illinois team; Captain Bob Brown, a center, and the powerful tackles, Tom Edwards and Harry Hawkins, were other Wolverines considered to be of All-America caliber.

The Michigan team of 1926 was not quite so strong as the previous one, although it, too, turned in a 7–1 season record. It was fortunate in defeating Minnesota in the last game of the season for each. The powerful Gophers had much the better of the contest, making 22 first downs against Michigan's 3. They were leading, 6–0, midway through the last quarter when a back fumbled. Oosterbaan picked up the ball and ran 60 yards to a touchdown. Captain Bennie Friedman converted to bring the count to 7–6 and enable Michigan to tie Northwestern for the conference championship. Oosterbaan and Friedman were popular All-America choices. The sole loss that season was to Navy. The game was played at Baltimore, but the Wolverines ate lunch at the Naval Academy mess. According to a story that still rates laughs among the old-timers at Annapolis, the visitors were fed with such lavish hospitality that they were logy at game time. Friedman threw 31 passes, and the Midshipmen broke up 24 of them. Navy won, 10–0, and went through the season unbeaten, although tied by Army.

Elton E. Wieman relieved the great "Hurry Up" Yost as coach in 1927. Michigan lost two games, and with them the conference championship, but Bennie Oosterbaan, now captain, enjoyed another great year. Of 15 All-America teams published, he appeared on every one to become the first Wolverine to win first-team All-America honors for three straight years. Already recognized as the finest receiver in the game, against Ohio State Oosterbaan threw the football 50 yards to Louis Gilbert, who ran five yards to a touchdown.

Oosterbaan was a good-looking fellow with a genial personality; gentle of manner and soft of speech, with a somewhat diffident air, he was a good mixer and very popular. When his playing days were over, the noted Detroit sportswriter H. G. Salsinger classed him as the greatest end since the introduction of the forward pass, and George Trevor of the *New York Sun* called him "probably the greatest of all pass receivers." He could go high or low for the ball with equal facility, and often grabbed it with one of his hands, which were almost as large as those of Brick Muller. His skill in handling the ball was the result of endless hours of practice both on and off the field. He was an excellent runner on end-around plays, being shifty, with a nice change of pace. He also did some kicking and was a fine blocker.

His football sense was so keen that Yost allowed him to use his own judgment on defense, and he smashed, waited, or floated as the spirit moved him. The result was that he had a reputation for being an unorthodox player, but he was never known to be outguessed, sucked in, or boxed. He was strong and agile enough to keep his feet and fight off the interference. Bob Zuppke was quoted by George Trevor as saying that he was not foolish enough to allow his Illinois teams to try to circle Oosterbaan's end. Curiously, Bennie seldom tackled below the waist. He would seize the runner around the shoulders and slam him to the ground.

Oosterbaan had a keen sense of humor. His smiling face and cheerful words inspired and relaxed the players. Bennie Friedman's well-known story of the 1926 Ohio State game is a case in point. The Buckeyes were ahead 10–7. Michigan had scored on a fake place-kick formation when Friedman passed 38 yards to Oosterbaan, who had outmaneuvered the defense and stood alone in the clear. With a few seconds remaining in the second quarter, Friedman decided to try a place-kick from the 44-yard line. As the Wolverines scattered to position, Oosterbaan brushed past Louis Gilbert, who was preparing to hold the ball for the kick, paused briefly and whispered something to him. The act did not go unnoticed. The Buckeye rooters were on their feet imploring their heroes to watch for a fake. "Watch Oosterbaan!" they cried. The Ohioans watched Oosterbaan, and Friedman kicked the goal that was the turning point of the game. Later it came out that Oosterbaan, after taking a look at all those yards stretching between them and the goalposts, had whispered to Gilbert that he was praying for a strong wind to blow the ball over. That was his "important message."

Bennie is one of the few Wolverines ever to win nine major letters. In basketball he lived up to his advance billing and made the team, as a forward, in his sophomore year. The next season he led the conference in scoring field goals with 50, and his work with rebounds was considered the best in the circuit. In his senior year he topped the conference in total points scored (129) and in field goals scored (57) in twelve games. He was All-Conference and All-American in both 1927 and 1928. Under Coach E. J. Mather, Michigan tied for the conference title in 1926 and won it outright the following season. Though Oosterbaan was considered a top Olympic prospect with the discus, he preferred to play baseball even though he had never played regularly prior to enrolling at Michigan. His coach, Ray L. Fisher, named him and another football man—Jack Blott, a catcher—as the greatest baseball players he had ever coached. Bennie started as an outfielder but was moved to first base, and according to Fisher he was the best in the conference in 1927 and 1928. During his last year he led the conference batters with an average of .469, getting 23 hits in 49 times at bat. Michigan was champion in 1926 and 1928.

After graduation, Oosterbaan turned down pro offers, to remain with Wieman as tutor of the ends. The next year (1929) Harry G. Kipke became head coach and retained Oosterbaan on his staff. In 1930 and 1931 Michigan tied for chief conference honors and was in sole possession of the title for the next two years. Oosterbaan developed Bill Hewitt and Ted Petoskey, ends whose ability was well recognized in college football. Hewitt went on to become a pro great with the Chicago Bears (see Chapter 8, "Great Pros").

Herbert O. "Fritz" Crisler took up the coaching reins in 1938. Under him, Oosterbaan coached ends, then backs, and then became senior assistant. In 1945 Crisler and his staff introduced the two-platoon system that is now so popular in school and pro ranks. During the ten years that Crisler and Oosterbaan were associated in coaching, Michigan tied with Purdue for the championship in 1943, were second four times, and tied for second twice. In 1947 the team won all games, including an awesome drubbing of Southern California, 49–0, in the Rose Bowl, and was considered by many to be the strongest in the nation. The long list of All-America and near All-America ends and backs that Oosterbaan helped develop include: Tommy Harmon, Forest Evashevski, Robert Westfall, Elroy "Crazy Legs" Hirsch, Elmer Madar, Robert Chappuis, Chalmers "Bump" Elliott, Robert Mann, and Leonard Ford.

Following the great season of 1947 when he was elected "Coach of the Year," Crisler decided to rest on his laurels and devote full time to his duties as Director of Athletics. Oosterbaan became head coach and lost no time in making the most of his opportunity. Most of the headliners of the previous season had been graduated, but he proceeded to mold the material at hand into another perfect team, which won all nine games played and was rated first in the nation. The team, champion of the conference, was deprived of the privilege of going to Pasadena because, by the terms of the Big Nine and Pacific Coast Conference pact, a college was ineligible to appear in the Rose Bowl twice in succession. However, Oosterbaan had his chance later, with his 1950 team. On New Year's Day, 1951, it beat California 14–6.

Although he produced other strong teams, Oosterbaan never scaled the heights he did in 1948 when he received the award as the outstanding coach of the year. Michigan divided the conference spoils with Ohio State in 1949 and was champion in 1950, the Rose Bowl season. It placed second in 1956 and shared that spot with Wisconsin in 1954. Bennie coached the Wolverines for 11 seasons through 100 games. They won 63, lost 33, and tied

4. He produced another flock of stars; high on the list were Richard Rifenburg, Ronald Kramer, and Thomas Maentz, ends; thirty-three-year-old Alvin Wistert, third brother to win All-America laurels for Michigan; R. Allen Wahl and Arthur Walker, tackles; Dominic Tomasi, a watch-charm offensive guard; Pete Elliott, quarterback; and Chuck Ortmann and James Pace, backs.

Oosterbaan retired from coaching after the 1958 season, but he continued to serve his beloved alma mater on a full-time basis in public and alumni relations.

DONALD MONTGOMERY HUTSON

(6:01; 190 in college, 185 as a pro)

A few years ago, at the suggestion of the late Herman Hickman, the editors of *Sports Illustrated* magazine inaugurated the practice of publishing an annual "Silver Anniversary All-America team," composed of those former players who had made the most out of life during the quarter of a century that had elapsed since the termination of their college playing careers. On the list for 1959 appeared the name of the old "Alabama Antelope," now owner of Don Hutson, Incorporated, a lucrative automobile agency dealing in Chevrolet and Chrysler cars, located in Racine, Wisconsin, not too far from Green Bay where his name is still spoken with reverence.

No one could belittle Hutson's offensive skill, but he had an undeserved reputation of being a weak defensive end. Josh Cody, Vanderbilt's greatest tackle, who frequently scouted Hutson both in college and pro football, said, "If he had a defensive weakness we were never able to effectively capitalize on it." The story seemed to have its origin in his last appearance in a college game, in the Rose Bowl. Stanford employed a power smash at end which required a team effort to stop. An end, by himself, was at a great disadvantage against it, and the Alabama wingmen were no exceptions. The faulty evaluation gained credence when he embarked on a professional career. Earl "Curly" Lambeau, the Green Bay coach, took full advantage of Don's speed, sure tackling, and uncanny ability to judge the flight of a thrown ball to use him as safety man on defense. Here he was of greater value than he would have been playing on the line. The scheme had the added advantage of keeping him relatively fresh for his offensive chores. He was fundamentally a good blocker, but for similar reasons he was usually spared the severe body beating that falls to the lot of a blocker. On one memorable occasion in the Rose Bowl, when a "perfect play" sprung Dixie Howell loose on a 67-yard touchdown run, it was Hutson who blotted out the Stanford safety man.

Saving him on defense was sound logic. He was such a wonderful pass catcher it would have been foolish taking chances and having him injured. But he never spared himself. In going after a ball, he fearlessly leaped for it regardless of the proximity of opponents ready to crash into him. No end, certainly none since Frank Hinkey, has been so feared and respected. He was such an awesome threat that, in both college and pro football, two defensive players were usually assigned to cover him even before the ball was snapped. Naturally, that gave his team a great advantage, and many of its plays were designed to use Hutson as a decoy.

Don came from Pine Bluff, Arkansas, where he was born on January 31, 1913. At school he was a tall skinny lad, a talented ballplayer but considered too frail for football. It was not until his senior year that he made the high-school grid team. He went to Alabama as a baseball player on a partial scholarship. His lack of weight almost caused him to be passed over when he turned out for football. Harold "Red" Drew, end coach at the time, was intrigued by the deceptive manner in which Hutson ran, with a smooth, effortless stride, as though he were loafing or, as Coach Frank Thomas expressed it, "shuffling along." Yet he invariably came in first in the wind sprints—small wonder, since he was a 9.8-second man in the 100-yard dash. Drew retained him on the squad, and he and Head Coach Frank W. Thomas, former Notre Dame quarterback, worked hard to develop the youngster.

Hutson weighed only 160 pounds when he turned out for the team at Alabama. In his senior year he was listed at 190, but he played with the professionals at 185, according to his own statement. Soft-spoken and retiring, he was somewhat of a lone wolf. His poker face and utter relaxation stood him in good stead going downfield. With a deceptive twist of his torso he could feint a defensive back bowlegged. His several gaits and changes of pace drove them to distraction. While seemingly running his fastest, he could suddenly turn on an additional burst of speed that would shoot him into the clear. He had an unerring instinct at following the ball, a keen sense of timing, and was a good broken-field runner when the ball was once in his big, sure hands. The "Wonder Worker," as Arthur Daley once called him, was also outstanding going down under punts. Even as a sophomore, in 1932, his punt coverage contributed largely to Alabama's upset victory over Vanderbilt.

Hutson progressed slowly at college. He was promising but not particularly impressive either on the freshman team or as a sophomore. In his junior year (1933) he played extensively, but it was not until late in the season, for the Kentucky game, that he made the starting lineup at left end. Against Georgia Tech he recovered a fumble to set up the winning touchdown, and by the end of the season was listed as one of the team's better players along with Tom Hupke, guard; Millard "Dixie" Howell, halfback; and Bill Lee, tackle.

In 1934 Alabama, with a veteran team, retained the conference crown, and Hutson reached the heights of glory. Dixie Howell got in the habit of passing to him in a pinch. Against Clemson, Don snared six, two for touchdowns. Probably the most spectacular catch he made during the entire season was against Georgia Tech when he leaped high in the air, while traveling at top speed, to haul down a 30-yard pass, after which he ran ten yards to a score. Nor was pass-catching his only claim to fame. Coach Thomas devised an end-around play for him. In the Tennessee game Don caught a pass to put the ball on the Volunteers' nine-yard line. On the next play he swung around end, cut back sharply between end and tackle, and dived over the goal line for the touchdown that gave Alabama the game 13–6 and, as events turned out, the championship. In a similar manner he scored against Kentucky after a 20-yard run, and while playing with the College All-Stars against the champion Chicago Bears, in the late summer of 1935, the same play enabled him to get away for a substantial gain.

Even before the Rose Bowl the Associated Press called Hutson "a sensational wingman," and he was on the All-America team of almost every nationally known agency. Every Alabaman who took part in the epic game against Stanford, before 84,474 screaming fans, must always rank it as the supreme game of his college career, and it was so with Hutson. Although the Indians were watching his every move, and in Bobby Grayson and Bones Hamilton had two of the leading pass defenders in college football, Don caught six passes for 165 yards and two touchdowns. His second score came after a short toss from Howell in the fourth quarter, but the first was a thriller. With a minute left in the second period, Riley Smith intercepted a pass on his own 46-yard line. On the next play Joe Riley, Howell's understudy, whipped a pass to Hutson. Don grabbed it on Stanford's 30 and dodged his way into the end zone.

Alabama won the game 29–13. It won all ten games that season and in national ratings was generally placed close behind all-victorious Minnesota. Hutson, Howell, and Captain Lee were on many All-America teams, and Riley Smith was to crash the select circle the next year. Charlie Marr, a guard, was an All-

Southern choice, while Paul "Bear" Bryant, an end who became a famous coach, and Joe Demyanovich, fullback were also highly regarded.

The following season (1935) Hutson wore a Green Bay Packer uniform, and it is difficult to believe that anyone could have made a more auspicious debut. Curley Lambeau had him sit out the opening game, against the Chicago Cardinals, in order to get the feel of the pro game and gain confidence. The next game was against the dreaded Chicago Bears. Green Bay had not beaten the "Monsters" in three years, and had lost seven straight games to them. Don started at his old position, left end. The Bears kicked off, and the Packers had the ball on their own 17-yard line. On the first play Arnie Herber faded back and threw the ball 50 yards to the rookie. Don left the Bears flat-footed and went on to a touchdown. Green Bay won, 7–0. In his first year, Don was chosen for the second All-Pro team.

The next year he was advanced to the first All-Pro team, and Green Bay won the world championship. The play-off game with the Boston Redskins had not been in progress three minutes when Herber shot a 45-yard pass to Hutson, who kept right on going to score. He caught five passes during the course of the game, which the Packers won, 21–6.

The season of 1937 seems to have been an off year. The Bears nosed out Green Bay for the Western Division title, and Hutson was relegated to the second All-Pro team. It began to look as though the smart pros were getting on to his style. But he was still improving and was again on the first All-Pro team in 1938. The Packers got the better of the Bears, but the New York Giants defeated them in the championship playoff, 23–17. Hutson, who was bothered with a bad leg, played little in that game.

For the next seven years, Hutson was on the All-Pro team each year, making it nine times in eleven years. He was a unanimous choice in 1941, 1942, and 1944. In 1941 and 1942 he received the Most Valuable Player award. That trophy has been discontinued, and Don is the only man in history to win it twice.

The Packers were again world champions in 1939 and 1944, defeating the Giants each year. In the 1944 game, which Green Bay won, 14–7, Don caught a pass to put the ball in scoring position. He then decoyed the Giants' secondary out of position so that Ted Fritsch was alone on the five-yard line when Irv Comp passed to him for the winning touchdown.

Probably Hutson's most famous battery mate was Cecil Isbell, the former Purdue star. Curiously, they were not on friendly terms, although each lauded the other as "tops" in his line. In an exhibition game with Los Angeles in 1939, Isbell passed from eight yards behind his own goal line, 69 yards to Hutson. When the latter scored, the play had covered 108 yards. Don could pass, too, although that was not what he was getting paid to do. Against the Giants, in 1942, he started on an end-around play but suddenly stopped to pitch a 40-yard touchdown pass to Harry Jacunski, the other Packer end. During the early fall, after each championship year, the Packers played the College All-Stars, and Hutson enjoyed a good day each year. In 1940 he scored three touchdowns, one after he took a 60-yard pass from Isbell and ran 30 yards. The others resulted from passes over the goal line, one 35 yards and the other 29. In 1945 Don ran 85 yards after intercepting a pass, and in addition booted a field goal and two conversions.

Hutson later claimed that he reached his peak in 1941 when he was twenty-eight years old. After that, he began thinking of retiring from the game and getting along in business. He was all set to get out after the 1943 season, but because of the shortage of personnel owing to the war he was persuaded to stay with the Packers. After 1945, when he was still good enough to be on the first All-Pro team, he retired and took with him twenty records. Following are the marks he set, many of which have now been broken: Most passes caught, career (11 years), 489; one season, 74 in 1942; one game, 14 against New York in 1942. Most touchdown passes caught, career, 101; one season, 17 in 1942; one game, 4 against Detroit in 1945. Most yards gained, career, 8,010; one season, 1,211 in 1942; one game, 237 against Brooklyn (on eight passes) in 1943. Shortest completed pass, four inches, from Cecil Isbell against Cleveland Rams in 1942. Most touchdown passes caught, championship play-off games, 9 in 4 games. Most points, career, 825; one season, 138 in 1942, and in addition he tallied the second highest total for a single game, 31 against Detroit in 1945. Most consecutive games scoring one or more points, 41 (1940 to 1944). Most touchdowns, career, 105; one seaon, 17 in 1942. For a single game he was again second with 4 against Detroit in 1945. Most points after touchdown, career, 174. Most years led league in scoring, 5; in pass receiving, 8.

Don had also been an accomplished baseball player and sprinter at Alabama. Taking advantage of his athletic reputation, he opened a dry-cleaning establishment in Tuscaloosa, but in 1939 he sold it and moved to Green Bay where, for a time, he was employed in a paper mill between seasons. Later he operated the Packer Palladium, a bowling alley, and upon his retirement from playing went into the automobile business in Racine. His coaches will never forget him; it would be very strange if they did. Curly Lambeau calls him the greatest pass receiver that ever lived, and Frank Thomas said Hutson was the best end he ever saw.

DAVID COLIN CAMPBELL

(6:00; 171)

In 1904 Walter Camp selected an All-Time team for a magazine, *The Independent.* It was composed exclusively of players from the "Big Three"—Princeton, Harvard, and Yale. With Frank Hinkey at end, he paired Dave Campbell of Harvard.

Campbell had to work for a living several years before entering college, and as a result he was a mature man of twenty-eight when he captained the Harvard team of 1901 that won all its games and overwhelmed Yale 22–0. He proved to be a shrewd, resourceful leader. In a game with Army, he improvised a form of buck-lateral play that sent Bob Kernan 60 yards to the winning touchdown just as the game was ending. Another valuable asset was his dependability—and availability; he was steady, consistent, and perservering, was seldom injured, and possessed almost un-limited endurance. He had the strength to box a tackle and to drag the ballcarrier. On defense, he was difficult to fool, used his hands well in fighting through interference, was fairly fast down under punts, and was usually a good tackler. In the slow, grinding mass play of the period, he would sometimes climb on top of the struggling linemen to clamp a headlock on the enemy ballcarrier and yank him backward.

In his first year at Harvard, Campbell failed to make the varsity squad. He captained the freshman team that defeated the Yale cubs 6–0. The next season (1899) he was proclaimed the best end in the country by all the leading critics. Caspar Whitney called him "pre-eminent," and Walter Camp thought his work was "almost without a blemish." That proved to be Campbell's most satisfactory season. Camp loyally retained him on his All-America team for the two remaining years, but others were not so generous.

The 1901 champion team, coached by Bill Reid, a former Crimson fullback, was well stocked with stars and played through the entire Yale game without a substitution. In addition to Camp-bell, Camp named Oliver Cutts (who, to Harvard's embarrass-ment, was later shown to have been a professional physical-training instructor) at tackle; William Lee, guard; Robert Kernan, halfback; and Thomas Graydon, fullback; with Edward "Pete" Bowditch, end; Crawford Blagden, tackle; Charles Barnard, guard; and Albert Ristine, halfback, on the second team. Camp-bell assisted with the coaching at Harvard on various occasions and was a member of Percy Haughton's original coaching staff that developed the champion team of 1908.

During the early days of World War I, Campbell engaged in

the manufacture of explosives, but after the United States entered the war he served with the 304th Tank Corps in France. After the Armistice he devoted his attention to engineering and later became an investment broker in Boston, where he died in 1949 at the age of seventy-five.

WESLEY EUGENE FESLER

(6:00; 188)

Grantland Rice, who succeeded Walter Camp in making the annual All-America selections for *Collier's* in 1925, picked several all-time teams during his long career as a sportswriter. He changed his mind with disconcerting frequency. In 1928 he named Muller at one end with the other a tossup among Hinkey, Shevlin, and Hardwick. In 1939 he paired Fesler with Muller, and in 1952 he replaced them with Don Hutson and Bennie Oosterbaan, both of whom had completed their college playing careers prior to 1939, although at that time Hutson was still a professional star.

Fesler was a Phi Beta Kappa student and an athlete of remarkable all-around ability. In addition to football, he played on the Buckeye basketball and baseball teams. Helms Athletic Foundation named him as a guard on its All-America basketball team in 1931, and he was good enough at baseball to warrant a tryout with the St. Louis Cardinals. In 1931 Parke H. Davis called him "the most versatile end the game has ever known."

During his years on the varsity, Ohio State produced no outstanding team, never finishing higher than fourth in the conference, yet he made the *Literary Digest* consensus All-America team each of the three seasons he played. In 1929, when a Northwestern back fumbled, he made an almost miraculous catch before the ball touched the ground, and ran 96 yards to score. Against Michigan, he grabbed a pass from Al Holman to score the winning touchdown. In his senior year (1930) he captained the team. After the Buckeyes suffered several defeats, he was moved into the backfield on offense. From then on, Ohio State was unbeaten, tied Wisconsin, and defeated Navy, Pittsburgh, and Illinois. Fesler called signals and did much of the passing, kicking, and ball carrying. On defense, he starred either at end or as a linebacker.

After his graduation, Fesler coached the ends at Harvard (1933 to 1941) and at Princeton (1945). At both places he also served as head coach of the basketball team. His tenure of office as head football coach included 1942–1944 at Wesleyan; 1946, Pittsburgh; 1947–1950, Ohio State; and 1951–1953, Minnesota. The first year he took over at Ohio State, the Buckeyes finished last in the conference; they tied for first in 1949 and were a close second in 1950. He produced some fine players: George Toneff, guard; Jack Lininger, center; and Jerry Krail, halfback, in 1949; and Vic Janowicz, halfback; Bob McCullough, center; Bill Trautwein, tackle; and John Biltz, guard, in 1950. At Minnesota he handled such stars as Paul Giel, back, and Jerry Helgeson, center.

Fesler retired from coaching after the 1953 season and is now a sales manager for Investors Diversified Services in Minneapolis. An interesting sidelight to his career opened in 1943 when the much-decorated General "Wild Bill" Donovan, the former Columbia University quarterback (1904) who headed the Office of Strategic Services in World War II, asked Fesler to establish and operate a recreational and physical program for the O.S.S. in Washington. It proved to be a fascinating assignment.

◆ ◆ ◆

AWARD-WINNING ENDS

Lawrence M. Kelley, *Yale*	HEISMAN, 1936
Kenneth Kavanaugh, *Louisiana State*	ROCKNE, 1939 (initial)
Robert L. Dove, *Notre Dame*	ROCKNE, 1942
H. Richard Duden, *Navy*	ROCKNE, 1945
Burr Baldwin, *U.C.L.A.*	ROCKNE, 1946
Leon J. Hart, *Notre Dame*	HEISMAN, MAXWELL, ROCKNE, 1949
Ronald G. Beagle, *Navy*	MAXWELL, 1954
Max Boydston, *Oklahoma*	ROCKNE, 1954

2

TACKLES

CAMP, 1910	DeWitt, *Princeton*	Fish, *Harvard*
YOST, 1920	Hart, *Princeton*	West, *Colgate*
TREVOR, 1927	Henry, *Wash. & Jeff.*	West, *Colgate*
GULF, 1933	Henry, *Wash. & Jeff.*	Cowan, *Princeton*
SHAUGHNESSY, 1943	Henry, *Wash. & Jeff.*	Nagurski, *Minnesota*
A.P., 1951	Henry, *Wash. & Jeff.*	Nagurski, *Minnesota*
RICE, 1954 *	Henry, *Wash. & Jeff.*	Stydahar, *West Virginia*
WEYAND, 1955	Henry, *Wash. & Jeff.*	Nagurski, *Minnesota*
HELMS, TO DATE	Henry, *Wash. & Jeff.*	Wildung, *Minnesota*
ADDITIONAL	Newell, *Harvard*	Fincher, *Georgia Tech.*
	Hubbard, *Centenary & Geneva*	

* Rice placed Nagurski at fullback.

❖ ❖ ❖

HECTOR WILLIAM COWAN

(5:10; 189)

Hector Cowan was a stern, big-jawed, scowling man who looked fierce because he was fierce, in a gentlemanly sort of way. A simple country boy of lofty principles, full of fun and high spirits, on the football field he played as rough as the rules permitted but he played clean. As his three-year opponent, George Woodruff of Yale, expressed it, "He did not play roughly for the sake of roughness itself." That was not the usual practice of his day. When there was no neutral zone and linemen played head to head, there was considerable infighting. No one ever accused Cowan of slugging, but by the legitimate use of his hands he earned a reputation as one of the "toughies" of the gridiron. When he became a divinity student, it was said that he feared the Lord and nothing else. His violent play prompted a battered opponent to exclaim, "Keep your hands for pounding on your Bible, and don't keep sticking them in my face!" At a time when profanity was considered a sign of virility, his language was above reproach. If sufficently aroused he might explode with such a violent expression as "Oh, sugar!" or "By Dad!"

Cowan once remarked that he never deliberately tried to put a man out of action but that he did not mind hurting one. Tackling between the waist and the knees was first authorized in 1888. Edgar M. Church, Pennsylvania's three-time captain, remembers tackling Cowan at the knees. Although that style was something new, the big Tiger had already acquired the knack of falling with his full weight on the tackler's back. Church felt as though his backbone were broken. When Cowan showed no inclination to remove his weight, Church yelled in exasperation, "Get off me, you ————!" To his amazement, a gentle voice replied, "Please do not use profanity in my presence; I'm a divinity student." The same story, with appropriate change of personnel, has been told at other colleges, so one gathers that Cowan made frequent use of the admonition.

It was unfortunate for Cowan that the tackling rule was not amended a year earlier. In a game against Harvard in 1887, when Cowan tackled Albert Holden, Harvard's captain and star half-back, his hands slipped below the waist. He promptly released his hold, but Holden fell and claimed a foul. Wyllys Terry of Yale, the umpire, disqualified Cowan, which was then the penalty for a foul. Harvard won, 12–0, and Princeton never forgave Terry, nor did Cowan, who was proud that he never intentionally fouled a man. Princeton couldn't do anything about it, but Cowan had an opportunity for vengeance. A few years after the game, he played with the Cleveland A.C. against the Crescent A.C. of Brooklyn for which Terry performed at halfback. Cowan did not turn the other cheek. When he tackled Terry, he took unholy delight in slamming him to the frozen ground and at least once he managed to toss him over his head.

It was on a day in late November, 1884, when Princeton was holding its next-to-the-last scrimmage prior to the Yale game, that the call came for Cowan. On that occasion, Jim Robinson the trainer, was annoyed because only ten of the scrubs were present. A guard, apparently feeling that he had contributed enough, failed to appear. As Jim looked over the crowd of students ranged along the sidelines, his gaze rested on a towheaded, rawboned farm boy with a good pair of shoulders and a fighting face. That was Freshman Cowan. He knew practically nothing about the game because it had not yet been introduced at Delaware Academy at Delphi, New York, where he had prepped for Princeton. However, he liked what he saw and needed no urging to turn out with the other students to cheer the team in the closing days of practice before it left to battle Yale in New York.

Robinson collared the surprised freshman and hustled him to the locker room where he was dressed in cast-off bits of uniform. Cowan recalled that his shoes were three sizes too small. After Robinson gave him a few pointers, he took his place in the scrub line opposite Tracy Harris. He must have acquitted himself reasonably well because Robinson urged him to come out the next day. That time he had the honor of facing Captain Clinton Bird, probably the best guard in the country. Again he did not do badly. After practice, Bird and Robinson held a consultation. Football was a relatively simple game in those days, but even so it was obvious that Cowan was too inexperienced to face the well-trained giants of Yale, and no time remained for coaching; so, regretfully, they had to let him go with the advice to turn out for the team the following year.

When the fall of 1885 arrived there seemed to be no further question concerning Cowan. He was given Bird's place at left guard; the former captain having been graduated. One of the greatest thrills of his playing days came to him that season in his first game against Yale. With time running out and the Elis leading 5–0 (on a field goal, which then counted five points), Princeton held and Yale punted. Henry "Tilly" Lamar got the ball and ran 80 yards to a touchdown. The conversion was kicked by Dick Hodge, and Princeton won the game, 6–5, and the championship. Charles "Reddy" DeCamp, an end, captained that formidable Tiger team, which rolled up 637 points in 9 games, averaging over 70 points a game.

Cowan continued playing guard the next two years, and his fame steadily increased. After he was graduated, Cowan entered the Princeton Theological Seminary and captained the Tigers for the 1888 season. He shifted himself to right tackle. The captain was the coach in those days, and Cowan advanced the game in several respects. Usually signals were given by the captain, but Cowan installed the quarterback as field general and adopted number signals, which Pennsylvania Military College had introduced the previous year. He perfected wedge play, and his team brought out a "split-the-line-open" play that was the original attempt at boxing a tackle. In spite of his efforts, Yale again triumphed, on a pair of field goals by Billy Bull. About that time, Yale's famous captain, William "Pa" Corbin, was quoted as comparing Yale's success to a righteous life, "Monotonous but satisfying."

Cowan still craved a victory; so, in 1889, he was back in uniform, at left tackle. Princeton was quite naturally disturbed by Yale's monopoly. Walter "Monte" Cash, a former Pennsylvania tackle, was lured from his home in Wyoming. He and Benjamin "Sport" Donnelly, an end who according to Heffelfinger could slug and still keep his eye on the ball, appeared in Princeton uniforms only that season. Roscoe H. Channing, a splendid halfback who became a noted mining engineer, was another special student. Knowlton "Snake" Ames, who Harvard claimed was a professional baseball player, was the fullback, and twenty-eight-year-old William "Pop" George held down center. The captain of that swashbuckling aggregation was eighteen-year-old Edgar Allan "Peter" Poe, grandnephew of the poet and himself later Attorney General of Maryland. That year an All-America team was selected for the first time, and Cowan, George, Poe, Ames, and Channing were on it, with Donnelly, Hugh "Horse" Janeway, 204-pound guard, and Jeremiah Black, halfback, listed as reserves. Ralph Warren, end, and Jesse Riggs, guard, were first-team choices the next season.

Before opposing Yale at Berkeley Oval in New York, Prince· ton had defeated Harvard 41–15, after trailing at half-time 10–15. Yale had lost only 2 games out of 110 played since 1876 and now had not been beaten in 49 consecutive contests. On the day of the great game, some 25,000 people turned out, which enabled the two schools to split a record sum of $11,200. On a decidedly swampy field the teams battled through a scoreless first half. Midway through the second half, following a 30-yard run by Cowan, a kicked ball was fumbled by a Yale back and recovered by Princeton for a touchdown. The Elis redoubled their efforts, but Ames' punting gradually drove them back.

Yale had the ball on its own five-yard line. Bill Wurtenberg, the quarterback, turned to check the position of the backs, and Joe Thomas, a substitute Princeton guard, slipped an arm around the hip of Bert Hanson, the Yale center, and gave the hand signal for putting the ball in play. Hanson snapped the ball, which bounced off Wurtenberg's leg into a good-sized mud puddle. Now came Cowan's supreme moment. He fell on the ball while Blue jersies swarmed over him. He struggled to his feet, shaking off mud, water, and Elis, and fought his way across the goal line. Princeton won, 10–0. At last Yale had been humbled, and Hector felt free to relinquish his post to a younger man.

For five years Cowan had performed in the Princeton line. He never left a game or a practice scrimmage because of injury. John Heisman, the famous coach, wrote in 1928 that Cowan "was probably the greatest of all tackles," and Billy Bull, Yale full-back, said he "could walk through a line as though it were paper." Helms Athletic Foundation named him to its all-time team until 1942. Parke H. Davis thought him every bit as valuable as Heffelfinger. Even with his gorilla-like strength, speed of hands and feet, and fighting spirit, it seems doubtful if a man his size could have handled the ponderous pros of the present. It is well, though, not to lose sight of the fact that a 187-pound Jack Dempsey all but annihilated a 245-pound Jess Willard. Cowan could run the hundred in 11 seconds and was famous as a ball-carrier. During his career, he scored 79 touchdowns. In today's game he might well have been an ace fullback.

At Princeton, Cowan was also on the lacrosse and track teams, was a member of a debating society, and vice president of his class in his junior year. At the close of the 1889 season, he was invited to organize football at the University of North Carolina and he is now listed as the Tar Heels' first coach. He was ordained a Presbyterian minister in 1891 and became pastor of a church in St. Joseph, Missouri. While there, he served as director of athletics and football coach at the University of Kansas, in 1894, 1895, and 1896. His Jayhawker teams won 15, lost 7, and tied 1. Two years later, after he had answered a call from a parish in Buffalo, New York, he held a similar post at the State Normal School at Potts-town, New York.

In 1906 Cowan resigned from the ministry and purchased a dairy farm near Hobart, New York, where he had been born on July 12, 1863. After he had given all seven of his children a college education, he sold the farm and, although in his sixties, embarked in business as a dealer in feed and fertilizer and as an agent of the Farmers Cooperative Association. He made a distinct success of that late venture and held such positions as director of the County Farm Bureau and president of the Dairymen's League. He reached the end of his long and interesting life at Stamford (New York) Hospital on October 19, 1941. William Lyon Phelps, Yale's distinguished Professor of English, said of Cowan, "I never knew a man of finer character."

JOHN RIEGEL DEWITT

(6:02; 198)

It was as a guard that DeWitt made his reputation, but football had opened up considerably by 1910 when Walter Camp expressed the opinion that DeWitt would make an "ideal tackle for the modern game." A few years later (1913) Herbert Reed, the sportswriter, noted that DeWitt's build was "ideal for the tackle position." In the still more modern game of the present, he would probably have been a fullback. He was big enough, and powerful, especially in the arms and shoulders; he was fast, active, and agile both mentally and physically. Reed felt that, until the coming of Jim Thorpe, DeWitt was the most dangerous runner from kick formation that had yet appeared and that he was the best punter and goal kicker of his period. DeWitt studied the game and put everything he had into his play. He was what the pros call a "money player," at his best when the stakes were highest. Leadership, courage, and versatility were among his chief attributes.

John was born in Phillipsburg, New Jersey, on October 29, 1881, but spent much of his early life in Riegelsville, Pennsylvania, founded by his mother's ancestors who were in America before the Revolution. She died when he was quite young and he was raised by two aunts. His father also passed away before he was graduated from Princeton, leaving him several million dollars and sole ownership of the Riegel Sack Company in Jersey City. John bought a Lozier, an expensive American car. Years later, Mrs. Elizabeth Robbins, who had been postmistress of Riegelsville, recalled that, when the horn of DeWitt's car heralded his approach, every man, woman, child, and animal hastily cleared the street because there were no traffic regulations then and John always seemed to be in a hurry.

DeWitt's life followed a pattern. He had a few *close* friends and a somewhat wider circle of less close ones. He showed little or no concern for other people. For those he liked, he was a warmhearted friend and they thought him a grand person. To the rest he appeared cold and arrogant, although as a rule he was courteous to everyone. But even his best friends knew better than to ask him personal questions. He was quite certain to tell them it was none of their business.

His indifference toward the bulk of mankind made him merciless on the football field. Harry Von Kersburg, later an All-America guard at Harvard, was a sixteen-year-old, 165-pound guard at Lehigh when he opposed the mature Princetonian who had no compassion for him but beat him to a pulp. Joe Gilman of Dartmouth recalled that when he lined-up against DeWitt in 1903, the latter growled, "There are two ways to play me—stay out of my way or get hurt." To illustrate the point, on the first scrimmage he clouted Gilman on the jaw. Gilman, who was also an All-American that year, gave DeWitt quite a tussle.

At Lawrenceville, DeWitt captained the football team and won fame as a weight thrower. Princeton fans waited eagerly for his appearance on the gridiron, but they had to be patient. He broke bones in both hands his freshman year and was out for the season. The following year (1901) DeWitt was installed at right tackle, but his line play was nothing exceptional. He shone to far greater advantage in kicking and carrying the ball. From kick formation he made many long runs, and in the last three minutes of the contest with Lafayette he ran 50 yards to the winning touchdown, tearing loose from three tacklers along the way. At the end of the season, during which the Tigers lost to Yale, 0–12, Walter Camp described DeWitt as "most versatile"; but Charles Patterson in *Outing* called him only a fair tackle, and advised playing him at guard.

After a few games in 1902, John was shifted to right guard, and was soon recognized as the mainstay of the team. Against Columbia he drop-kicked a goal from the 45-yard line, scored all of Princeton's points in a 10–0 victory over Cornell by means of two field goals, and all five points against Yale with a beauty from the 50-yard line. Although constantly rushed by the big Blue linemen, he averaged close to 50 yards a punt. He could kick both a spiral and an end-over-end ball, depending upon which type the opponent found most difficult to handle. His weakness here was that, occasionally, he forgot his own strength and outkicked his ends even though he kicked a high ball and had a fast pair of ends going downfield for him.

The great guards of the season, along with DeWitt, were Yale's Ned Glass and Cornell's Bill Warner, younger brother of the celebrated Pop. DeWitt won a "newspaper decision" over Warner but met more than his match in the rawboned Yale giant. Glass gave DeWitt a hectic afternoon, but when the supreme moment was at hand he could not budge the Princetonian. Yale won, 12–5, on two long runs. Otherwise the Elis had but one scoring opportunity. With a first down on the 2-yard line, they hurled three plays behind Glass, but each time DeWitt beat his rival to the charge and piled up the play. Princeton took the ball, and DeWitt kicked it out of danger. Big John might not have been the best guard in the country, but in a crisis there was none better. Glass and DeWitt were Camp's All-America selectees, and the famous expert judiciously remarked that, without other duties, DeWitt would be "a formidable player."

The next year (1903) DeWitt was captain; despite that added burden, his line work "improved very much," according to Camp. Certainly there was no deterioration in his running and kicking. In a fierce struggle with Georgetown, he plunged to the only score of the game. He scored by means of a dropkick against Brown, and kicked a pair against Cornell. Against Dartmouth's formidable team, he ran 70 yards. The Big Green, which later defeated Harvard, outplayed Princeton that day and would probably have won had it not been for the individual brilliance of DeWitt and the Tiger ends. Against Lafayette, John plunged to a touchdown and drop-kicked a 40-yard field goal. Princeton won all those games, and in addition defeated Carlisle, Lehigh, Bucknell, Swarthmore, and Gettysburg. Going into the Yale game, the Tigers had not yielded a point, and it was for the Elis that De-Witt was saving the fireworks.

In those days the captain was still the boss. According to the recollections of Donald Grant Herring, then a freshman and later a star tackle, DeWitt dismissed Arthur "Doc" Hillebrand and the assistant coaches a week before the big game. He thanked them for all they had done in helping to develop the team and said it was now up to him to get the players in the proper frame of mind. It didn't help when Walter Foulke, a strong halfback, was injured to the extent that he would be unable to play. Princeton, with a team composed of five seniors, two juniors, and four freshmen, would be called upon to face Yale's veterans, six of whom were, or would be, first-team All-Americans and four second-team choices. Yale had by far the stronger material and was a two-to-one favorite, but DeWitt had succeeded in arousing his team to a high emotional pitch.

Yale was the first to score and seemed on the way to another touchdown, but the Tigers held. Ralph Davis blocked a drop-kick, and DeWitt picked up the bouncing ball and ran over half the length of the field to a touchdown. Joe Vetterlein, the clever freshman quarterback, usually kicked the conversions, but in that tense situation the captain himself took over. The kick was good, and the score was tied at 6–6. DeWitt's punts (one of 70 yards) and runs from kick formation forced the Elis back. With the game almost over, Yale had to punt. With the ball on the 43-yard line, at a difficult angle and with a tricky crosswind blowing, John decided to try a field goal. So powerful was the kick that it was estimated it would have been good at 75 yards! Princeton was ahead, 11–6, and after a few more plays the game was over.

John DeWitt's team had accomplished its mission. It was the champion. Every selector of All-America or All-Eastern teams listed the big captain. Camp called him the hero of the year. Camp also honored Howard Henry, end, and J. Dana Kafer, halfback, on his All-America team. Other critics gave first-team nominations to Ralph Davis, end, who had been Camp's first-team choice in 1901 and Princeton's captain in 1902; Harold Short, center; Jim Cooney, the big freshman tackle; Joe Vetterlein and the injured Walter Foulke. Davis and Sumner Rulon-Miller, freshman fullback, were on Camp's second team.

DeWitt's fame was not confined to the football field. For four years he was the Intercollegiate champion hammer-thrower. He broke the association record in 1902. Alfred Plaw of California, the first to use three turns in the ring, held the All-America College record, but in time DeWitt topped it by heaving the iron ball 166 feet 5 inches, a record that would stand for six years. During the summer of 1904, following his graduation, he kept in training, and at the Olympic Games at St. Louis he placed second to his countryman, John Flanagan, holder of the world record. DeWitt also won the shot put at most of the college dual meets, but here, again, he could not beat Edgar Glass. The discus throw was not yet on the collegiate programs, which was unfortunate because, while at Lawrenceville, DeWitt made the second-best throw in the nation.

DeWitt's strength and poise also came in handy off the athletic field. Jack's, a night spot and rendezvous for monied college men who chanced to be in New York, was famous for its bouncer, whose specialty was ejecting young college gentlemen who were "going large" a bit. Such a performance was a feature of any night. The boys bet on the length of time it would take, particularly if the victim was a noted athlete such as Tom Shevlin. One night DeWitt and his friends were at Jack's. He was behaving himself, but the bouncer, probably egged on by the betting crowd, tackled him. DeWitt unceremoniously threw him out the front door into the gutter. Nothing like that had ever happened before. The magnitude of the feat impressed even the Yale men, and DeWitt became the hero of intercollgiate café society.

Following his graduation, DeWitt was anxious to get on with his business. He assisted with the coaching at Princeton to some extent during 1904, but after that he turned his full attention to his work and eventually gained the reputation of being a keen businessman. He became president of the National Bag Company in New York and was director of several manufacturing corporations. On July 28, 1930, he left his home in Fairfield, Connecticut, for New York to visit a heart specialist under whose care he had been for some time. As the train was pulling into the Grand Central Terminal, he suffered a fatal attack.

HAMILTON FISH

(6:04; 200)

The Fish family came to America about 1637. Nicholas Fish was a lawyer, soldier, and politician. During the Revolution he fought at Saratoga, Monmouth, Yorktown, and in other battles and became a lieutenant colonel. He brought the "Ham" into the family by naming his son after his good friend Alexander Hamilton. The first Hamilton Fish had a distinguished career. He served in public office for over thirty years, as a member of Congress, as lieutenant governor and then governor of the State of New York, as a United States senator and, for eight years, as President Grant's Secretary of State. His son, also Hamilton, after serving as speaker of the New York Assembly and Assistant Treasurer of the United States, was elected to Congress. On December 7, 1888, at Garrison, New York, he became the father of "Ham," the hero of this sketch.

Our "Ham" was a man of parts, as Joseph Addison might have described him, but some of the parts did not mesh to form a homogeneous pattern. Smart, energetic, and ambitious, he entered Harvard, from St. Mark's School, in the fall of 1906 when he was only seventeen years of age. Not only did he excel on the gridiron; he was also *cum laude* for three years. Coming from such a prominent family with wealth and prestige that accumulated through the years, and meeting success at every turn, a youngster would have to be extremely level-headed not to become affected. Even in football, a member of his family had distinguished himself. His father's brother, Stuyvesant, had captained Columbia's first team in 1870. Ham was opinionated and lost no opportunity to express his views. In certain quarters he gained the reputation of being a haughty, condescending individual.

From a football standpoint, Ham's arrival at Cambridge did not seem to come at a propitious time. Harvard had not beaten Yale since Dave Campbell's team turned the trick in 1901. Hopes were high in 1906, but Yale won again. The tall, slim, youthful Fish played left tackle on the freshman team, that being the first year that freshmen were ineligible for varsity competition. They took a 28–10 beating from the Eli first-year men, which did not bode well for the Harvard future. As a sophomore in 1907, Fish moved to the varsity right-tackle position, where he was a regular during the balance of his college days. Harvard accounts class him as only "fair" that year, but already there were flashes of brilliance. The press reported that he played "a whirlwind game" against Williams, did "excellent work" downfield against Navy, and "showed to advantage" against Brown. But all was forgotten when, late in the season, Harvard was blasted by Carlisle and Dartmouth and received another trouncing from Yale—the sixth straight victory for the Blue, during which period proud Harvard had not registered a single point.

But that unhappy season proved to be the proverbial darkness that preceded the dawn. The new captain, twice All-America guard Francis "Hooks" Burr, secured the appointment of Percy Duncan Haughton as head coach for 1908. Haughton was a busy man, and Harvard had to reimburse him for time lost from business, thus making him the first professional coach in the storied "Big Three." Haughton wanted Lieutenant Ernest Graves, a former West Point player, as a line coach, but Secretary of War William Howard Taft, Yale, '78, frowned on the suggestion. Undismayed, Haughton carried the matter to the President, Theodore Roosevelt, Harvard, '80. The latter approved the request with a note to the Secretary that stated, "I was a Harvard man before I was a politician."

Getting Graves to Cambridge was a clever move, and under his coaching Fish improved immeasurably. His aggressive defensive play featured every game. He gained the reputation of being an unorthodox player because, as a shrewd play diagnostician, he was permitted to rove from his position in the line. It was almost impossible to fool him. On straight smashes he invariably was there to turn back the play. On offense, despite his size, he crouched very low, and with the snap of the ball sprang forward as though jet-propelled. In 1908 Howard Leslie's touchdown in a 6–0 victory over Dartmouth was made through a hole opened by him. In the push-and-pull style still authorized, Ham dragged and shoved the ballcarrier most effectively. On occasion he ran with the ball (gains of five and ten yards against Yale in 1908), and his blocking was excellent.

In the open he was always conspicuous. He frequently beat the ends downfield under punts and he was a sure tackler. The only game Harvard did not win in 1908 was against Navy. The Midshipmen had scored early. At midfield one of them bored into the line. Joe Nourse, Harvard center, stole the ball and started for the goal line with a Navy man in pursuit. Seemingly from nowhere, Fish came up and blocked the Middie so hard that the latter turned a couple of somersaults. Nourse's touchdown enabled Harvard to even the count at 6–6. In the following year Fish performed a somewhat similar stunt against Brown.

Haughton worked out a play that made Fish eligible to receive a forward pass. It developed from kick formation. The man in kicking position ran to the right after receiving the ball. Fish drifted farther to the right so that the ball would cross the line of scrimmage at least five yards from where it had been put in play in order to comply with the prevailing rules. The big fellow set himself firmly before jumping for the ball because, in those days, a receiver could be pushed or knocked down. Ham was not bothered very often, but Walter Camp recalled with amusement a time when he was bowled over. Sitting on his broad posterior, Ham stretched his long arms heavenward and hauled down the ball. In 1910 Camp maintained that Fish was the best receiver of the forward pass yet to play.

In practically every game, Fish's proficiency with the thrown ball helped his team at some critical time. In 1907 he caught a pass from Hooks Burr to set up the touchdown in the 6–5 victory over Brown. In 1908 his catches highlighted victories over Carlisle and Dartmouth, and in the following year, against Army, he caught three passes, a feat remarkable for that time. Such a phenomenal performance made him the most feared man on the team, and future opponents devised special defenses to stop him. In a game with Cornell (in 1909) he made a beautiful catch, but because it was behind the Cornell goal line it was not allowed, for in that year a passed ball crossing the goal line, on the fly, resulted in a touchback.

That Army game of 1909 ended on a tragic note. Alix Byrne, Cadet tackle, met his death trying to stem Harvard's power smashes. As a result "push-and-pull" football was abolished in the following year. As captain of the Harvard team, Fish attended Byrne's funeral, and he took steps, through his family, to secure an appointment to West Point for Byrne's younger brother.

Fish was a natural-born leader, dominating and aggressive. When Burr was injured in 1908, Ham was appointed acting captain even though he was only a junior, and a young one at that. Fish led Harvard to a historic victory over Yale. Harvard's most consistent gains were through holes opened by Fish. When Yale overshifted by playing both tackles against him, Harvard sent Ernest Ver Wiebe, usually a blocking back, for repeated gains through the weakened side. Harvard marched fifty-five yards before the Elis were able to stop them. From the 23-yard line, Vic Kennard, a left-footed kicker, drop-kicked a field goal. The 4–0 victory gave unbeaten Harvard the best claim to the national championship. When Secretary Taft learned the result of the game, he is reported to have said, "Oh, pshaw!" President Roosevelt canceled an appointment in order to get the results at the White House. What he said has not been recorded; probably it was "Bully!"

Fish and Nourse were on Walter Camp's All-America team, with Ver Wiebe and John Cutler, the quarterback, on the second team and Sam Hoar, a guard, on the third. Although he had missed the big game, Hooks Burr was named on several honor teams, and the backs Ham Corbett and Bob White were also highly praised.

As was to be expected, Fish was elected captain for 1909. As that season progressed it seemed like a replay of the previous one. Harvard and Yale, adhering to power football, whipped all rivals. Each had won all its games when they faced each other in what was called "the Battle of the Giants." Harvard outgained Yale, 207 yards to 88, but penalties, Ted Coy's kicking, and Yale's close-in defense prevented a Harvard score. Two field goals and a safety gave the Elis the game, 8–0. The value of a field goal had been reduced to three points that year.

Harvard had a new quarterback, and some of the experts were of the opinion that Fish militated against his team's chances by interferring too much with the youngster in calling signals. But even his most severe critics had to admit that he played a wonderful game in the line. In the two games under his leadership, the Harvard forwards had prevented the great Ted Coy, Steve Philbin, and the other Yale backs from scoring a touchdown. Fish was again All-American, and so was Wayland "Dono" Minot, the plunging fullback. Paul Withington, center, and Bob McKay, tackle, were on Camp's second team, and Lothrop Withington and Bob Fisher, guards, and Ham Corbett, halfback, on the third. McKay and Fisher were first-team men the next season.

Fish loved the game. Following his graduation he wrote feature football articles for the *New York World* and occasionally crossed the Hudson from his home in Garrison to assist his old coach, Pot Graves, with the West Point tackles. He organized and played with all-star teams that played for charity. In 1914 Carlisle was beaten, 13–6, at Boston, and the next year the All-Stars lost to Rutgers, 28–7, at the Polo Grounds, New York. After the armistice that ended World War I, he was appointed captain and coach of the 4th Division team in the Army of Occupation of Germany. It reached the Third Army finals, where it was eliminated by the ultimate A.E.F. champion, the 89th Division, by a score of 14–0. The latter team was coached by Ham's former teammate, Paul Withington.

During the war, Fish had commanded a company of the 369th Infantry, 93rd Division, composed of Negroes. It engaged in the Champagne offensive as part of the French IX Corps, and suffered heavy casualties. The French Government decorated Fish with the Croix de Guerre for valor at the capture of the village of Séchault. Later he was transferred to the General Staff of the 4th Division and promoted to the grade of major. After the armistice he helped organize the American Legion.

Fish entered into the general insurance business and became vice president of John C. Paige and Company in New York. He served in the New York Assembly from 1914 to 1916 and, as representative of the 26th New York District, in the Congress of the United States from 1919 to 1945. He will go down in history as one of the first figures of national prominence to speak out on the danger of Communism. Now past seventy, he is still very active in matters pertaining to football and in patriotic organizations such as the American Legion and the Order of Lafayette.

EDWARD JOSEPH HART

(5:11; 210)

While playing at Exeter, Eddie Hart sustained a total fracture of one of the wings or flanges of a vertebra in his neck by plunging into one of the goalposts, which at that time were set on the goal line. But he was so heavily muscled as to be almost a freak, and was able to continue his gridiron career without interruption. In fact, it is not definitely known whether he received the injury in a game with the Yale Freshmen in 1905 or against Andover in 1907. He played out his freshman year at Princeton in the fall of 1908. In the following winter he experienced difficulty in putting the shot; a "click" was heard when he turned his head in a certain way. It was not until then that the extent of his injury was discovered. X-ray pictures revealed that the fractured vertebra had never healed. Doctors pronounced him fit to continue playing provided he wore a specially constructed steel and leather headguard and harness designed to take all strain off his neck. It weighed about fifteen pounds. Subsequently he was able to discard it. During his three varsity years he played sixty minutes in every game that he started.

Eddie was born in New York City on May 22, 1887, of Irish parents of humble circumstances. They raised him well. He was straightforward and honest. A mutual friend told me that he thought Eddie never told a lie in all his life. A decent boy with a minimum of ego, but ambitious and persevering, his genuine friendliness made him popular everywhere, and few were jealous of his success. His parents moved to Exeter, New Hampshire, and he attended Phillips Exeter Academy in that town as a day boy. From there he went to Princeton.

Hart had quick reflexes and amazing speed for a heavy man. He could beat most of the backs and ends off the mark and stay ahead of them for ten or fifteen yards. Although not a good student, his mind worked fast in an emergency, as on the football field, but it was his abnormal strength that attracted the most attention. Sportswriters hazarded the opinion that he might well be the strongest man in America, if not in the world. Stories of his feats of strength have become legendary at Princeton.

While walking along the street, he heard someone shout, "Catch me, Eddie!" and he looked up as a man leaped from a second-story window. The man supposedly weighed 195 pounds, but Eddie caught him. After a discussion with three other football men, each an All-American, he stood on one foot while the three, attacking in unison, tried in vain to bowl him over or force him to put down the other foot. A few years after graduation, he attended practice at Princeton in street clothes and shoes. To settle a question concerning the use of hands, he was pressed into service. For over an hour he held off Gru Ballin, twice All-America tackle, and Bev Lonstreth, another established veteran. They worked together, but neither could gain contact with his body. After the war, at the Cirque de Paris, a European strong man offered a purse to anyone who could stay a minute with him. Before a crowd of 40,000, many of whom were jubilant American G.I.'s, Eddie pinned the strong man's shoulders to the mat. At one time he kept in condition by working out at the Chicago Athletic Club where Jack Curley brought his wrestlers to train. After he worked with the wrestlers for a while, he was urged to turn professional, but he was not interested.

Hart made the Tiger team at fullback in his sophmore year, 1909. Navy was defeated, 5–3, through a touchdown plunge by Eddie, but the team did not win any of the other important games, and as a result he received few All-America honors. Camp placed the captain, the 223-pound tackle R. C. Siegling, on his third team, and the *Brooklyn Daily Eagle* experts liked Eddie's playing well enough to give him a place on their first team. He was a strong line plunger, but it was probably his linebacking that stood out most prominently. At the end of the season, Eddie, a sophomore, was signally honored by being chosen captain for the next year.

Bill Roper was secured as head coach for 1910, and conditions began improving. There had always been agitation among the coaches to put Hart at tackle. After Princeton squeezed by Lafayette, 3–0, Eddie went to left tackle. There he played in victories over Carlisle and Dartmouth. His defensive work in both games was headlined. Against Dartmouth, Tol Pendleton, the Princeton speedster, caught a punt and ran 85 yards to the winning touchdown after Hart had given him his start by blocking out two Dartmouth men. Princeton had shown little offensive strength in those games, and Hart was moved to fullback for the Yale game. Princeton was the favorite, but the Elis sprang the "Minnesota shift," brought east by Tom Shevlin, and won, 5–3. Pendleton made Camp's All-America team, while two of the newspapers placed Hart at fullback and two at tackle on their honor teams.

One wonders what thoughts were in Eddie's mind when he accepted reelection as captain. During his three years at Exeter, Andover had triumphed each year. In his freshman year the Yale cubs had won, and now, after his two seasons on the big team, Yale had two more victories to her credit. It seemed as though Fate had decreed that he play on beaten teams.

The 1911 season did not get off to a good start. Hart injured a leg and missed early games in one of which Lehigh held the Tigers to a 6–6 draw. He was supposed to sit out the game with Navy, but when the situation looked dark he went in, and Princeton managed to escape with another tie, 0–0. Ahead loomed Harvard, on the schedule for the first time since 1896, a strong Dartmouth team, and the nemesis, Yale. Somewhere along the way, Hart took complete charge. The fiery Bill Roper was still head coach, but it became apparent that Eddie was in command. Grantland Rice was to call him "the last captain that ran his own team."

Harvard had another superbly coached Haughton team that went to Princeton "expecting to tear the Tiger line to shreds." Apparently Haughton reasoned that if Hart could be liquidated, the team would fall of its own weight. Time after time, Percy Wendell and the other strong-running Cantab backs piled into Eddie, but the Tiger line held firm. Late in the second quarter, redheaded Joe Duff blocked a Harvard dropkick. Sanford "Sam" White grabbed the loose ball and ran 85 yards to a touchdown, after which Pendleton kicked the point. Later, White, in covering a punt, tackled a Harvard man on the five-yard line. Then Hart, who went downfield almost as fast as the ends, roared up, and the whole mass toppled over the goal line for a safety. The final count was 8–6, Harvard having scored late in the game after a long forward pass had put the ball on the two-yard line—the only time the Tiger line yielded all afternoon. After the game, Hart was dubbed "Hercules" by sportswriters.

The week after the victory over the Crimson, the line contained Dartmouth's attack, but the game would have resulted in another stalemate but for a freak goal. Wallace DeWitt dropkicked from the 45-yard line. The ball hit someone in the line, rolled along the ground, struck something, and bounced freakishly over the bar to give Princeton a 3–0 victory and cause the rules to be changed. Now only Yale stood between Princeton and the championship—only Yale!

The previous year, Rufus Stanley Woodward, father of the present day well-known sportswriter of the same name, wrote that "Harvard courage oozes when they see Blue stockings." He probably felt the same about Princeton. Since the American colleges adopted Rugby in 1876, down to and including 1910, Yale had been beaten by Princeton only eight times and by Harvard four, and several of the beaten teams were substantial favorites when they opposed the Blue. It was not that the courage of the Johnnys or Tigers oozed. They wanted to win badly enough, and fought to the limit of their ability. The reason was largely psychological. To offset the prestige that Yale enjoyed in those days, it was necessary for a team to play well over its head in order to win. It took a captain of supreme personality, courage, and spirit to whip his team into the winning frame of mind. The last such paragon at Princeton had been John DeWitt in 1903. Now Hart grimly determined that his would be another winning team.

The game with Yale was played on a field deep in mud and slime. There were no forward passes or onside kicks, it was fierce, savage, old-fashioned he-man football, reputedly the hardest-fought contest Yale and Princeton had yet played. At one stage Joe Duff hobbled up to Hart and said he couldn't stand on his left leg. "Play on your right leg," Eddie growled back. Duff played the game of his life, and the same flaming spirit carried him to a hero's death in World War I. Hart absorbed an enormous amount of punishment, but he also dished it out. Several Yale tackles opposed him before the day was done. With such an example, the Tiger linemen played dedicated football. It was an application of the old infantry slogan "Follow me!"

The break came early when a pass from center eluded the Yale fullback. Again it was Sam White to the rescue! He sloshed sixty yards through the muck to a touchdown, and when the game ended Princeton was ahead 6–3. "We had to win," said one of the Princeton players, "We were more afraid of Eddie than we were of Yale!" Bruised and battered, Hart played, according to the *New York Times,* "as great a game as has ever been seen on Yale Field."

For a few days the critics argued whether it was luck or fight that enabled the Tigers to defeat three of the most powerful teams in the nation on successive weekends. They came to the conclusion that it was fight that had prevailed—the fight that Hart had inspired in his team. The Tigers carried the fight to their opponents and kept it there all afternoon, and when the breaks came they were prepared to take advantage of them. Hart, White, and Duff were practically unanimous All-America choices. All were on Camp's first team, but Arthur Bluethenthal, the center, who also picked up a large popular vote, made only Camp's second team. Hobey Baker, halfback, and Tom Wilson, guard and later mayor of Binghamton, New York, secured votes from other critics.

Hart had the Celtic temperament of being emotional, uninhibited, and loyal to his friends. A few years after his playing days were over, he and Heff Herring attended a game at Princeton. Eddie spotted one of his players, a little substitute quarterback named Thornton Emmons. He reached over, plucked the man out of his seat, and kissed him on the cheek. The crowd laughed, but sobered when Hart said to Heff, "That's what I think of the fellows on my team," and he added, "That little guy had guts." They all had to have guts to be on Eddie's team.

After being graduated, Hart worked for the Booth Fisheries. He was sent to Alaska to learn the business, and was then given an executive position in the Chicago office. At the outbreak of World War I, he was the second man in Chicago to enlist. He joined the U.S. Marines and rose from private to captain. He served chiefly at Bordeaux, France, in charge of railroad facilities under the direction of General Charles Dawes, but he took time off to coach the Saint-Nazaire Marine football team, which lost only to the 89th Division, the champions of the A.E.F. Following the war, he was in real estate and the insurance business in New York and was reputed to be one of the few men to write policies in the million-dollar class. As a hobby, he raised dogs. He was back in Marine green in World War II, and served as athletic officer for the First Amphibious Corps in the Pacific. When he was inactivated in January, 1946, he was a lieutenant colonel. After his retirement from business, he made his home in Toronto, Ontario, where he died on November 28, 1956.

D(AVID) BELFORD WEST

(6:02; 194)

George Trevor, the most lyric of all sportswriters, past or present, wrote a long time ago, "Fair Chenango's sun-kissed valley is famous for its sweet apples and sweeter football players." The sweetest of them all was Belf West, son of Banker William W. West. Belf was born on May 7, 1896, and raised in Hamilton, a small community in upstate New York that centers upon Colgate University. His father was treasurer of the university from 1896 to 1910. Belf attended Colgate Academy until that famous old school closed its doors at the end of the 1912 term. He remained a year at Phillips Andover, long enough to help win the traditional football game with Exeter, and finished his preparatory work at Peddie Institute in Hightstown, New Jersey. He entered Colgate in the fall of 1914.

Larry Bankart, former Dartmouth All-America end, who had coached Colgate in 1910 and returned in 1913 to mold a great team, was pleased to see the rangy Andover veteran. Freshmen were then permitted to play at Colgate, and West was installed at right halfback on the big team. Although 1914 was supposed to be a rebuilding year, the team in its second game defeated Cornell 7–3. The Big Red, studded with future All-Americans, was just one year short of being the national champion. Colgate's touchdown came when West threw a pass to C. E. Stewart. With West backing up the line, Colgate four times stopped Cornell within the 25-yard line. The team failed against Army and Yale but rallied at the end of the season to tie Syracuse, even though outweighed eighteen pounds per man.

Bankart's system was built around the tackles. Both on offense and defense they were the key men. They had to be good—and always were! He gave them first priority. In 1915 Joe Brooks, the famous left tackle, had been graduated. The best man to replace him was West, so Belf found himself in the line, paired with Earl

Abell, the captain. He learned fast, but Abell received the most publicity that year and was Camp's choice for All-American. That Colgate team looked powerful as it beat Army for the first time in Colgate's history. Yale, which had been defeated by the 1913 team, was again conquered. A century score, 107–0, was accumulated against Rensselaer Poly. Unbeaten and unscored upon, Colgate was overconfident and complacent when they faced another gigantic Syracuse outfit. The Saltine warriors, sparked by Chick Meehan could do no wrong that day; they started rolling and nothing could stop them. Colgate was overwhelmed, 38–0.

West was kept at tackle in 1916. His partner was Clarence "Steamer" Horning, the team captain who had been moved into the vacancy created by Abell's graduation.

Under Bankart's careful tutoring West developed into a great tackle, "a polished stylist," as he was called. Both Walter Camp and George Trevor pronounced him ideally built for a tackle—of that period, at least. Larry Bankart recently expressed the opinion that he would have made an excellent corner-post linebacker with a present-day pro team. He was a quick starter with a terrific charge and fine speed downfield; he ranged laterally as far as any tackle ever has done; he had rare intuition, was an unerring tackler, could use his hands most effectively, and was courageous under pressure. In addition, he was a long-range punter, place-kicker, and passer. In the days when the ball went to the opposition where it was thrown out of bounds, instead of kicking, he would pass sixty or seventy yards and over the sideline—frequently down in the "coffin corner."

Colgate startled the football world when it defeated Illinois, champion of the Western Conference for two straight years, 15–3. Busy otherwise as he was, West found time to kick two field goals to help the scoring. Yale proved a stumbling block, winning 7–3. Colgate outplayed the home team most of the game, but was frequently stopped by penalties; the only score was the result of a place kick by West. Against the Syracuse giants, practically the same array that had humiliated them the year before, the outweighed Colgate boys ground out a 15–0 victory. In that game, in rain and mud, West booted his famous 52-yard place-kick. He also kicked another field goal against the Orange to bring his season total to seven—the two not previously mentioned were against Springfield. Colgate played through the Syracuse game without a substitution. Those "Little Giants," as they were now being called, were iron men, ten having played the full game against both Illinois and Yale.

The last game of the season was against Brown, on Thanksgiving Day, at Providence. In Fritz Pollard the Bruins had the fastest and most elusive halfback of the year. He had run wild against both Yale and Harvard. Unbeaten and untied Brown was already looked upon as the logical recipient of the national championship. No student of football had any doubts concerning the outcome of the game with Colgate. On a muddy field, the New Yorkers played an inspired game. The tackles clinched their All-America rating. They flawlessly executed the cross-checking by which Colgate gained so much ground over tackle, and they were largely instrumental in holding Pollard down. Colgate scored four touchdowns, and but for the phenomenal defensive work of Pollard, the score would have been larger. West figured prominently in every score. Oc Anderson slipped through a hole West opened for the first touchdown, which climaxed a 60-yard march. The second came after Horning had blocked a kick and West recovered the ball on the 26-yard line. Gains behind him set up the third touchdown, and the fourth he made by himself. He picked up a fumbled ball and raced 28 yards to pay dirt. Though the ball was wet and heavy, he kicked all four points after touchdown to bring the score to 28–0.

As a result of the downfall of Brown, Pittsburgh was favored for the national title. Colgate, "the last word in football efficiency," was rated second, third, or fourth by various critics. In addition to West and Horning, Walter Camp placed Oscar Anderson, the quarterback, on his All-America team, thus making Colgate the only college to place three men. Camp claimed that West

FOOTBALL IMMORTALS

FRANK HINKEY: "He had the combative instincts of a leopard. . . . A murderous glare appeared in his eyes. . . . Even his own teammates feared him. . . ."

Courtesy of University of Michigan

GERMANY SCHULZ: Big, strong, and full of energy, he never wore out.

Courtesy of University of Michigan

WILLIE HESTON: "Heston's name never dies."

Courtesy of T. T. Hare

T. TRUXTON HARE: He was "a heroic figure."

JIM THORPE: In later years talking to Pop Warner (left), the coach who helped guide him at Carlisle. Below, as an undergraduate, young Thorpe poses formally. Below right, as an outfielder for the New York Giants.

"No feats on the athletic field seemed beyond his powers."

Fats Henry (*below*): "He looked like blubber, but it was all muscle."

Brick Muller (*center*): "Enormous hands, speed and power."

George Gipp (*right*): "Win one for the Gipper."

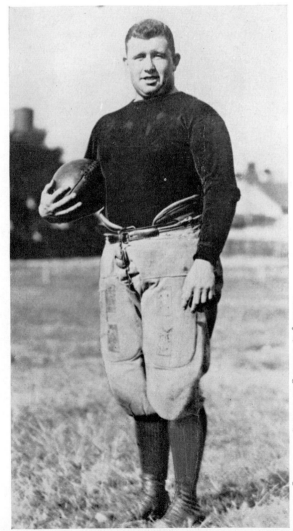

HAROLD "Red" GRANGE: "The greatest broken-field runner in history." The famed "Galloping Ghost" was also known as the "Wheaton Iceman." *Right*, Number 77 leaves the field after his last game as a college player.

BRONKO NAGURSKI: He confused the selectors. A great tackle, Big Nag was also a great fullback. *Right,* as a Chicago Bear he's set to plunge into the New York Giant line.

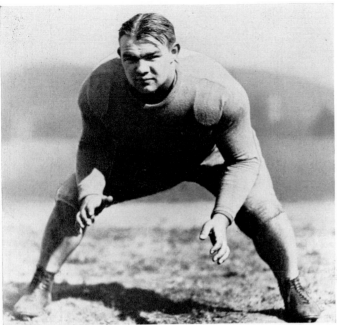

HERMAN HICKMAN: He had brains and brawn and plenty of both.

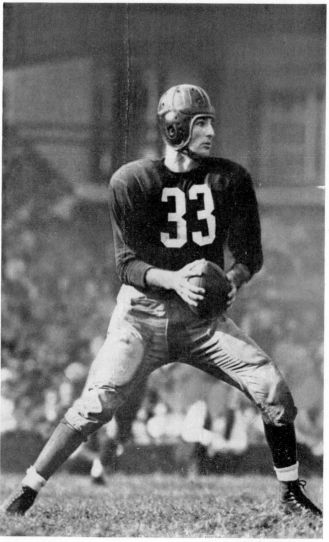

SAMMY BAUGH: Slingin' Sammy was a Washington Redskin for sixteen years.

CAL HUBBARD (*right, above*): Later he became a Major League baseball umpire.

DON HUTSON (*right, below*): As a Green Bay Packer, he set a pass-catching standard.

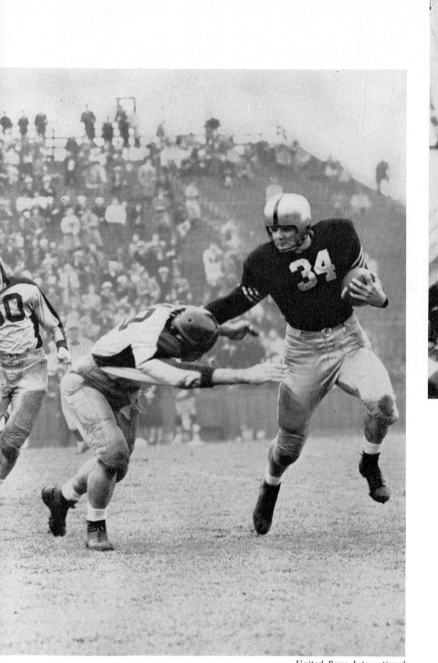

GLENN DAVIS (*left*): West Point's Mr. Outside shows his broken-field style to a Columbia tackler.

DOC BLANCHARD (*above*): Mr. Inside was the perfect complement to Davis. Here Blanchard hits the middle of the Penn line.

outclassed all tackles of the year. All-Eastern selections included
Mike Good and Biff Barton, guards, and Chuck Hubbell, halfback.

West was elected captain for 1917, but when the war came he
left college to join up. At Camp Dix, New Jersey, in 1917, when
the army was flexing its muscles, he played with the 307th Field
Artillery, which tied the 311th Infantry for the camp championship. Curiously, his quarterback was Anderson, while the dough-
boys were led by Ellery Huntington, Colgate's All-America
quarterback in 1913. Naturally, West made the camp team that
defeated Percy Haughton's team at Camp Devens, 19–0. Walter
Camp for *Collier's* and Paul Purman for Newspaper Enterprise
Association picked All-America Service teams. Each named West
to his first team. Anderson was Purman's choice for quarterback,
but Camp found still another Colgate star to pilot his mythical
team, R. A. Watkins of Mineola Air Field, who had played halfback on the 1916 Colgate team.

The 78th Division, to which West's regiment belonged, was in
the front lines in France a total of thirty-eight days, and participated in both the Saint-Mihiel and Meuse-Argonne offensives. It
advanced about 13 miles, captured 432 prisoners, and suffered
7,245 casualties. After over a year and a half in military service,
Belf West was discharged as a first lieutenant. In the fall of 1919,
he again appeared on the Colgate campus, along with nine other
veterans of the 1916 team who had returned to earn a degree and
play more football. West was chosen captain. He had injured a
knee, and by now was playing with a steel brace. Undoubtedly
that affected his kicking, because he began missing attempted
field goals, but for short kicks such as conversions, he was still
deadly and, during the season, made good on all thirteen tries.

Colgate began with victories over Susquehanna, Brown, Cornell, and Princeton. When they met Dartmouth, critics felt that
this game would decide the championship. The Big Green, like
Colgate, was well stocked with hard-bitten war veterans—tough
linemen such as "Swede" Youngstrom, Gus Sonnenberg, who became a professional wrestling champion, "Cuddy" Murphy, and

Bill Cunningham, who became a noted newspaper man. Dartmouth had downed Penn State and Cornell, among others, and was unbeaten. In the memorable meeting, West was just about everywhere; he opened a hole for Hank Gillo to score and he kicked the conversion. Time and again he stopped Dartmouth plays behind the line, and he frequently beat his ends going down under kicks. Colgate seemed to have the game in the bag with a minute remaining. The Maroon attempted to punt with the kicker too close to the line. Youngstrom, bloody and muddy, burst through, blocked the kick, and took the ball over for a touchdown. When the conversion was made, the score was tied 7–7. It now appeared as though championship honors would have to be shared.

Colgate defeated Rochester while Dartmouth downed Pennsylvania, but on the same fateful Saturday afternoon both "big fellows" were beaten. Syracuse downed Colgate 13–7, while underrated Brown squeezed by Dartmouth 7–6. Ranking the teams was a problem. The *New York Times* solved it by bracketing Penn State, Syracuse, Colgate, and Dartmouth for first place in the East. Camp again placed West on his All-America team with Gillo on the third team. Of the thirty-six All-America and All-Eastern teams published, West was on thirty-four.

West was an excellent all-around athlete. For several seasons he was Colgate's best pitcher, and he also played center on the basketball team. He excelled at tennis, track, ice hockey, and golf and was an ardent hunter and fisherman. After graduation he played professional football with the Canton Bulldogs in 1921 and then settled down to a business career. From 1927 to 1934 he served as manager of the Better Business Bureau in Buffalo. After a few years in the investment business, in 1937 he established and became a partner in the Smith-West Company of Buffalo, dealers in machinery and industrial equipment. The pressure of business does not prevent him from devoting time to civic affairs in Buffalo and alumni and athletic matters at Colgate. Recently he was elected to the University Board of Trustees, and he served as a member of the Colgate Athletic Council for several years. A kind man with a keen sense of humor, West is an outstanding citizen and family man. "One of the most remarkable characters I have ever known," said Everett D. Barnes, Director of Athletics at Colgate.

WILBUR FRANCIS HENRY

(5:10; 230 in college, 245 as a pro)

In the days before the pros began assembling beef on the hoof, when the popular concept of an athletic hero was a tall man with broad shoulders, slim flanks, and a flat stomach, the appearance of "Pete" or "Fats," as Henry was variously styled by his friends, aroused sportswriters to speculate whether by chance he was a throwback to the early Paleolithic Age. Henry was thickset, like a caveman, and he had the courage, cunning, and strength that enabled those hardy ancestors of ours to cope with the hairy mammoth and the giant cave bear with few weapons besides their hands. They are considered to have been brutal, a word that exactly describes the manner of Henry's charging, blocking, and tackling. But there the similarity ends. Pete was good-looking, with a cheerful round face; he held his head high, was very intelligent, a good student at college, and could hold his own in conversation; he was agile enough to be a basketball star, and as Grantland Rice said (and we don't insist that you believe it), he was as fleet "as a bounding deer." In a game he was never known to lose his temper or use profane language.

Henry, who was born on a farm outside Mansfield, Ohio, on October 31, 1897, had the distinction, because of war conditions, of playing on the Washington and Jefferson varsity for five seasons, and he was the first student to win major letters in four sports—football, baseball, basketball, and track. He entered

Washington and Jefferson College in the fall of 1915. The Presidents were about to complete a glorious regime under Bob Folwell. Pittsburgh had been humbled three times in a row, and during two seasons Washington and Jefferson lost but one game—by a point, to the champion Harvard team of 1914. Many of the men who had made that record possible had been graduated, among them "Brit" Patterson, greatest W.&J. tackle—up to that time. The seventeen-year old freshman from the Ohio farmlands stepped into his place.

Pete's running mate was Maurice Witherspoon, who also received some All-America recognition that year, as did Fritz Heyman, the demon pass catcher and "Scrubby" McCreight, a clever passer particularly adept at making the short over-center pass that W.&J. featured. Folwell built his 1915 team from fairly light and inexperienced material, but at that it lost only to Pittsburgh. Too much reliance had been placed on a passing attack, and Pop Warner had taught Bob Peck and the other Panthers how to break it up. Yale, Lafayette, and Lehigh were among the teams beaten. W.&J. joined Harvard, Princeton, and Army as the only schools to defeat Yale in successive years. The Presidents' line became famous after the Yale game when it held the Blue once on the five-yard line and again on the one-foot line. Obviously, the green country boy had not been found wanting.

For the next two seasons, Sol Metzger handled the football destinies of W.&J. and, under him, Henry matured and developed into a formidable tackle. Metzger's teams did not quite equal the record of those of the Folwell administration, but they were noted for their powerful lines. Henry, who bounded around like "a human rubber ball," to quote Rice again, was a conspicuous figure in every game, particularly in 1917 when Penn State was held to two first downs. In the same year he loomed large in a heroic goal-line stand against Pittsburgh, in a long march against West Virginia, and by blocking kicks against Washington and Lee. Already he was gaining recognition outside the state. Walter Camp gave him honorable mention in both 1916 and 1917, and

Frank Menke had him on his third All-America team in 1916 and on the first in 1917. Because of the war, Camp picked only an honorable mention list in 1917. Nine All-America teams appeared in the *Spalding Guide* that year, and Henry was on a majority of them.

R. F. Hutchinson coached during the war year 1918. Fats captained the team, which did not go very far in an abbreviated schedule. George Orton wrote that Henry "played magnificently all season." Walter Camp seized upon the occasion of the Armistice on November 11th to resume publishing his All-America selections. Possibly because of W.&J.'s indifferent record, Camp placed Henry on his second team with Jack Tressell, another good pass receiver, at end on the third. The only other selectors of All-America teams that year, Frank Menke and Robert W. "Tiny" Maxwell, both found a place for Henry on the first team.

David C. Morrow, former W.&J. star, took over the coaching reins in 1919, Fats' last appearance in college competition. It was to be a good year for W.&J. and a good one for Fats. Little was expected of the team, and the victory over Syracuse, 13–0, in the fourth game of the schedule was one of the big surprises of the season. The Orange, with a line buttressed by Joe Alexander, a Hall of Fame guard, and H. J. Robertson, one of the best centers of the year, was a two-to-one favorite. The work of Henry in that game was spectacular. Some of the quotes from the newspapers are expressive: "head and shoulders over the other forwards," "he was everywhere," "excellent tackling," "opened up big holes," "never let up a minute all afternoon," "marvelous at interfering in the open," "phenomenal endurance," "faultless diagnostician," "non-stoppable charge." He kicked off twice; each time the ball sailed 70 yards and over the Syracuse goal line. This was the sole reverse suffered by Syracuse during the regular season.

It was unfortunate that Henry or Edgar Garbisch did not do the goal kicking after touchdown, because the miss cost the Presidents the game with Pittsburgh, 6–7. West Virginia also nosed out W.&J., 7–0, in the Thanksgiving Day finale. In ranking

the teams of the East, Dan Daniel of the *New York Sun* placed
W.&J. fourth, following Syracuse, Penn State, and West Virginia.
Camp and the great majority of experts had Henry on their All-
America teams. Receiving honorable mention were Captain Elmer
Carroll, end, and Harry Erickson, former Great Lakes halfback,
whose running back of punts settled the Syracuse game. Russell
Stein, the other tackle, became an All-American in 1921, and
Edgar Garbisch, a guard, went to the Hall of Fame as a West
Point center.

Grantland Rice, in 1954, stated that Henry "probably never
had a superior at tackle play," and in 1943 Clark Shaughnessy
agreed with John Heisman's estimate that Henry was "the perfect tackle in every phase of the game." Gil Dobie thought he was
the greatest tackle he had ever seen, and marveled at his being
as active as a small man. Pop Warner, Big Bill Edwards, Wilmer
Crowell, and Chick Meehan were others who considered him
"tops." George Trevor quoted Camp as saying of Fats, "the
greatest tackle I ever saw in action," while Ed Garbisch calls his
old teammate "by far the greatest." One of his numerous assets
was blocking punts. Trevor thought he must have blocked more
than any other player in history. One of those resulted in a most
unusual play. Against Westminster, in 1919, he broke through
so fast that he actually took the ball off the toe of the kicker and
ran 36 yards to a touchdown.

Pete looked fat, but most of what appeared to be blubber
was hard muscle. He was a quick thinker, well coordinated, and
excelled in several sports. He was a member of the W.&J. basketball team that was champion of the western Pennsylvania and
West Virginia area in 1919. The following year, when he captained the quintet, he was named on a regional All-Star squad
selected by H. A. Stansbury, Director of Athletics at the University of West Virginia. Mr. Stansbury had Henry's teammate,
Elmer Carroll, on the first team. Henry's talents at baseball were
varied; he caught in 1917, played left field in 1919, and first base

in 1920. He also won his letter as a weight thrower on the track and field team when he was not playing baseball.

In 1920 Henry went into pro ranks with the Canton Bulldogs. During the decade he played, no All-Pro teams were selected, but his standing among his contemporaries is established by the fact that, in 1952, Roger Treat, after consultation with leading authorities, selected Henry as one of the tackles on an All-Time, All-Pro team, which he published in his encyclopedia. Pete still holds two league records. In 1923 one of his punts against Akron traveled 94 yards through the air. The year before, against Toledo, he had drop-kicked a field goal from the 50-yard line. That record has been equaled, but because of the shape of the ball now in use, it will probably never be broken. It seems strange that he was not more conspicuous as a kicker while in college.

Fats was in good company at Canton. Playing left end was Bob Higgins of Penn State, another 1919 All-American, while Albert G. Feeney of Notre Dame, later mayor of Indianapolis, was at center. In the backfield was a trio of fabulous Indians, Jim Thorpe, Joe Guyon, and Pete Calac, although Thorpe was slowing up perceptibly. On December 4, 1920, the Bulldogs played the Buffalo All-Americans at the Polo Grounds in the first real game of professional football ever played in New York. A gathering of 15,000 saw Buffalo block one of Old Jim's kicks for a touchdown, and win, 7–3. The *New York Times* singled out Henry above all linemen, and commented upon his "fancy playing." Canton won a return match at Buffalo, and a third game ended in a tie. Both teams, as well as Akron, claimed the professional championship.

With the National Football League in operation, Canton officially captured the title in 1922 and 1923. Those were great teams, coached by Guy Chamberlain, former Nebraska end. Another distinguished Cornhusker, Link Lyman, teamed with Henry at the tackle slots to form what may have been the greatest pair that ever played together. Neither of those teams was beaten.

In 1924 Cleveland bought the champion team, lock, stock, and barrel—but not Fats. He became involved in a salary dispute and joined the independent Pottsville Maroons in the Pennsylvania coal region. When Pottsville entered the league in 1925, Henry came to terms with Canton and was then sold to Akron. He wore the uniform of the New York Giants in 1926. For the next two years, he and his associates attempted to revitalize the Maroons. Pottsville was a red-hot football town, but it did not have a large enough population nor the ready access from outside to support a major professional football team. Fats and his companions worked hard. In 1928, with a fourteen-man squad, they played five important games in ten days. After that season, the team was forced to disband, and Fats retired. But he was lured back for one more season (1930) with the Stapletons of Staten Island.

In 1932 Pete accepted the post of Director of Athletics at W.&J., and he retained the position until his death on February 7, 1952, from complications arising from diabetes. During his long term in office, he frequently assisted with the football coaching and, in 1942, the year before W.&J. discontinued football for the duration of the war, he filled in as head coach. Henry was a friendly man who took his football fame in stride and was well liked by his associates.

BRONISLAW NAGURSKI

(6:04; 203 in college; 238 as a pro)

Here is an old chestnut, one of Dr. Clarence Spears' favorite after-dinner stories while he was coaching at Minnesota. He assumed his duties in the fall of 1925 and, according to his tale, the next summer he began combing the back country for husky farm boys to bolster his football squad. When he saw a likely-looking prospect working in the fields, he would stop to inquire the way to town. If the lad pointed with his hand, Doc drove on, but if he picked up the plow and pointed with it, Doc got out and discussed the advantages of a college education. Some say that is the way he corralled Nagurski. In fact, sometimes he said so himself. Nagurski came to the university in the following fall, 1926.

Bronko was a native of Canada, born on November 3, 1908, at Rainy River, Ontario, where his parents had settled after coming to America from the Polish Ukraine. When Bronko was little—he once was little—the family moved to International Falls, Minnesota, where Mr. Nagurski opened a grocery store and where the boy grew up and went to school. There he made a reputation as a fullback, and at Minnesota he played end, tackle, and fullback. Moving him from position to position did not disconcert his coach, because, as Doc Spears was to say, Big Nag could have been All-American at any position.

Bronk was a good-natured, undemonstrative, unassuming sort of fellow with a high-pitched voice something like Jack Dempsey's. Although he was ready with a smile and had a friendly manner, he was not at ease among strangers. On the playing field he concentrated on the task at hand, and rarely spoke. And he had a certain air of reserve that, backed by his amazing physique, discouraged people from taking liberties with him. It has been said that when he worked in the woods of northern Minnesota as a boy, mature lumberjacks stood somewhat in awe of him, and his friends and teammates at college or in the pro ranks never made him a party to horseplay or practical jokes. He was not unlike a smoldering volcano. People thought it advisable not to arouse him.

There will always be those to argue as to where, in the galaxy of football immortals, Nagurski belongs—among the tackles or with the fullbacks. There have been faster backs than Nagurski. If a man broke through quickly he could nail Nagurski, but if the lines locked long enough for him to take the few steps necessary to generate momentum, he was almost unstoppable. It was then that he "ran his own interference," as Steve Owen put it. His fake kick, jump-pass became famous, and he was fast enough to run the ends from kick formation. As a tackle, his devastating charge and use of hands, his smart and aggressive play, made him a standout. In the open he did not tackle; instead he threw a body block to smash the ballcarrier to earth.

In 1929, when Grantland Rice picked his All-America team, he thought Bronko better at tackle than at fullback, and George Trevor wrote, "He is an infinitely better lineman than he is a carrier." Clark Shaughnessy, Pudge Heffelfinger, and others have been of the same opinion. His coach, Dr. Spears, insisted that he was the greatest tackle that ever played, while Clarke Hinkle, who for several seasons was his greatest rival on the pro field, called him the greatest fullback of all time. And, in his final all-time selection, Rice moved him to fullback. You can take your pick. Bernie Bierman hailed him as "the greatest player of all time"; Steve Owen called him "the one and only"; and Dick Hanley, another noted coach, claimed that he never saw an individual who possessed so much all-around ability. Grantland Rice thought a team composed of eleven Nagurskis could have beaten eleven Thorpes or eleven Granges.

Probably more stories have been told about Nagurski than about any other football player excepting Jim Thorpe. Jim is dead and Bronko has been retired for almost a score of years, but the public never seems to tire of hearing of their incredulous exploits. Their fame increases with the years, and it is already becoming difficult to tell where fact ends and fancy takes over. Eventually we may see Bronko enshrined with that legendary hero of the north country, Paul Bunyan. Dr. L. H. Baker, a leading football authority, started one of the Nagurski fables when he stated that the *New York Sun,* in 1929, had picked Bronko on its All-America team as both a tackle and as a fullback. Now, a ten-man team that included Nagurski could undoubtedly defeat many full teams, but no one would be foolish enough to propose a ten-man All-America team. The *Sun* placed Nag at tackle, with Thomas "Tug" Parkinson of Pittsburgh at fullback.

On the freshman team and for the first three varsity games in 1927, Nag was at right end. The third game resulted in a 14–14 tie with Indiana. Bronko, who had caught several passes and performed well on defense, was benched by a charley horse. Minnesota had a strong line, but the left tackle, Al Maeder, was a little light for the sort of game played by the Gophers. When Nag was able to get around, Spears had him understudy Maeder. The game with Notre Dame started him on the road to fame. The powerful Irish were leading 7–0, and the game was almost over when, as Maeder's substitute, Bronko burst through the line, hit the runner so hard he dropped the ball, and Nag fell on it on the 15-yard line. From there the Gophers scored— touchdown and conversion—and the game ended 7–7. It was one of the few times that a team came from behind against Knute Rockne, and it marked the first time in twenty-two years that the Irish had not won on their home field. That game established Nagurski. He was the starting left tackle in the remaining games, but the draw with Indiana had cost Minnesota the conference championship, for Illinois had a perfect record. It is strange that even though Nagurski had played sensationally in the last few games, he did not receive even third-team All-Western honors. The most widely recognized of his teammates were Captain Herbert Joesting, fullback; Harold Hanson, guard; and Harold "Shorty" Almquist, halfback.

Joesting having been graduated, Spears placed Nagurski at fullback for the 1928 season. Bronko usually played that position, but occasionally he was shifted back to left tackle. His heavy line plunging was a source of wonder, but it was his defensive work that excited the most admiration. Sometimes he played forward as defensive tackle; sometimes he backed up the line. In one of the late-season games he injured his back and probably should not have been permitted to play in the finale against

Wisconsin. A special protective brace was made for him, and he went in and played the full sixty minutes. At the time of the game, Wisconsin was unbeaten and needed only a victory over Minnesota to gain the undisputed conference championship. The teams were very evenly matched; the difference proved to be Bronko. He recovered a fumble on Wisconsin's 17-yard line, and in six plunges carried the ball over for the only touchdown of the game. With time running out, he overhauled a Badger on the eight-yard line when the latter appeared to have a clear field, and just before the final whistle he intercepted a pass. Earlier in the season, the Gophers dropped games to Iowa and Northwestern, by one point each, and those reverses pushed them into third place in the conference. Again Nag was overlooked by the selectors of "all" teams. They preferred Captain George Gibson, guard; Kenneth Haycraft, end; and Fred Hovde, quarterback. The last named is president of Purdue University.

In his senior year (1929) Nagurski continued to alternate between tackle and fullback, and he distinguished himself in each position. The Gophers' two defeats kept them in third place. Dr. Spears developed several powerful teams, but they were not overburdened with luck. During 1928 and 1929 they lost four games by a grand total of five points—three through failure to convert after touchdown. Iowa and Michigan were the teams that halted the Gophers in 1929, and in both games Nagurski was a standout. He started at tackle against Iowa, but toward the end was moved into the backfield, and went 45 yards to a touchdown. His line smashing set up the touchdown against Michigan. He closed his college career brilliantly against Wisconsin. Twice he bulled his way across the Badger goal line, and, as in every game in which he participated, his defensive play was probably the outstanding feature of the game.

That year the burning question among the arbiters was not whether or not Nagurski belonged on an All-America team but at what position to place him. In the Associated Press poll, 65 voted for him as a tackle and 50 as a fullback. Rice, who placed him at tackle, rated him 100 percent in tackling, use of hands, and charging, and 90 percent in interfering and diagnosing. After Nagurski, the leading Gophers were Robert Tanner, end, and Arthur Pharmer, quarterback. Bronko played in the Shrine game at San Francisco on New Year's Day, 1930, and in 1945, when all-time Shrine teams were selected, he was placed at tackle on the All-East team.

In 1930 Nagurski wore the colors of the Chicago Bears. Red Grange, who also played with them, pointed out that Bronko's smashing power raised the team from ninth in the league in 1929 to third in 1930. It was again third the following year, when in a game with the Chicago Cardinals, Nag showed his speed by running 65 yards to a score. In 1932 the Bears clashed with Portsmouth for the title, and Nagurski passed to Grange in the end zone for the winning touchdown. The present system of play-offs between the champions of the two divisions was inaugurated in 1933. The Bears were opposed by the New York Giants, who had beaten them in an earlier game. In the play-off, Nagurski kept the Bears in the running, not only through his line smashing but also through his passing. On a fake buck he jump-passed to Bill Karr in the end zone. The most spectacular play, and the one that gave the Bears the game 23–21, occurred when he jump-passed to Bill Hewitt and Hewitt lateraled to Karr, who ran 25 yards to score.

The Bears boasted of a string of 18 consecutive victories when they again squared off against the Giants in the title play-off in 1934. The game was played on a frozen ice-covered field, which gave the Bears a slight advantage. After Bronko plunged to a touchdown, they led at half time, 10–3. At the suggestion of Ray Flaherty, Steve Owen, the Giants coach, borrowed a supply of sneakers from Manhattan College. They arrived during the intermission, and this made the difference in the second half. The Giants ran away from the slipping, sliding Bears, and won, 30–13. That was the famous "basketball-shoes game."

The following year Nagurski was slowed up considerably by

arthritis, and this was the only season he was not an All-League choice, either on the first or on the second team. His illness affected the Bears, and they did not have championship teams in 1935 or 1936. They came back to win the western crown in 1937, and lined up against the Washington Redskins in the play-off on another icy field. Both teams played in sneakers, but Sammy Baugh's passing more than offset Nagurski's line crashing, and the Redskins won, 28–21. After the season, Nagurski announced his retirement. He had won a place on the All-League team in 1932, 1933, and 1934 and gained second-team honors in 1931, 1936, and 1937. No team was selected for his first professional season, 1930.

Football did not provide his only source of income. During the winter of 1933–1934 he took up professional wrestling, and during his career in the ring won over three hundred matches with his football flying block. Upon his retirement from competitive sports, he purchased a 200-acre farm near International Falls. But he was not through with football yet.

In 1943, with the war on and manpower at a premium, the Bears prevailed upon Nagurski to rejoin the team after a layoff of six years. After his crops were harvested, the big farmer came to town. He played tackle and helped the Bears to another world championship. The Redskins were beaten in the play-off, 41–21, but the game the fans still tell about is the one with the Cardinals when Bronko took his old position behind the line and ground out 84 yards and a touchdown in 15 carries. In his nine years in professional football he gained 4,031 yards in 872 attempts. That is not the league record only because official figures were not kept in 1930 and 1931. The season of 1943 was his last in football. He has since devoted his attention to his large farm, and watched Bronko, Jr., grow up to play tackle at Notre Dame and later with the pros in his native Canada.

JOSEPH LEO STYDAHAR

(6:04; 215 in college; 230 as a pro)

Grant Rice sometimes quoted Thomas Gray's immortal lines to the effect that "full many a flower is born to blush unseen" when teased about omitting from his All-America selection some player who later won recognition as a great star. Something like that might have occurred to him when he named the All-Time team that appeared in his autobiography in 1954. Rice stated that his linemen were named because of their college play, and the sad truth is that, when he picked All-America college teams he did not give Stydahar so much as honorable mention.

West Virginia University is not a small or unknown institution whose stars would normally blush unseen, and "Jumbo Joe" could hardly have been mistaken for a shy violet. In other years, Mountaineer elevens had ranked among the best in the nation, but by the time Joe matriculated, material had run low. Greasy Neale, one of the best coaches, could give them but three victories against five defeats and three ties in 1933, Stydahar's first year on the team. Neale moved on to Yale, and Charles "Trusty" Tallman, a member of the state legislature and a former All-America end, who took his place, guided the team to a six-four record in 1934. But the next season (Stydahar's last) West Virginia was back in the slough with three victories, four defeats, and two draws. Under such circumstances selectors of All-America teams were not likely to turn their gaze in the direction of Morgantown. In later years West Virginia would produce other great teams and many fine linemen, but Joe Stydahar is still the finest.

Stydahar was born at Kaylor, Pennsylvania, on March 17, 1912, but he lived most of his early life in Shinnston, West Virginia, and always called that place his home. While still a freshman at the university (in 1932), he was listed as one of the leading players in the state. For the next three seasons he was varsity left tackle, and captain in his senior year. Among his specialties was blocking punts. This was one of the chief reasons West Virginia had a winning team in 1934. That year, at Forbes Field, Pittsburgh, he blocked one on Duquesne's 15-yard line, picked up the ball, and ran to a touchdown that enabled the Mountaineers to beat the Dukes 7–0, for the first time since 1931. His blocked kick set up a touchdown in the victory over Washington and Lee, and in a hard-fought game lost to Pop Warner's Temple Owls he threw his huge bulk in front of a kicked ball; Charley Goodwin, an end, grabbed it, and scored.

Joe was a big, likable fellow, but tough and aggressive. He was high-strung, and according to Steve Owen, would throw up at game time. The tension passed when he began bumping into people. His competitive spirit may be judged from the fact that when he was playing pro football against the Detroit Lions, he had four teeth knocked out and played thirty-five minutes with the exposed nerves causing him untold agony.

Though Stydahar missed All-America rating in college, his fine playing did not go unnoticed. In 1934 Andy Kerr, Pop Warner, and Eddie Casey, all celebrated coaches, picked him for their All-Eastern teams, and the next year Kerr and the *Football Annual* again so honored him, while the Associated Press and International News Service gave him a place on their second All-Eastern teams. Andy Kerr, coach of the East team in the Shrine game at San Francisco, invited him to play with his squad, which was composed of players from east of the Mississippi. "Name" players started the game. Stydahar got in for only seventeen minutes, but he was one of the few linemen cited for having "turned in a brilliant performance," as the East won, 19–3. Joe was also invited by Bernie Bierman to play with the College All-Stars against the professional champions, the Detroit Lions, in the fall of 1936. Again he went in as a substitute, but especially distinguished himself in the epic 7–7 tie, during the course of which the collegians registered nine first downs and the pros only one.

Stydahar is one of the sixteen men to be enshrined in the

State Athletic Hall of Fame. He is also a member of the All-Time All-West Virginia University football and basketball teams. In 1933 the Eastern Basketball Conference was formed by Pittsburgh, Temple, Carnegie Tech, Georgetown, and West Virginia. Bucknell and Penn State later joined. West Virginia finished last the first season, but the next year, with Stydahar leading the conference with 100 points in ten games, the Mountaineers placed second. "Jumbo Joe" won a place on the All-Conference and on the All-Pittsburgh Area teams and was given honorable mention by Les Gage in his selection of an All-America team for the *Literary Digest*. In 1935 he failed to lead the scorers but sparked the team to a tie with Pittsburgh for the title. The Panthers were fortunate in the play-off game, and Stydahar was again chosen for the All-Conference team.

Upon completion of his college career, Stydahar signed to play professional football with the Chicago Bears, "the Monsters of the Midway." He quickly became just about the fiercest monster of them all. At the end of his first pro season, in 1936, he tied with Ernie Smith, former Southern California All-American, for a tackle berth on the All-Pro team. Smith was given the nod because of his greater value as a place-kicker. While place-kicking had nothing to do with line play, it was probably as fair a way as any to break the tie. The next year (1937) it wasn't close. Not only did Joe lead all tackles; the 43 points voted him were more than any other player received regardless of position. The Bears won the division title but lost the championship play-off to Sammy Baugh and the Washington Redskins.

In 1938, 1939 and 1940 Stydahar was again on the All-League team. In 1940 he played a conspicuous role in the stupendous 73–0 play-off victory over the Redskins. The best he could get in 1941 was honorable mention, although he helped the Bears win another world championship. He served as a substitute for the Bears in 1942, but he was far from through. In the play-off, lost to Washington 14–6, of all the Bear linemen "only the veteran Styhadar caught the eye," according to the *New York Times*.

During his seven-year stint with the Bears, he had been chosen for All-Pro-League honors four times and had played on two world-champion teams and two that won the Western Division title. After World War II he returned to the Bears and was a substitute in 1945 and 1946.

Stydahar had accepted a commission as an ensign in the Naval Reserve and was called to active duty in March, 1943. He was assigned to the armed guards. While on duty at Fleet City, California, in the fall of 1944, he played with the Bluejacket football team and won a place on the All-America Service team. After that, he went to sea on the USS *Monterey* and served in the American, European-African, and Asiatic-Pacific theaters of operation. He reached the grade of lieutenant, and was relieved from active duty on December 1, 1945, but remained in the Reserve, subject to call, until 1954.

Following the season of 1946, Joe accepted an offer from Clark Shaughnessy to become line coach of the Los Angeles Rams. In those days the Rams were a cantankerous crowd, full of dissention. Every year or two, Owner Dan Reeves would fire the coach. In 1949 the Rams won the Western Division title but faltered in the championship play-off, losing to Philadelphia 14–0. When the familiar bleat was heard, Shaughnessy received his walking papers and Stydahar was elevated to the hot seat. Shaughnessy was furious with his former assistant for accepting the position, and boasted that he could take a high-school team and beat the Rams under Stydahar's coaching, but Joe did well that year. His pass-happy team finished the regular season deadlocked with the Chicago Bears. In a play-off for the western title, Joe's team won, 24–14. But that was as far as they advanced. In the championship play-off, they lost a tough one to the Cleveland Browns, 30–28.

Stydahar enjoyed a prosperous year in 1951, although the season did not open happily. Some of the players expressed their rugged individualism by breaking training, and Joe promptly imposed fines on twenty-eight of them amounting to approximately

$7,900. The fines were later rescinded, but the players knew who was boss and realized they might not be so fortunate the next time. When people, including his players, got to know Joe, they respected and admired him and he became one of the most popular men in Los Angeles.

That year, he had a happy hunch. One of his halfbacks was Elroy Hirsch, who had starred at both Wisconsin and Michigan. The famous "crazy legs" had taken such a beating over the years that Hirsch was about ready to quit. Stydahar moved him to end, where he not only continued in the game for several more seasons but became an even greater star than he had been as a back. With his aid and that of Bob Waterfield, Norm Van Brocklin, Tom Fears, and other outstanding players, the Rams again swept to the division championship. That time they did not falter in the finale. The Cleveland Browns were beaten 24–17, and Stydahar's team was champion of the world.

However successful he had been at Los Angeles, Stydahar had just about stayed his limit. When the 1952 edition of the Rams got off to a poor start, he joined the "alumni"—he was fired on September 30th, and was very unhappy about it. Stydahar had given freely of his time to football, but he had other interests. He had gone into the corrugated box and container business in Chicago. After serving as head coach of the Chicago Cardinals in 1953 and 1954 with fair success, he devoted full time to his business. Since early 1959 he has been president of the Big Bear Container Corporation. He lives in nearby Glencoe and is active in community affairs. He has been as successful off the field as he was on it, and was chosen for *Sports Illustrated*'s Silver Anniversary All-America team in 1960.

RICHARD KAY WILDUNG

(6:00; 214)

No one could ever accuse Dick Wildung of being a "showboat." He was no dashing charger, but rather the wheelhorse type. A quiet, self-effacing team man, he might have lacked color with which to fire the imagination of the sportswriters, but he was nearly perfect in the technique of tackle play, and he so overwhelmed all opponents that he could not fail to win acclaim. He was a power in the big Minnesota lines, a solid, unbreakable man who, in most important games, went the full sixty minutes. He was never injured in four years of college play. It was claimed that his strongest points were downfield blocking and diagnosing opponents' plays but his paralyzing tackling was also outstanding. Despite his bulk he was generally one of the fastest men on the team, both in pulling out of the line and in going downfield. But what especially endeared him to his teammates and fans was that he was at his best in rough going.

Dick was born at St. Paul, Minnesota, on August 16, 1921. His family later made its home in Luverne, Minnesota, where he attended high school and was an All-State choice in football and All-Division in basketball. He also competed in track, but at the university he confined himself to football. He earned his meals by serving as cashier at a downtown restaurant and he also held down a position at the Northwest National Bank in Minneapolis, a job that tied in with his course in business administration at the university. During the summer of 1942, he served as counselor at a boys' camp in northern Minnesota where one of his companions was his keen football rival David Schreiner, an All-America end from Wisconsin. Wildung was a model tackle, and he came close to being a model youngster off the field. Bernard Swanson of the *Minneapolis Tribune* called him "the finest type of boy." Conscientious, ambitious, and hard working, he neither drank nor smoked.

It is said that Dick made the team the first day he walked on the field, as a sophomore in the fall of 1940. That Bernie Bierman team relied chiefly on a rushing game, and passed less than any other team in the conference. It was undefeated, and generally considered the strongest team in America. Ohio State, Iowa, Northwestern, Michigan, Purdue, and Wisconsin within the conference, and Washington and Nebraska, outside, were beaten. In six of those games, the Gophers came from behind to win. The line performed prodigiously, especially in the vital game with Michigan. Four times the Wolverines had a first down inside Minnesota's five-yard line, and despite the presence of the All-America backs Tommy Harmon and Bob Westfall, they were able to score only once—on a forward pass. In that game Wildung blasted a hole in the right side of Michigan's line, which Bruce Smith broke through and raced 80 yards to a touchdown. Joe Mernik converted, and Minnesota took the Little Brown Jug game 7–6. That rugged line also halted Washington within the five-yard line with the score 19–14, and held Ohio State on the one-yard line in the Gophers' 13–7 victory. People raved about Minnesota's great pair of tackles, but the truth is that Wildung was overshadowed that year by Urban Odson, 247-pound veteran. Odson and George Franck, a halfback, were on many All-America teams.

The next year (1941) Minnesota enjoyed another perfect season and was again a unanimous first choice in the national ratings. Odson was still an outstanding performer, but that time Wildung was not taking a back seat for anyone. He and the halfback Bruce Smith appeared on most All-American selections. Other outstanding players were Helge Pukema and Butch Levy, guards; Gene Flick, center; Bob Fitch, end; Bob Sweiger and Bill Daley, backs, and Wilford Garnaas, the blocking sophomore quarterback. The team, which compiled the best record in the conference in both offense and defense, is considered one of the greatest teams in all history.

In order, the Gophers defeated Washington, Illinois, Pittsburgh, Michigan, Northwestern, Nebraska, Iowa, and Wisconsin. The game with Michigan was witnessed by 85,753 people. Critics were of the opinion that Wildung gave his best performance against Nebraska, but there was little to choose between his games; they were uniformly superior. Minnesota, noted for its power, downed Northwestern through a ruse that was more like Rockne than like Bierman. A forward pass by Otto Graham to Bud Hasse had put the Wildcats ahead. Minnesota lined up hurriedly with the seven linemen indifferently strung along the line of scrimmage. Without signal or huddle, before the Wildcats could get set, Gene Flick suddenly passed the ball to 155-pound Bud Higgins, who slipped around his own right end and ran all the way to the score that gave the Gophers the game 8–7, and kept them on the road to the championship.

It was expected that halfback Bill Daley, very popular with his mates, would be elected captain for 1942, but the honor went to Wildung. According to all accounts, Wildung turned out to be an excellent leader, although his team lacked the success of its immediate predecessors. With the war on, Bierman had left the campus to return to the U.S. Marines, with whom he had served in World War I. Dr. George Hauser, his chief assistant, took over. Although handicapped by injuries to key players throughout the season, he produced a good team; but certain opponents, namely the Iowa Naval Preflight Seahawks, Illinois, Indiana, and Wisconsin were better, at least on the day they met the Gophers. Minnesota won from Pittsburgh, Nebraska, Michigan, Northwestern, and Iowa.

Minnesota did not win the championship, but Wildung made All-America again. Even in defeat, Wildung had stood out. Francis J. Powers, of the *Chicago Daily News,* called him "the country's outstanding lineman"; Bob Otto, of Iowa, said, "Wildung is the greatest tackle of all"; Harry Stuhldreher, Wisconsin coach, rated him "as good as they come"; while Roundy Coughlin, the humorist-sportswriter from Madison, wrote in his droll way, "Wildung is the most marvelous lineman I ever *seen.*" Bierman, who placed him on his All-Time All-Minnesota team, said he was "as good a tackle as I've ever coached."

Dick was selected to play with the East team in the Shrine game on January 1, 1943, and the following summer he played with the College All-Stars against the pro champion Washington Redskins. In each case he was in the starting lineup. The All-Star line stopped the pros cold. The Redskins had to depend almost entirely upon Sammy Baugh's passing, but at that, the collegians, coached by Harry Stuhldreher, won, 27–7.

In August, 1943, Wildung was called to active duty with the Naval Reserve. He served as an ordnance instructor at Albert Hall in Chicago until December of 1944, when, after attending school at Melville, Rhode Island, he went to the Philippines. There he skippered a PT boat of the same type that President Kennedy had commanded. Later, Wildung acted as squadron operations officer. When he was discharged in March, 1946, he was a lieutenant, junior grade.

From 1946 through 1951, and again in 1953, Wildung played professional football with Green Bay; unfortunately, those were comparatively lean years for the Packers; no championships were won, and most of the critics looked elsewhere for their nominations for the All-Pro team. After his retirement, Wildung was in the insurance business in Minneapolis for a time, but he is now living in Redwood Falls, Minnesota, and has opened a large and highly successful hardware store.

MARSHALL NEWELL

(5:07; 168)

Camp's All-Star team in 1904 had Ma Newell teamed with Cowan at the tackles. Newell seemed ridiculously small for the position, but he was built like a tree stump. As late as 1931,

Parke H. Davis considered him one of the strongest tackles ever to play. With fast hands, an unusually powerful arm-thrust, and great driving power in his short legs, he could jolt a much heavier man back on his heels. His low-slung weight enabled him to block with authority. Full of fire, rugged, fast, and agile, he was selected by Caspar Whitney four times for the All-America team, beginning in 1890 when Harvard defeated Yale, 12–6, for the first time since 1875, and won the championship. Newell was considered the bulwark of the line, but to beat Yale required a real team effort. Whitney gave first or second All-America honors to Captain Arthur Cumnock and Frank Hallowell, ends; Newell and Joshua Upton, tackles; John Cranston, center; Dudley Dean, quarterback; John Corbett and James Lee, halfbacks, and Bernard Trafford, fullback.

Newell became Cornell's first professional coach in 1894. His team won from Michigan, Lafayette, Lehigh, and Syracuse, scored on Princeton, 4–12, and Harvard, 12–22, and held Pennsylvania to 0–6. Herbert Reed, who played under him at Cornell and became the famous sportswriter "Right Wing," recalled that on occasion, in practice, Newell would line up against the varsity and single-handed outplay an entire side of the line. During the two years he coached the Ithacans, he helped develop such All-Americans as Pop Warner, guard; Joe Beachman, end; Clinton Wyckoff, quarterback; and William Ohl, fullback.

Newell also rowed and was at bow in the famous crew that defeated Yale by ten lengths in 1891. At Harvard, he is remembered as much for his magnetic personality and fine character as for his athletic ability. A farm boy from the Berkshires, Newell willingly went out of his way to help others. Even the freshmen, affectionately and respectfully, called him "Ma." He was a tremendous influence for good, and he left a lasting impression on everyone with whom he came in contact.

On Christmas Eve, 1897, he was killed in a railroad accident. In his memory, Harvard erected a gate at the entrance to Soldier's Field.

WILLIAM ENOCH FINCHER

(6:00; 190)

In picking his all-time teams, Grantland Rice remained loyal to "Fats" Henry throughout, but seemed to have difficulty finding a suitable partner for him. In 1928 he left the place open with Cowan, Fish, and Hart named as the most deserving candidates. In 1939 he decided upon Fincher, but then came Hubbard in 1952 and Stydahar in 1954.

Because of war conditions, Bill Fincher had the opportunity of playing on five football teams at Georgia Tech. As a freshman, in 1916, he played on the team that rolled up the record 220–0 score against Cumberland University whose fullback was George E. (*Presidents Who Have Known Me*) Allen. Fast enough for an end, strong enough for a tackle, and agile enough, as a guard, to become a key man in the complicated "Heisman shift," Fincher played all three positions with distinction. He was a unanimous All-Southern choice as a guard in 1917, end in 1918, and tackle in 1920. In 1919 he also received votes for the honor team as an end. Camp preferred him as an end, and placed him, at that position, on the second All-America team in 1918 and on the first in 1920.

In 1917 the famous Golden Tornado team, coached by John W. Heisman, overwhelmed Pennsylvania 41–0, Auburn 68–7, and all other rivals. Because Pennsylvania held Pittsburgh, the East's best, to a 6–14 score, and Auburn had played a scoreless tie with Ohio State, Western Conference champion, Georgia Tech was generally recognized as the Number One team in the nation. Tech scored 491 points against 17 in nine games, and Fincher, who had only one eye, contributed 49 conversions to swell the total. Five members of that great team, which averaged only 177 pounds, appeared on All-America selections: Everett Strupper and Joe Guyon, halfbacks; Captain Walker "Big Six" Carpenter, tackle; George "Pup" Phillips, center; and Albert Hill, quarterback. In addition, Fincher and the ends M. G. Guill and R. S. Bell were named on various All-Southern teams.

Heisman built his 1918 team around Fincher, who was captain, and Guyon, the Indian, reinforced by Ashel "Bum" Day, an All-America center, and other experienced players who were transferred to Tech in order to take military training. The Yellowjackets lost only to Pop Warner's Pittsburgh team in a game that settled the national collegiate championship. After a mediocre season in 1919, Tech came back in Fincher's last year (1920) and regained the Southern title by beating Bo McMillin and his Centre team 24–0. That Tech team also lost only to Pittsburgh. With Fincher appeared such All-America or All-Southern stars as Captain Buck Flowers, Red Barron, and Judy Harlan in the backfield, and John Staton, end. After graduation, Fincher became affiliated with the Coca-Cola Company in Atlanta. He retired from business in 1961.

ROBERT CALVIN HUBBARD

(6:05; 240 in college; 265 as a pro)

Mild-mannered Cal Hubbard, whose size, playing ability, and dominating personality made him a commanding figure, is considered by most authorities as the greatest tackle ever to play professional football. He could go "the hundred" in close to eleven seconds, was mobile, aggressive, and hit extremely hard. In 1922 he appeared as a tackle at Centenary College in Louisiana. That was the first year that Bo McMillin, the former "Praying Colonel" from Centre, coached the "Southern Gentlemen," as he called his team. It won the championship of the Louisiana Intercollegiate Association. The ambitious Bo arranged some intersectional games for 1923. Cal played end, most of the time, as Centenary won ten and lost only to Boston College. It defeated all sectional rivals as well as Texas Christian, 23–0. In 1924 Hubbard shifted between tackle and end while "the Gentlemen" beat Boston College 10–9, St. Louis 23–13, and defeated a number of other good teams. Hubbard was the outstanding performer for Centenary, and McMillin proclaimed him the greatest football player he had ever seen. Less partial critics were fully as enthusiastic. Bill Alexander, Georgia Tech coach, who had seen Hubbard play as a tackle at Centenary, declared him the best lineman he ever saw, and that was the opinion of Professor Lacy Lockert, the South's foremost football historian who chose him as an All-Time college tackle. But Centenary was too small and too far off the beaten path to be noticed by many of the experts, and no All-American or even All-Southern honors were forthcoming for Hubbard.

McMillin moved to Geneva College, in Pennsylvania, in 1925, and Hubbard dropped out of sight, but in 1926 he materialized at right end for Geneva. Geneva lost a tight game to Cornell, 0–6, and won a beauty from Harvard, 16–7. Charles Parker of the *New York Evening World* placed Hubbard on his All-America team for 1926. Others, because of the small size of Geneva or the fear that Cal might be classed as a "tramp athlete," placed him on substitute elevens or gave him honorable mention. He was so superior on both offense and defense that he could not be overlooked entirely. Hubbard excelled as a blocker—leading the runner and mopping up the secondary—and he was deadly at boxing any tackle he opposed. He could reach high above the defenders to grab a forward pass. On defense he backed up the line and it was almost impossible to get past him. In 1948 H. G. Salsinger of the *Detroit News* conducted an investigation to determine the greatest linebacker of all time. When his search narrowed down to Cal Hubbard and Germany Schulz, he decided to let it go at that, because a team required at least two linebackers. He thought they were the best.

For the next two years, 1927 and 1928, the New York Giants teamed Cal at tackle with another rugged customer, Steve Owen.

The Giants took advantage of Hubbard's unique ability and installed a screen-pass play with him eligible to receive. From New York, Cal moved to Green Bay where Earl L. "Curly" Lambeau was building a champion organization. The Packers won twelve and tied one to win the world title in 1929. They remained at the top in 1930 and 1931. It was a wild, boisterous crew; every man loved the game and played it up to the hilt. All-Pro teams were not selected prior to 1931. For that year, Hubbard and Mike Michalske were selected for the honor team along with Laverne Dilweg, a 60-minute end and former Marquette All-American who later was elected to the Congress of the United States, and John McNally, a spectacular, unpredictable halfback who played under the name of Blood.

In those days, prior to unlimited substitution, a professional club carried a "policeman"—a strong man who was level-headed and even-tempered. It was his duty, when an opponent was getting away with "dirty" playing, to convince the culprit of the error of his ways. Hubbard was the Green Bay "policeman." He was so highly respected by both teams, by the fans and the officials that, when he took summary action, it was recognized that the victim merited the punishment that befell him.

Hubbard was again All-League in 1932 and 1933. He continued playing regularly with the Packers through the season of 1935. In 1936 he became an umpire in the American Baseball League. His baseball duties kept him from early football practice, and the Packers placed him on the inactive list. The New York Giants secured him on October 29th, and three days afterward he played against Detroit. Later he was sold to the Pittsburgh Steelers, and quit playing at the end of the season. He became almost as famous as a baseball umpire as he had been as a football player, and in 1958 was appointed umpire-in-chief in the American League.

◆ ◆ ◆

AWARD-WINNING TACKLES

Donald B. Whitmire, *Navy*	ROCKNE, 1944
George Connor, *Notre Dame*	OUTLAND, 1946 (initial)
William Fischer, *Notre Dame*	ROCKNE, Outland, 1948
Robert Gain, *Kentucky*	OUTLAND, 1950
James Weatherall, *Oklahoma*	OUTLAND, 1951
Richard Modzelewski, *Maryland*	ROCKNE, Outland, 1952
Stanley Jones, *Maryland*	ROCKNE, 1953
Robert Reifsnyder, *Navy*	MAXWELL, 1957
Louis Michaels, *Kentucky*	ROCKNE, 1957
Alexander Karras, *Iowa*	OUTLAND, 1957
Mike McGee, *Duke*	OUTLAND, 1959
Merlin Olsen, *Utah State*	OUTLAND, 1961

3

GUARDS

CAMP, 1910	Heffelfinger, *Yale*	Hare, *Pennsylvania*
YOST, 1920	Heffelfinger, *Yale*	Hare, *Pennsylvania*
TREVOR, 1927	Heffelfinger, *Yale*	Hare, *Pennsylvania*
GULF, 1933	Heffelfinger, *Yale*	Hare, *Pennsylvania*
SHAUGHNESSY, 1943	Heffelfinger, *Yale*	Hare, *Pennsylvania*
A.P., 1951	Heffelfinger, *Yale*	Suffridge, *Tennessee*
RICE, 1954	Heffelfinger, *Yale*	Hickman, *Tennessee*
WEYAND, 1955	Heffelfinger, *Yale*	Hare, *Pennsylvania*
HELMS, TO DATE	Heffelfinger, *Yale*	Hare, *Pennsylvania*
ADDITIONAL	Glass, *Yale*	Cannon, *Notre Dame*

❖ ❖ ❖

WILLIAM WALTER HEFFELFINGER

(6:03; 206)

"Pudge" Heffelfinger was born on December 20, 1867, in Minneapolis. Sixteen years later he helped to organize a football team at Central High School there. Over the next fifty years, Pudge continued to play football, for the last time when nearing his sixty-sixth birthday. During the course of this fifty-year period he helped to write some of the greatest legends in football history. When he died at the age of eighty-six, the football world lost one of the most memorable figures ever to draw on a jersey.

Eligibility rules being what they were, Heff was permitted to play occasionally with the University of Minnesota varsity in the fall of 1887, although he was still in high school. He earned the reputation of being a pile-driving halfback. He was handy with an ax and he enjoyed wrestling and skating. Such exercise gave him great strength in his limbs and back without interfering with his speed or agility. But there must have been some surprise when Pudge put in an appearance at New Haven in the fall of 1888. He weighed only 178 pounds. Even though he was superbly coordinated, he had, and retained throughout his life, an awkward way of standing and walking and a shy manner, although, when aroused, he could become quite aggressive. George Woodruff took one look at him and called him "a ridiculous example of the rawboned Westerner." They put meat on his big frame at the Yale training table, and that year he played at 192.

Yale needed linemen more than backs, and William H. "Pa" Corbin, the captain, paired Heffelfinger with Woodruff as the guards. Corbin, who was tall and dignified with a handlebar mustache adorning his horselike face, was a great center and a stern disciplinarian. Under his rough treatment, Heff was worked over plenty before Corbin was satisfied, if indeed he ever was. In later years Heff remembered Pa calling him an old cow because he did not play rough enough to suit him. Corbin made a lasting impression on Heff. In talking to the author, some sixty years later, he casually mentioned "the captain." "Which captain do you mean?" I asked. Heff looked surprised. "Why, Pa Corbin, of course." There was only one "captain" in his long life.

Under the coaching of Corbin and Walter Camp, Heffelfinger evolved his celebrated semi-erect stance. As he explained it, he stood more or less erect, knees bent in a slight crouch, body leaning forward from the hips, feet about three feet apart, left foot advanced. That looked all right for defense, but, I argued, a man should play lower on offense. "Stand up and I'll show you," he said. With hands clasped in front of his chest, he pivoted like a hammer thrower and struck me with his shoulder so hard that it was all I could do to keep my feet. I might add that at that time he was eighty-three while I was a slip of a lad at fifty-eight. When I told Red Blaik, then Army coach, about it, he said it was possible that Heff had something that had been lost through the years. He planned inviting him to West Point in order to take moving pictures of the shoulder lunge, but I don't believe he ever got around to it.

Heffelfinger was in excellent company his freshman year at Yale. In addition to Corbin and Woodruff, there were such famous players as Amos Alonzo Stagg and Frederick Wallace, ends; Charles Gill, tackle; William Wurtenberg, quarterback and the kicking fullback, Billy Bull. Harvard was not played because of a disagreement as to the site, but Yale won 13 games and scored 698 points while holding opponents scoreless. No All-America team was selected that early, but several survivors of that season have assured me that Heff was the outstanding guard in the land. It was he who wrecked the Princeton wedge Hector Cowan had worked so hard to perfect. When the wedge got underway, Pudge took a running leap and, with knees drawn up, struck the apex man on the chest. That usually halted the wedge in its tracks. He varied his style, when the apex man crouched, by diving over his head and landing on top of the ballcarrier.

Heff had a problem his first season in collegiate football. I asked him if he had ever slugged a man in a game. Shamefaced, he admitted doing so once. As he recalled, it was in a game with Pennsylvania his freshman year. His personal opponent, A. C. Bowser, weighed 220 pounds and had been overpowering all rivals. The gangling freshman was a match for him when Bowser lost his temper and clipped Heff on the jaw. The latter was nonplused. "That's not the way gentlemen play," he said, but on the next play Bowser slugged him again. As Heff explained it, the man wouldn't listen to reason, so he drove his great bony fist into the Quaker's midsection. Bowser passed out, but he recovered and continued in the game. "And do you know, after that he played like a gentleman," said Pudge virtuously. "No one else ever slugged me," he added thoughtfully—obviously, for a good reason.

The next two years were not so happy for Yale; the championship was lost to Princeton in 1889 and to Harvard in 1890, though neither could gain consistently through the Eli line. Princeton, with a superior kicking game, scored through fumbles, while Harvard's touchdowns came after long runs. Those were the only games lost of the fifty-seven played by Yale during Heffelfinger's four years. Heff was the backbone of the Blue team. With his fast start and tremendous power, he was a devastating line plunger, and in runs in the open he was faster than most halfbacks. As a result, he carried the ball frequently. When he played in the line, he spearheaded the attack, smashing ahead like a bulldozer, with the ballcarrier hanging to a strap on the back of his uniform. Incidentally, when Yale was within scoring distance, Heff usually played in the line. On defense, he was smart, and his speed and strength enabled him to brush aside blockers and get at the ballcarrier.

In 1890 Yale introduced a new feature to increase Heffelfinger's effectiveness. His former teammate, George Woodruff, conceived the idea of a guard coming out of the line to head the interference. Camp was doubtful, but he consented to try it against Pennsylvania. Pudge, pivoting out of his position at left guard, took three steps to the right and then swung in front of the ballcarrier and mowed down would-be tacklers with a rolling shoulder block while keeping his feet. It was to revolutionize end-running. Near the end of the game with Harvard that year, Heffelfinger cleared the way for Ben Morison, who turned a Harvard end. They were in the open and had covered 40 yards when Bernie Trafford and Dudley Dean closed in on Morison from different angles. Unfortunately, Heff could not divide himself. He put out Dean, but Trafford nailed the runner and saved the day for Harvard.

In the spring of 1891, Heff won a seat, Number 5, in the Yale crew. Harvard took the race for the first time since 1885, and Pudge was now out for revenge on two counts—football and rowing. He had completed the three-year course at Sheffield Scientific School and enrolled in the Law School, so he was again available for football in the fall of 1891. Bum McClung was captain, and Walter Camp continued as advisory coach. They stressed teamwork, and developed what Camp enthusiastically maintained was the greatest team yet to appear. It won all its games and amply atoned for past indignities at the hands of Princeton and Harvard. Heff had his revenge, and was again a member of a championship team.

That year (1891) was the third that an All-America team had been selected. Heffelfinger had made it each year. Every All-Time All-America selection the writer has ever seen has included him. It will probably be so until the end of time. Heffelfinger has become a legend. Great guards will come and go, but it is inconceivable that any critic, however "progressive" he might be, would ever rate any of them above the man "with frame of iron and heart of steel," as Grantland Rice wrote. The Elder Statesman, Bernard M. Baruch, who often saw Heff play, called him a "One-Man Army." During the unsuccessful agitation to pressure him into playing another year, one of the papers published a sentimental ballad which closed on the plaintive wail, "Linger, oh, linger, Heffelfinger."

He lingered the next year (1892) long enough to create a diversion at the Yale-Harvard game. In his enthusiasm, he wandered out on the field, and it took three policemen to get him back to the sideline. That fall he played with the Chicago Athletic Association, which on a trip East played six games in twelve days.

In the fall of 1893, after playing a few games with the Chicago A.A. and assisting at Lehigh for a short time, he coached at the University of California. Later that same season, he went to Portland, Oregon, and helped with the Multnomah Athletic Club team. The next year he was back at Lehigh, that time as head coach. His team closed strongly with victories over Lafayette and Cornell, although in justice it should be said that the game with Cornell ended in a fight, and the Ithacans also claimed the victory. In 1895 he was in charge at Minnesota. Under him, the Gophers defeated Wisconsin and Chicago but lost to Purdue and Michigan. After that he quit as a head coach and joined his father in the latter's flourishing shoe business. The three college teams of which he was head coach won a total of fifteen games, lost twelve, and tied one.

Although Pudge no longer sought a head coach's portfolio, he was far from through with the game. It was while he was assisting Dr. Henry L. Williams at Minnesota, in 1903, that he made what was probably his greatest contribution to coaching science. In those days of mass play and no forward passes, teams frequently lined up on defense with nine men, shoulder to shoulder, in the line. When a hard-hitting speed boy like Willie Heston cracked the right spot, he was likely to break through and keep on going. Because Minnesota had a date with Heston and his highly proficient playmates, Pudge conceived the idea of using a seven-man line with three linebackers—in other words, two lines to be broken through. The results were startling. Michigan was held to two first downs and one touchdown. The game ended in a 6–6 tie, and that was one of "Hurry Up" Yost's famous point-a-minute teams. Both Minnesota and Michigan won all other games and were rated among the top teams of the nation.

Heff had another colorful and highly publicized coaching experience. In the fall of 1916, he returned to New Haven to help whip the line into shape for the big games. He put on a suit and scrimmaged against the varsity. There are different versions of the story but sure facts are that Malcomb Baldridge, 196-pound tackle, sustained two broken ribs, and Clinton Black, 210-pound All-America guard, a badly bruised leg before Tad Jones, the head coach, ordered Heff out of action. Pudge was then a month short of forty-nine. After World War I, in 1920, Heff came back, but when Tad Jones refused to allow him to scrimmage for fear of injuring his linemen, the aging Heff was so disgusted that he took the next train back to Minneapolis, and never again volunteered his coaching services to his alma mater.

By 1922, Heff was approaching fifty-five. That year, he captained an all-star team that played Ohio State Alumni in a charity game. Bo McMillin, former Centre College All-American, who was Heff's quarterback, told Grantland Rice that it was unbelievable the way the old guard came out of the line to lead the interference, and Bo had reason to remember. On two occasions, Heff took out the end unaided and sprung Bo loose for long touchdown runs. During the course of action, Pudge sprained a shoulder, but he stuck out fifty-one minutes of the game, which his team won, 16–0. And, on Armistice Day in 1933, when he was just short of sixty-six, he played for nine minutes in a snowstorm in a charity benefit game at Minneapolis, and again his team won, 6–0.

In addition to business and football, Pudge was active in politics. In both 1904 and 1908 he was a delegate to the Republican National Convention. Theodore Roosevelt singled him out for special greeting when he went to Sagamore Hill with the committee to notify T.R. of his nomination for the Presidency, in 1904. In 1924 Pudge was elected to the Hennepin County Commission and served as its chairman for a number of years. He was later active in the advertising business in New York City, and spent the last years of his life at Blessing, Texas, where he passed away on April 5, 1954.

T(HOMAS) TRUXTUN HARE

(6:02; 198)

Hare was the Chevalier Bayard of football players, a knight without fear and without reproach. Tall and handsome, with deep-set expressive eyes, wavy hair and clean-cut features, soft of speech, dignified of bearing and with a magnificently proportioned physique, he had the air of a patrician. He was called the "British type" of gentleman athlete. There was a certain aloofness about him, but it seemed to accentuate his sterling character and quality of leadership. He was personally very popular among his fellow players, who twice elected him captain. In his senior year his classmates elected him "spoon man," one of the highest class honors.

Hare was modest almost to a fault. He would not push himself forward or scheme for his advancement. He was very successful in later life, becoming an attorney for the United Gas Improvement Corporation of Philadelphia, with a big house on the exclusive Main Line. In addition he was a civic leader, author of eight books and some poetry, a popular and respected figure everywhere; but his closest friends professed to be somewhat disappointed. He was considered one of the ablest lawyers in Philadelphia, and it was felt that he should have risen to the very top of his profession, with no national office beyond his reach. But Trux was not built that way.

Hare assured the writer that he never weighed as much as 200 pounds for his championship games, but his coach, George Woodruff, claimed that he was "certainly ten pounds heavier than Heffelfinger," which would have made him about 215. When Grantland Rice visited him, he was in a hospital recovering from a long illness. He was emaciated and, in his usual self-effacing manner, seemed inclined to belittle his exploits. Rice left with the conviction that such a man was not of all-time caliber. But Granny was wrong. Walter Camp called Hare "a heroic figure" in every game he played and said that he was the only man who could have made the All-America team in any position. Camp selected him for the All-America all four years and so did everyone else. Trux was considered to be the most powerful man then playing the game. He called signals, punted, kicked goals, ran with the ball and, in the interference, ranged far on defense and never met his match in line play.

Hare was born in Philadelphia on October 12, 1878, into a family that had been in America since 1773. His father was a prominent attorney. After attending St. Mark's School at Southboro, Massachusetts, he entered the University of Pennsylvania in the fall of 1897. He then weighed 178 but built up to 185 before the end of the season. Woodruff said that Hare never expected to be much of a player in college and was quite surprised when he was asked to play with the varsity.

But all bashfulness left him when the game got under way. In that rough-and-tumble age, he could rough it with any of them. Years ago, I heard a story that I have been unable to verify as to date, although some oldtimers with whom I spoke remembered having heard it. The incident occurred in a game with Carlisle. Hare's personal opponent was not one of the grim, silent redmen. He enjoyed heckling palefaces, particularly those from the big universities, and most particularly a dignified individual like Trux Hare. He began riding Hare, and when he saw that the latter was paying no attention to his banter, he emphasized his point by playfully spitting tobacco juice in Hare's face. Ralph Morgan, long-time Penn athletic authority, said that, as he heard the story, "There was no immediate retaliation on Hare's part." Certainly it would have been out of character had he engaged in a brawl on the field. In those days it was legal to hit an opponent with anything except the clenched fist. The Indian was big and knew all the tricks, but he was not nearly so fast or as strong as Hare. Coldly and methodically, the Pennsylvanian smashed him. When Penn had the ball near Carlisle's goal line, Hare went into "guards back" formation and, taking the ball himself, drove straight at the Indian and bowled him over the goal line.

That "guards back" formation was the latest word in offensive football at that time. George Woodruff had introduced it at Pennsylvania in 1894 and, during the next three seasons, the Quakers had won forty games and lost but one—to Lafayette in 1896. In the original formation, both guards dropped back, one a yard and a half behind his normal line position and the other a yard behind him. The backs were in T-formation with the fullback about four yards behind the quarterback. A wide variety of plays was possible from that formation. The most consistent gainer called for the forward guard to take the ball and be pushed by those behind him. The repertoire included a quick kick by the quarterback, which served much the same purpose as the forward pass of later date because the men to the rear of the quarterback when he kicked were eligible to catch the ball on the fly.

Year after year Hare was Pennsylvania's most dependable ground gainer. Not only did he excel in carrying the ball; he was also a devastating blocker. He was fast enough to turn an end, and his powerful legs made him an ideal man for plowing through a line. In his last game against Harvard, in 1900, he ran 35 yards to a touchdown, dragging opponents most of the way. When he crossed the goal line he had five Harvard men clinging to various parts of his anatomy. Despite his size, he could hurdle a would-be tackler, and he had a trick, when tackled low, of turning a complete somersault that either broke the hold of the tackler or enabled him to pick up a few extra yards. Woodruff played him deep when Pennsylvania received a kickoff so that he had a better chance for a runback.

The same year Woodruff introduced "guards-back" he brought out a short-end defense that put as great a burden on the guards as did the offensive play. In this defense the guards played back, not unlike modern linebackers except they were a little closer up. The ends smashed in, and it became the responsibility of the guards to cover the flanks as well as to plug holes in the line. Hare's tackling on the ends against Harvard as a freshman elicited raves from the sportswriters that did not abate until he was through playing. Camp marveled at the way he caught fast backs from behind.

Once, when Hare was in an expansive mood, he told me of his most unusual play and, I imagine, the one of which he was proudest. Charlie Daly, Harvard's great quarterback, swung wide around an end. Hare went out to meet him. Because Daly was adept at hurdling, Hare tried to tackle him high. As Hare left his feet in a flying tackle, Daly dropped to the ground. In that split second when he saw Daly disappear from in front of him, Hare thought to thrash his feet. As luck would have it, a foot anchored on Daly's shoulder, and the good big man fell on the good little man.

Walter Eckersall told of seeing the 1899 Chicago-Pennsylvania game while still a schoolboy. With time running out and the score tied 5–5, Chicago had the ball a few feet from the Quaker goal line. Eckersall remembered Hare, his jersey torn to shreds, daring the Maroon quarterback to send the play at him. There was nothing reticent about him then. In those days personality played a larger part in the game than now, and Walter Kennedy, the Chicago quarterback, refused to take a dare. Besides, he had some rugged boys up front, and in Frank Slaker the best linebucker in the West. Three times, Slaker crashed into the Red and Blue line. Each time, Hare parted the Chicago line with his big hands and stopped Slaker. That stand saved the game—the ball was eighteen inches from the goal line when Pennsylvania took possession. Eckersall, looking backward, did not think Kennedy exercised good judgment.

After Jack Minds, the 1897 captain, was graduated, Hare added punting to his already crowded schedule. His kicking into a sharp wind carrying snow and sleet, on a field almost ankle deep in mud and slush, held off Cornell in 1898 and enabled the Quakers to win, 12–6. In 1899, in a famous punting duel with Charlie Daly, the efforts of both were called magnificent by sportswriters. After that performance, he seems to have punted only at critical times, when an extra effort was necessary. He took up drop-kicking, and was used to kick goals after touchdown. In 1899 he registered Pennsylvania's only score against Carlisle by means of a field goal from the 25-yard line at a difficult angle. That same year, after scoring a touchdown, he converted to give the team a draw with Brown, 6–6. He scored field goals against both Cornell and Chicago in 1900.

In 1897, Hare's freshman year, Pennsylvania won all sixteen games played and received Number One rating. Harvard, Cornell, Carlisle, Brown, Dartmouth, Wesleyan, Penn State, Lafayette, and Lehigh were among those beaten. It was the only undefeated team that Hare was to play on. He was already the most celebrated player in school, but there were a number of outstanding men on the team. Captain Jack Minds, fullback, and John Outland, tackle, were also on Camp's first All-America eleven; Sam Boyle, end, was on the second, and Josiah McCracken, guard, and Peter Overfield, center, on the third. S. Goodman, tackle, and J. Hedges, end, received recognition from other sources. McCracken and Overfield were first-team choices in later years.

In 1898 Harvard found a way to stop "guards-back," and gave Pennsylvania its sole defeat of the season, 10–0, although the Quakers outgained the Crimson 340 yards to 225. The fact that the hitherto invincible "guards-back" could be stopped was of momentous importance, particularly at Pennsylvania. Almost overnight the famous system became obsolete, but Coach Woodruff refused to admit it. He clung faithfully to his tarnished brainchild. In 1902 Pennsylvania obtained another coach, but that was too late to help Trux Hare's two teams. In his first year as captain,

1899, the Quakers had, for them, a disastrous season, losing three games and tying two. Cornell and Michigan were among the eight teams beaten. The next year, 1900, when Hare again led the Red and Blue, he took on still more work, and conditions improved. A hard-fought game was dropped to Harvard, but the Quakers won all the others, from Columbia, Cornell, Chicago, Carlisle, Brown, Navy, Lafayette, Lehigh, Penn State, Dickinson, Haverford, and Franklin and Marshall, and were rated third in the nation.

Josiah McCracken, who spent most of his adult life as a medical missionary in China, and Hare were among the best hammer throwers in the world. In the Intercollegiates, McCracken won the championship in 1899 and was second the other three years. Each time, Hare was just behind him, but at the Olympic Games in Paris in 1900 Hare reversed the order. He placed second to the world record holder, John Flanagan, with a throw of 151 feet 9 inches. McCracken was third. Hare won the event at the Pan American Exposition at Buffalo in 1901. He kept in condition after his graduation and placed third in the All-Around Championships of the Amateur Athletic Union held in conjunction with, but not as part of, the Olympic Games at St. Louis in 1904. He was also good at golf and tennis, and later became fond of archery. For a time he was president of the United Bowmen of America. As a student he had also been active in dramatics, music, and literature.

Truxtun Hare retired from the practice of law in 1941 and served as managing director of the board of Bryn Mawr Hospital, outside Philadelphia. After a prolonged illness he died at his home, at Radnor, Pennsylvania, on February 2, 1956.

HERMAN MICHAEL HICKMAN

(5:10; 239)

Do you remember when you were a freshman at high school and met Friar Tuck wandering through the pages of *Ivanhoe*— a rotund fellow—strong, agile, and cunning, seemingly always ready for a fight or some other form of fun? Some people claim to see a resemblance between the good friar and Hickman. Herman's squat, bulky figure made him a rock on defense. On attack, he could rip an opponents' line apart or pull out fast enough to lead the interference on end sweeps. He was not a great downfield blocker, but in the close attack he could block with great force and keep his feet well. Paul Parker, the line coach at Tennessee during Herman's playing days, maintained that only Gene McEver, the All-America halfback, could beat Hickman in the 10- to 50-yard "wind sprints." Understandably, Colonel Parker rated his protégé as the greatest guard he ever saw.

Hickman was born in Johnson City, Tennessee, on October 1, 1911, the son of a well-known lawyer. After attending local schools, he enrolled at Baylor Prep in Chattanooga where he earned a reputation as a fullback, shot-putter, and wrestler, besides winning numerous declamatory and oratorical contests. But it was not as an orator that many colleges sought his services. Parker, who was recruiting for Tennessee, enlisted the support of Herman's mother, who then made her home in South Knoxville, and between them it was not difficult to convince young Herman to enter the University of Tennessee.

Frequently, muscle men experience difficulty amassing sufficient credits to enable them to enter college, but in Herman's case he virtually had too many. By the end of junior year in prep school, he had accumulated 18½, and all he needed for entrance was 15. The Tennessee coaches would have preferred him to round out his senior year at school, but with competition as keen as it was, they thought it wise to take him while he was in a receptive frame of mind or, as he himself used to say when coaching, "When we see a good prospect, we throw him, shoe him and carry him over the mountain." In the fall of 1928, when he was not quite seventeen and was a shadowy 203 pounds, he matriculated at Tennessee.

Herman made the freshman team and won his letter as a sophomore. The following season (1930) he was at tackle on the big team. He was really too short for the position, but it was hoped that his speed and strength might enable him to overcome that handicap. The fourth game of the season was with an unusually powerful Alabama squad that went on to finish unbeaten and win in the Rose Bowl. The Crimson Tide broke Tennessee's string of thirty-three consecutive games without defeat, by winning 18–6. That reverse was the only one suffered by the Volunteers during the four years that Hickman was in college. Tragic as the occasion was, it provided Herman with one of the funny stories that he was to tell at countless football gatherings. After the game, Bob Neyland, the head coach, criticized his playing. Herman stubbornly insisted that he had followed instructions—to get a yard and a half across the line of scrimmage and make a pile. Neyland growled, "I told you to make a pile but I didn't tell you always to be at the bottom." Herman usually added ruefully that, after the Alabama game, he was switched to guard.

Hickman learned his new position rapidly. The week after meeting Alabama, Tennessee defeated North Carolina 9–7 and the local papers commented that Herman was "much more at home" as a guard. He probably played his best game of the season against Vanderbilt. As usual he was a bulwark on defense, and on offense he knocked over opponents to enable speedy backs like Buddy Hackman to get under way. Bob Murphy, in the *Knoxville Journal*, wrote, "He rose to a pinnacle he has never occupied before." Herman played another great game against Kentucky. That year Tennessee opposed Florida in a postseason game for charity. With the Vols leading 13–6, Florida had a third down on the

1-yard line. Twice the Gator backs smashed into the middle, and Herman threw them back for a 1½-yard loss. Paul Zimmerman of the Associated Press wrote, "They will be talking about that Hickman until the cows come home." Colonel Parker insisted that this was the last time that any Southern team attempted to gain through Hickman.

Herman was only twenty years old in his senior year—still not old enough to vote. But he was maturing fast and had developed a Sherlock Holmes trait of observation and deduction. One of the greatest performances of his career was in the victory over New York University, 13–0, at Yankee Stadium on December 5, 1931, in a game to aid the unemployed. At that time, guards usually fought through on defense, but in the first half of the game in New York, Hickman was frequently observed sliding behind his own line. Parker was ready to yank him out at the first mistake, but Hickman made no mistakes—only tackles. Between halves, Parker took him to task for his unorthodox playing. "Coach," said the dutiful Herman, "their Number Three man points nearly every play. When I know where the play goes, I can't help going there too." Sportswriters who had submitted their All-America selections earlier, and who were seeing Herman in action for the first time, gnashed their teeth in frustration, but Grantland Rice could say, "I told you so." He had seen the big boy before and had picked him for his honor team.

Other top Vols that season were Eugene McEver and Beattie Feathers, backs; Ray Saunders, tackle; Captain E. S. Mayer, center; and O. M. Derryberry and V. H. Rayburn, ends. Tennessee was unbeaten but lost the mythical national championship because of a 6–6 draw with Kentucky. In the Shrine game at San Francisco, Hickman was at left guard in the East's starting lineup. The East won, 6–0.

Hickman had planned to study law, but his college years fell in the midst of the depression. Money was scarce and good business opportunities were difficult to find. Rudy Dusek, of the famous wrestling family, convinced him that the best and fastest way to make real money was in professional wrestling. In 1932 he joined a wrestling troupe. With his cherubic smile, restrained manner, and clean-cut appearance, he was usually cast as the "good guy," or hero, in the exhibitions. Because of his football reputation, the flying tackle had to be his pet "hold," although he later added a crowd-pleasing "belly-bounce." In the five years that he performed on the mat, he appeared in some 500 exhibitions.

In 1933 Herman signed with the Brooklyn Dodgers pro football team of which his erstwhile opponent, "Shipwreck" Kelly from Kentucky, was part owner and star halfback. From that association came another of Herman's delightful stories. On certain plays, he and Kelly were assigned to double-team an opponent. In one of the games, Kelly took one look at the monster against whom they would have to operate, and said, "You take him, Herman; I own the club." But Herman did not need much, if any, assistance in handling any man. In his "freshman" year he was recognized as the greatest guard in pro ranks, and was named on the All-League team.

In 1934, after playing awhile with the Dodgers, Hickman quit the pro ranks and began a coaching career. During the fall of that and the following year, he served as line coach at Wake Forest under James Weaver. He then moved to North Carolina State where he assisted Williams "Doc" Newton for six years. At State he developed Ed "Ty" Coon, a tackle of All-America caliber, and he also lectured the senior class in English on Kipling and Masters. Probably the happiest and most gratifying period of his adult life began in 1943 when Earl H. "Red" Blaik brought him to the banks of the Hudson. At West Point he fashioned lines for the formidable teams of the Blanchard-Davis era. His contribution to the All-America roster was amazing: Casimir Myslinski, center; Francis Merritt, tackle; Joseph Stanowicz, guard; John Green, guard; DeWitt Coulter, tackle; Albert Nemetz, tackle; Joseph Steffy, guard; Arthur Gerometta, guard; Robert St. Onge, center; and Goebel Bryant, tackle. Two more of his boys, James Henry, guard, and William Yeomans, center, were similarly honored the year after Herman left West Point. Coulter also became an All-Pro.

Herman's hillbilly drawl, quick wit, friendly disposition, fund of humorous stories and ability to recite appropriate poetry for all occasions made him a favorite with everyone. His enormous capacity for food also earned him a certain degree of fame. He thought nothing of demolishing several main courses along with the trimmings at one sitting. He was proud of his reputation as a trencherman and once attempted to arrange an international eating contest. Storing away such vast quantities of food built him up until there were some 310 pounds of him, but he could still move amazingly quickly. There was nothing sluggish about him. He admitted that he was probably the strongest fat man in the world. Good cigars were another of his weaknesses; he had special sizes and shapes made for each meal.

Herman was a great attraction as an after-dinner speaker. He had such a droll delivery that he could tell the same yarns over and over again and still get laughs. General Bob Neyland told me that he had heard some of Herman's stories at least forty times, but every time he heard Herman tell one Bob laughed as though he had never heard it before. Herman was probably at his best when talking about his kinfolk in the Tennessee mountains. Part of his charm lay in making himself the butt of some of his stories. Possibly he overdid that claim to modesty when he introduced himself as "Humble Herman" after he became a well-known radio commentator.

Hickman hated to leave Blaik and his friends at West Point, but when Yale offered him a three-year contract as head coach it was too good an opportunity to ignore. He took up his duties at New Haven during the fall of 1948. Yale was not blessed with much material in those days. Levi Jackson, the Negro halfback who captained the team in 1949, was about the only one to achieve national recognition. As a result of that situation, Herman's record for four years was not impressive—16 victories, 17 defeats, and 2 ties. His teams reached their peak against Harvard. The first year he lost, but then followed two wins, with a tie in his last year. Against other time-honored foes, Princeton and Dartmouth, Yale bowed four times. To show what he could do when he had the horses, he coached North to a victory over South, 20–14, at Miami in 1949, and prior to the opening of that season he handled the College All-Stars, which defeated the New York Giants 28–13, at the Polo Grounds, in a game for the *Tribune* Fresh Air Fund. His team consisted of men from twenty-two different colleges who trained together for eighteen days. According to the *New York Times*, the collegians were "beautifully coached." They rolled up the highest score ever accumulated by an All-Star team in eleven years. During the summer of 1951, Hickman headed a group of coaches that conducted a seminar for occupation troops in Germany.

During his years at New Haven, Herman became very active in radio and television. Yale liked him, as was evident by the new and more lucrative contracts he received, but after his 1951 team finished in the Ivy League cellar without winning a league contest, he was asked to decide between coaching and entertainment. He chose the latter, and tendered his resignation to the Yale authorities in August, 1952. He was soon one of the most widely known and well-liked men in his new field. His marvelous memory made him a sensation as a panelist. His comments on sports, current events, and poetry were followed avidly. He also wrote books and contributed to magazines. While driving through Maryland on his way to visit his mother in Florida, he suffered a gastric ulcer attack, and a month later, on April 25, 1958, he died in a hospital in Washington, D.C.

ROBERT LEE SUFFRIDGE

(6:00; 190)

For most of the transcendent heroes of the gridiron, a boy's coach becomes his most fervent booster, but Bob Suffridge seems to have provided an exception to the rule. He was not one of Coach Robert R. Neyland's pets. Suffridge, who was high-spirited and full of fun, and the trainer, Micky O'Brien, had a misunderstanding on the bus returning from practice just prior to the Orange Bowl game. Neyland sided with O'Brien, and despite Suffridge's marvelous playing and well-known loyalty to the school and the team, he was never able completely to work his way back into the good graces of the head coach. Neyland's senior assistant and West Point classmate, Bill Britton, who took over the head coach job in 1935 when Neyland was on Army duty in Panama, claimed that Suffridge was "one of the all-time greats." John Barnhill, line coach and later head coach at both Tennessee and Arkansas, said, "Bob was the best guard I have ever coached." Gus Manning, Director of Sports Information at Tennessee, rated Suffridge as "the greatest lineman ever to come out of Dixie," and he quoted Harvey Robinson as saying that Suffridge was "the greatest and, by far, the best" he had seen in twenty-seven years of coaching.

Suffridge was a native of Fountain City, Tennessee, born there on March 17, 1916. He came from a broken home and was taken care of and kept in school by relatives and friends. After playing on the Central High School football team for four years, he toyed with the idea of going to Southern California, but Howard Jones, the coach, did not seem interested. Other schools, particularly Alabama, wanted him, but eventually he followed his school friends to "the Hill." Bob was anxious to secure an education and was supremely confident that he could get ahead. John Barnhill considered that self-confidence one of his most important assets, not only on the football field but also in the classroom. At the university he made grades just good enough to get by, but he was never worried because he was confident that he would get through—and he always did.

At Tennessee, Suffridge made the freshman team, and the next season (1938) paired with Edward Molinski to form one of the finest pair of guards ever to play football. Molinski presented a most unusual case. As a freshman at Tennessee, he competed in the Golden Gloves boxing championships. In the finals, in Chicago, he suffered a broken nose and was knocked out. After that he quit college and returned to Massillon, Ohio, where his father worked in the steel mills. During the course of a strike, the Ohio National Guard was called out, and Ed, who was a member, found himself pointing a machine gun at the picket line of which his father was a part. After that sobering experience, he decided that he wanted an education after all, and wrote to Bob Neyland, who agreed to give him another chance. By hard work and determination he went to the top at football and in studies. He earned a Master's degree and made six A's during his last quarter in school. "Mo" did not stop there; he put himself through medical school and is now practicing in Memphis.

The 1938 team was the best yet to represent Tennessee. It won all games and rounded out the season by downing previously unbeaten Oklahoma, 17–0, in a rough game in the Orange Bowl. During the course of the season, Alabama was beaten, 13–0, for the first time since 1932, and Suffridge later said that this victory provided him with the greatest thrill of his football career. In that game, Tennessee's first touchdown was set up by George "Bad News" Cafego. The Vols were in single wing to the right with a balanced line and the left end playing wide. Cafego, in the tailback position, received the ball and started toward his right with Alabama's right end rushing in after him. Suffridge, playing right guard, pulled out and blocked that end while Cafego, on a "comeback" play, whirled and ran to his own left for 18 yards, to the 1-yard line, from which Tennessee then took it over.

After the Vanderbilt game, Ray Morrison, the Commodores'

coach, called Suffridge "one of the finest I ever saw." Bob improved with each game. Late in the season, Tom Anderson of the *Knoxville Journal* wrote, "Suffridge rose to new heights in his meteoric career as has been the case in all games." There seemed to be no limit to his capabilities, and he was only a sophomore. The United Press selected him for its All-America team. Captain and end Bowden Wyatt, present head coach at Tennessee, and George Cafego, a halfback, were other Vols considered for the highest honors, while Molinski and Babe Wood, S. Bartholomew, and L. Coffman, backs, gained All-Southern rating. The *Football Annual* considered Tennessee first in the nation, while the Associated Press placed the Vols second to Texas Christian.

In the rough work in the line, Suffridge reigned supreme. He possessed great speed and power, and his charge was described as explosive. Having the same sort of catlike reflexes as Bill Hewitt, the great pro, he shot across the line of scrimmage so fast that it frequently looked as though he were offside. His mind worked equally fast, and he was never trapped. Strong of arm and leg, he stunned an opponent with his forearm and hurled him backward or to one side so that he got into the enemy backfield almost as soon as the ball. He excelled in rushing passers and kickers and was almost unblockable. His lateral range was astounding.

Brilliant as he was on defense, Suffridge was probably even better in the close line play of the attack. In the high-speed plays and fast-breaking reverses employed by Tennessee, he was quick enough to get out and head the interference downfield. He was considered a perfect blocker, frequently upsetting opponents with a vicious shoulder block while keeping his feet. While there were guards who were faster than he in a straightaway run, he nevertheless blocked and tackled so often and so well downfield as to draw consistent praise. Rugged and aggressive, the dark-haired young man loved the game and never loafed either in a game or at practice.

Spring workouts in 1939 began shortly after the return from

the Orange Bowl. Neyland announced plans for converting his All-America guard into a Number One back, and Suffridge had to turn out to practice with the freshmen. Some thought that this was done as a disciplinary measure because of the incident with the trainer at Miami. Suffridge took it without complaint, and worked hard. Nothing came of the move. When the season of 1939 got under way, Bob was back in the line. Tennessee was again all-victorious during the regular season, but Suffridge did not participate in all the games. He missed three because of an injury to his left knee. After that he played with a cumbersome brace that cramped his style and prevented him from roaming and charging with his customary vigor.

The Vols had a string of 22 victories going, and had not been scored upon in their last 15 games when the long-hoped-for call to the Rose Bowl was received. Southern California was the opponent. Suffridge wanted to win that one badly, if for no other reason than to get back at Howard Jones, but it was not to be. Undermined by the exaggerated buildup that had been accorded the team, and faced by an alert, well-coached opponent, the Vols lost to the Trojans 14–0. Despite his bad knee, and playing on a losing team, Bob was hailed by Southern California as one of the outstanding players of the game, and the United Press, which that year picked an All-Bowl team, named him as one of the guards. Molinski shaded him for All-America rating, although both were chosen by many critics. Cafego and James Rike, center, also received much acclaim. Before the reverse at Pasadena, the Associated Press had rated Tennessee second and Southern California third.

Tennessee began moving again in Bob's senior year, and for the third consecutive season went through the regular schedule unbeaten to be rated at or near the top by most observers. It was a splendid organization, boasting such headliners as the wonderful guards Suffridge and Molinski; Marshall Shires, tackle; Ed Cifers, end; and Robert Foxx and Johnny "Gone with the Wind" Butler, backs. By going to the Sugar Bowl that season, Bob completed the circuit. He had appeared in a different major bowl in each of his three varsity years, and during that period he never played in a losing game against a Southern rival.

The Sugar Bowl game with Frank Leahy's unbeaten Boston College Eagles was one of the most thrilling in history. Suffridge got his team off to a good start. Going down under a punt, he hit a bean eater so hard that the latter dropped the ball. Tennessee recovered and pushed on to a touchdown: 7–0! For the first time in six years, a Tennessee punt was blocked. Boston capitalized on the break to score on a pass play from a spread: 7–7! Tennessee marched 55 yards after receiving the kick-off: 13–7! Not to be outdone, the Eagles drove 65 yards after taking the next kickoff: 13–13; It was now the Vols' turn, after taking the kickoff they reached the 7-yard line before the Eagles held, and Tennessee missed an attempt at a field goal. A few runs and five straight passes put the ball on Tennessee's 23-yard line. Suffridge, who had sat out a few plays, was about to go back in when Charlie O'Rourke, the slim Boston passer, faked a pass and then zig-zagged through the surprised and scattered Vols all the way to a touchdown. Final score, 19–13!

The spectators were enthusiastic over the brilliant runs and passes, but in the line, the play was fierce and rough and not always of the cleanest variety. But the linemen on both sides were so adroit in the practice of modified mayhem that few penalties were called. At Boston College they claim that Suffridge tossed sand in his opponent's face when he charged. Tennessee scornfully points out that he would have had to carry the sand with him, because the field was heavily sodded. Whatever happened, Suffridge was again one of the stars of the bowl games, and there was no doubt as to who was the top guard for 1940. Of the thirteen All-America teams examined by the writer, Suffridge was on all of them. Not only was he named on the Associated Press All-Time team; he also received more votes than any other guard when the Christy Walsh All-America Board polled sportswriters in picking its All-Quarter-of-a-Century team (1924–1948). The Washington

Touchdown Club awarded him the Knute Rockne trophy as the best lineman of the year, and he also received the Atlanta Touchdown Club award as the outstanding Southern player of the year.

In 1941 Suffridge played with the Philadelphia Eagles and received honorable mention for the All-Pro team. He reported for active duty as an ensign in the Naval Reserve in May, 1942, and the next fall was a member of the Georgia Navy Preflight Skyscrapers, one of the strongest football teams in the services. The United Press named him for its All-America Service team. He was transferred from the air arm of the Navy to the armed guards in June, 1944, and was released from active service, with the grade of lieutenant, in September, 1945, just in time to take another fling at professional football, again with the Philadelphia Eagles. After that, he retired from the game and is now with an insurance company in Knoxville.

EDGAR TOLL GLASS

(6:04; 210)

Ned Glass, a huge fellow from Farmington, Connecticut, was the other guard, with Heffelfinger, on the All-Star team that Walter Camp picked in 1904. Before entering Sheffield, Glass had played at Syracuse in 1898 and 1899 and at Mercersburg Academy in 1900. He was barred from the Princeton and Harvard games in 1901 because of the "one-year residence" rule, but he was eligible in 1902, the only year that he was allowed to play in championship games while at Yale. By that time he was a man of twenty-five, rugged, experienced, and abnormally strong, particularly in the arms and hands. He could bend an iron pipe into the shape of a pretzel. It is said that he never fully let himself out for fear of killing or maiming someone. Thin-lipped and firm-jawed, with cold blue eyes, he was an awesome figure. Fortu-

nately for all concerned, he was a likable man with no meanness
in his nature, although when an opponent became too obstreper-
ous or took liberties with him, he was not above taking a poke at
him with his fist—not too hard, just enough to bring the man to
his senses. At that, he was so rawboned that, as Charlie Daly once
said, it was necessary only to run into him to get hurt. Emory S.
Land (later a rear admiral) did just that when Navy played Yale
in 1901, and he came away with a broken collarbone.

Ned's ways were not orthodox, but because of his great
strength he was able to obtain peculiarly satisfactory results. In
the bone-crushing age, a defensive lineman's safety lay in keeping
close to the ground, but Glass played rather high, as Heffelfinger
used to do. Instead of a head-on collision with his opponent, there
being no neutral zone then, Ned would cuff him aside, knife
through the line, and seize the ballcarrier. His long, powerful
arms earned him the nickname "Cyclops." On offense he would
drag the Yale ballcarrier along for yards, with many of the opposing team ganging on him. On a trick play that ended in what
is now called a veer-buck, Yale's captain, George Chadwick, twice
went half the length of the field to touchdowns against Princeton.
All Glass had to do on that play was to block off three Prince-
tonians long enough for Chadwick to get through and away. Old-
timers like to include Glass with Heffelfinger, Hare, and DeWitt
at the top of the list of all-time guards. Although fast, Glass never
had an opportunity to show the versatility of the other three, but
for position play in the line it is doubtful if he ever had an equal.
He has been called a football genius, and not without cause.

Yale's 1902 team, although tied by Army, was unbeaten, and
downed Princeton 12–5 and Harvard 23–0. Glass was the keystone
in the famous "Irish line," probably the strongest in Yale annals.
Glass, Henry Holt, center; James Hogan and Ralph Kinney,
tackles; and Tom Shevlin, end, appeared on Camp's All-America
team with George Goss, guard, on the second team. The next
year the other end, Charles Rafferty, made the first team. The
1902 backfield was also all-star: Chadwick and Foster Rockwell,

quarterback, were first-team All-America, and Harold Metcalf, halfback, and Morgan Bowman, fullback, second.

Mike Murphy, the celebrated trainer, thought that Glass should have been the greatest shot-putter of history, but for some reason or other, Ned was never a champion, although he placed several times at the "Intercollegiates," both from Syracuse and from Yale, and he won the event at the Harvard-Yale dual meet in 1903. In the summer of 1904, he placed second to Tommy Shevlin in the hammer throw at the Oxford-Cambridge versus Harvard-Yale dual meet in London. There was no shot-putting event on the program.

Glass became district sales manager for a steel corporation in Cleveland, Ohio, and died there in 1944 at the age of sixty-five.

JOHN JOSEPH CANNON

(5:11; 193)

When he began selecting all-time teams, Grantland Rice strung along with Heffelfinger and Hare, but in 1939 he turned over the latter's place to Jack Cannon, who remained in favor until 1954, when he was dropped to make way for Herman Hickman. Cannon was a departure from Knute Rockne's normal preference for comparatively small "watch-charm" guards, but Jack was quick and Jack was nimble and Jack could get into the interference with the speed of a lighter man while his vicious charge and cagy play made him a bulwark on defense. Playing without a head guard, his close-cropped black hair conspicuous in every play, he was the happy-warrior type, kidding and talking and thoroughly enjoying a rough contest. In 1929 his magnificent playing made him the outstanding man on what might have been the strongest of all Notre Dame lines. The other guard was the captain, John Law, with Tim Moynihan at center. Ted Twomey was at one tackle post, the other being manned by Frank Leahy until he was injured. Cannon, Twomey, Moynihan, and Law appeared on various All-America selections.

Led by All-America quarterback Frank Carideo, Notre Dame won all nine games played that season and was generally rated first in the land. Like all the Irish, Cannon pointed for the game with Army in New York, and it was at Yankee Stadium on a frozen field before 85,000 spectators that Jack displayed his skill to the greatest advantage. Among other features, he kicked off four times and made the tackle three of those times. He was frequently the first man downfield under a punt. When Jack Elder intercepted one of Chris Cagle's passes and ran ninety-six yards to a touchdown, it was Cannon who threw a key block to get him started and it was Cannon who led the smashing line that kept the desperate cadets from scoring. Notre Dame took the game, 7–0. When the final whistle sounded, an unusual event took place. The beaten Army players crowded around Jack to congratulate him on his phenomenal performance.

At the Shrine game at San Francisco there were many famous players eager to see action, but Cannon was allowed to go the full sixty minutes. Jack McDonald, a San Francisco sportswriter, said that Cannon's line play was the best he had ever seen, and he quoted Bronko Nagurski, who also played with the East team in the Shrine game, as saying that Cannon was "a perfect guard." Bob Zuppke and Big Bill Edwards were among the experts who expressed the belief that Cannon was the best guard since Heffelfinger.

Jack now owns and conducts the Jack Cannon Flower Cart, one of the largest florist establishments in Columbus, Ohio.

◆ ◆ ◆

AWARD-WINNING GUARDS

Robert L. Suffridge, *Tennessee*	ROCKNE, 1940
Endicott Peabody, *Harvard*	ROCKNE, 1941
Joseph B. Steffy, *Army*	OUTLAND, 1947
Edward Bagdon, *Michigan State*	OUTLAND, 1949
Lewis McFadin, *Texas*	ROCKNE, 1950
Robert Ward, *Maryland*	ROCKNE, 1951
J. D. Roberts, *Oklahoma*	OUTLAND, 1953
William T. Brooks, *Arkansas*	OUTLAND, 1954
Calvin Jones, *Iowa*	OUTLAND, 1955
James Parker, *Ohio State*	OUTLAND, 1956
Robert M. Novogratz, *Army*	ROCKNE, 1958
R. D. "Zeke" Smith, *Auburn*	OUTLAND, 1958
Roger Davis, *Syracuse*	ROCKNE, 1959
Thomas Brown, *Minnesota*	OUTLAND, ROCKNE, 1960
Joseph Romig, *Colorado*	ROCKNE, 1961

4

CENTERS

CAMP, 1910	Schulz, *Michigan*
YOST, 1920	Schulz, *Michigan*
TREVOR, 1927	Schulz, *Michigan*
GULF, 1933	Schulz, *Michigan*
SHAUGHNESSY, 1943	Peck, *Pittsburgh*
A.P., 1951	Schulz, *Michigan*
RICE, 1954	Schulz, *Michigan*
WEYAND, 1955	Schulz, *Michigan*
HELMS, TO DATE	Schulz, *Michigan*
ADDITIONAL	Lewis, *Harvard*
	Hooper, *Dartmouth*

ADOLPH GEORGE SCHULZ

(6:04; 243)

It was something of a mystery to Germany Schulz that a normal, healthy, able-bodied man could get tired playing a game of football. Such an attitude is understandable when one surveys his background. He grew up in the steel mills around Fort Wayne, Indiana, where he was born on April 19, 1883. He began working in the mills as a boy whenever he could spare the time from school, and he continued working there during his vacations while at college. Steel mills are no place for weaklings, and at the turn of the century, when the hours were longer and working conditions more hazardous than they are now, it took a man of tough fiber and considerable stamina to perform the work six, or even seven, days a week. Under such conditions, young Adolph acquired a formidable physique, and by the time he was sixteen he was already a 200-pounder doing the work of a full-grown man.

When he entered high school, he experienced no difficulty making the football team. He also played on the town team. In those days the biggest and strongest men were usually the guards, and that was the position he filled. The only time either of his teams could play was on a Saturday afternoon. Each needed his services badly; besides, interest was so keen that the fans desired to see both teams in action. It was arranged that they play their games on the same field; alternating, the schoolboys playing a half and then the townies taking their turn. It was a break for the players, having such a nice long rest between halves, and it was a break for Adolph, too. It enabled him to play 140 minutes of practically continuous football, a half being then thirty-five minutes long. To improve his wind and speed, he took a long run every morning before breakfast. When he went to Michigan, where they played only one game an afternoon, he felt as though he were doing only a half-day's work.

The young man tapered off his weekend by playing with a semipro team on Sundays. In a game against a team of former college stars, he was opposed by Dick France, a former Michigan guard. France persuaded him to go to Michigan instead of Purdue, as he had planned, and in the fall of 1904 he reported to Coach Fielding H. Yost at Ann Arbor. Michigan's center was a swarthy veteran named Henry F. Schulte. The similarity in names caused some confusion, and presently Schulte was being called "Indian" and Schulz, "Germany." The latter became so widely known by that nickname that eventually he signed his checks and had his name listed in the telephone directory as Germany Schulz.

Yost was happy about his recruit who, despite his bulk, was faster than most ends and backs, with feline reflexes and the stamina to play a full game at top speed. His huge hands seemed specially designed to clamp onto a hapless ballcarrier. Schulz played guard until the fifth game, against Ohio State, when Yost had him change places with Schulte. Centers then played in the line on defense, so about the only new thing Schulz had to learn was passing the ball. Those were the days when Yost was earning his nickname "Hurry Up." A quarterback gave his signals for the next play while the players were still untangling themselves from the previous one, and the ball was snapped as soon as they lined up. The center had to be the first man in position, which was probably why Yost wanted the agile Schulz as the pivot.

Schulz "broke in" in 1904 with the mighty point-a-minute machine captained by Willie Heston. The first important game of the season was against Wisconsin, and Schulz was called upon to face the All-Western center Richard Remp. With no neutral zone, the lines virtually locked as soon as the ball was put in play. Germany hit upon a novel scheme. On defense, he dropped back about a foot, and when Remp charged he was in position to brush him aside and break through the line. Yost was amazed at such unorthodox procedure, but with Germany making many tackles behind the Badger line, he did nothing about it. Michigan won with surprising ease, 28–0, and Yost gave much of the credit for

the team's staunch defense to Schulz. After that, at Yost's suggestion, the big fellow dropped back a yard, and roved.

Yost has often been quoted as claiming that Schulz was the first
roving, or loose, center and the first to use a spiral pass to the
kicker. It is difficult to pinpoint such innovations, but it seems
that Pennsylvania's Bob Torrey roved against Columbia in 1903,
while Georgetown authorities insist that their Percy Given performed in like manner against Navy in 1902. Pot Graves, the famous old line coach, believed that the first center to pass a spiral
was M. L. Elliott of North Carolina in 1899. It is doubtful if Yost
or Schulz ever heard of those achievements. It seems quite likely
that such refinements of center play were devised at Ann Arbor
independently.

Be that as it may, Schulz was one of the pioneers in both
matters, and his spectacular success caused centers everywhere
to try to imitate him. Grantland Rice said that he saw Schulz and
all the good ones that followed him, and none, not even the
prodigious pro Mel Hein was quite his equal. Germany's hands
were so large that he needed but one to pass the ball yet Walter
Camp called his passing—and blocking—flawless. On defense,
he assumed a semi-erect stance. With his long and powerful arms
he brushed aside the interference and then moved in fast. He
would throw himself half sideways in front of the ballcarrier, seize
him around the knees, and allow him to topple to the ground.
Like Glass and other men of superstrength, he seemed afraid of
injuring an opponent, and never tackled viciously or slammed a
man down.

Schulz liked to box, and could mix it up when the occasion
demanded, but in general he played a strictly clean game, avoid-
ing all appearances of unnecessary roughness. Pat Dwyer, Pennsylvania center in 1907, recalled that he was instructed to slug
Germany every time the latter passed the ball. His hardest blows
served merely to annoy the big fellow, who growled, "Aw, quit
that and play like a man." Germany's only retaliation was to over-
whelm Dwyer as he did all opponents. Before a game, Schulz was

so utterly relaxed that he frequently took a nap in the dressing room while waiting for the call to the field.

The 1905 Michigan team, captained by Fred Norcross, the quarterback, lost its final game to Chicago 0–2, to terminate a fantastic string of fifty-six defeatless games. Walter Camp saw the game, and was not too impressed by the Wolverines. He put Joe Curtis, tackle, and Indian Schulte, guard, on his second All-America team, and the great halfback Tom Hammond on the third. He omitted Schulz, but the latter appeared on six of the eight All-Western teams that were published in the Spalding *Guide*. Well established, in the Midwest at least, Germany was obliged to leave college and return to the roller mills in order to earn funds with which to continue his education.

Schulz returned to Ann Arbor in 1907, and found a new game confronting him. During his year of exile, the forward pass and neutral zone between rush lines were brought into the game in an effort to open it up and remove some of its rougher aspects. The new style gave Germany a greater opportunity to display his speed, diagnosing ability, and cruising range. That was his "great" year when Walter Camp and most leading authorities recognized him as the most capable center in history. The Wolverines lost only to Pennsylvania, 0–6, but almost pulled the game out with one of Yost's tricks.

The play was used when it was Michigan's ball after having been kicked out of bounds. Schulz obtained the ball at the sideline (as it was then customary for the center to do) and ran back on the field. When he put it down, the other six linemen were in position, all on the same side, thus making Germany eligible to receive a pass. Usually he went downfield on one flank with Harry Hammond on the other. In an earlier game he had caught a 40-yard pass. In the critical play against Penn, Captain Paul Magoffin also went down. The pass was to him, while Schulz turned in and cut down the safety man. Magoffin scored, but the play was declared illegal because the pass had crossed the line of scrimmage within five yards of the point where the ball had been snapped by Schulz. It was a hard one for Michigan to lose. The playing of Schulz throughout was lauded as the outstanding feature of the game. And Penn did not forget it!

Germany captained the Wolverines in 1908. To a certain extent it was a rebuilding year, since six of the starting lineup of the previous season had been graduated, among them Harry Hammond, who had been the backbone of the team. Yost had some good prospects, but they were still a year from jelling. The team was built around the captain, who, unfortunately, got off to a late start because of scholastic difficulties, but when Michigan took the field against Pennsylvania both teams were unbeaten. The Quakers had an unusually strong team captained by Big Bill Hollenback and including several other All-Americans.

Against that talent, Michigan was obliged to play largely a defensive game, and the defense consisted chiefly of the big linebacker. At times during the bitterly contested first half, it seemed as though he were single-handedly holding back the furious Quakers. Hollenback stated that always two and sometimes three or four men were assigned to cover Schulz. They converged on him from different angles on every play, and it must be remembered that clipping was then perfectly legal. Still, sportswriters estimated that Schulz made 90 percent of the tackles as he roved from sideline to sideline. Yost maintained that it was Schulz's finest game, and Hollenback felt it was humanly impossible for a man to play better. People called him a marvel and said he had put on the greatest one-man defensive show ever seen.

Pennsylvania led at half-time, 6–0, scoring on a triple pass play. Shortly before the end of the half, Germany wrenched a hip and had to take time out for the first time in his career. As the second half wore on, the rough play took a further toll. He was kneed in the abdomen and injured a hand. He could no longer move well. On defense, Yost stationed the guards between the tackles and ends in an attempt to stop Penn's fast drives to the flanks. Battered as he was, Schulz held the center with five linemen opposing him, but he no longer could help to the outside, and the score mounted. With ten minutes remaining, Referee Lang-ford stopped the game and urged Yost to remove Schulz. The big fellow, half carried and half led, cried like a baby and begged to be allowed to continue in the game. The final score was 29–0. Walter Camp expressed the opinion that Schulz had been out of condition. He left him off his All-America team, but many others still regarded Schulz as the best center in the country.

After graduation, Schulz joined the staff of the General Elec-tric Corporation at Madison, Wisconsin, and in 1911 and 1912 coached the line at Wisconsin under John P. Richards. The Badg-ers captured the conference crown in 1912. For the next three years, Germany was back at Michigan with Yost. His linemen were all well grounded in fundamentals. He produced such All-America or All-Western stars as R. P. Butler, tackle; A. L. Buser and R. M. Keeler, guards; and T. E. Powell, center, at Wisconsin and M. H. Pontius, tackle; G. C. Paterson, center; and E. All-mendinger, and W. Cochran, guards, at Michigan. In 1916 he went to Kansas Agricultural College (Now Kansas State) as di-rector of athletics and football line coach. After four seasons, he accepted a similar post at Tulane, where he remained for two years. Next, he secured a position as insurance adjuster for the Medical Protective Society of Fort Wayne. He worked out of the Detroit office, and for one season, 1923, served as head coach at the University of Detroit. His Titans won their climax game with Gonzaga 13–7, to complete a season record of four victories, three defeats, and two ties. After that last fling at the game he loved, he devoted full time to the insurance business until his death, after a long illness, at the Henry Ford Hospital in Detroit on April 14, 1951.

Germany was big, cheerful, and full of energy. He always loved sports and was active in American Legion baseball in Detroit. He belonged to the Tribe of Michigamua, a University of Michigan alumni society that helped to obtain positions for recent graduates.

ROBERT DURHAM PECK

(5:08½; 179)

Bob Peck was just about the only college center any reputable critic has ever had the audacity to rank above Germany Schulz. A southpaw, who fairly reeked with color, his strident voice could be heard over the clash of conflict, urging his comrades to fight harder. He seemed always to be talking. Full of pep and exuding self-confidence, he kept his team alert and keyed to the highest pitch. He provided that intangible element, that extra element of spirit for any team he played with.

The slogan "When Peck fights, the team fights" meant that Pitt was "up" almost all the time. Bob was a terrific competitor, extremely aggressive, fast, strong, alert, and a keen diagnoser. He was particularly valuable in breaking up end runs and slashes just outside tackle and in defending against forward passes. In 1916 Carnegie Tech's famous speedster "Sunny" Kesner was unable to get away for any long runs, and several times Peck threw him for substantial losses as Pitt won 14–6. Washington and Jefferson, with its formidable passing attack, had flattened the Panthers three consecutive times, but in 1915 it was largely Peck's work in breaking up passes that enabled his team to triumph 19–0.

Bob was small and chunky, and one wonders how he would have fared against the giants of today. But don't sell him short. In 1916 Syracuse's captain, Harold White, weighed 256 pounds, and the other guard, Chris Schlachter, 245. The previous year, the latter had appeared on Camp's and many other All-America teams, and White had also gotten a number of votes. They constituted the most famous pair of guards in the country—or did until they encountered Pitt. The Panthers gained repeatedly through them. Agile and strong, charging very low and fast, it mattered not to Peck that he was outweighed seventy-five pounds or so. He nailed his man and opened holes for the hard-running Panther backs. Only twice during the game was Pittsburgh held for downs. Spectators were dumbfounded. Walter Camp was among those present, and after the game, he was beseiged by reporters asking for an explanation of the seeming miracle. Like the rest, the "Father" was nonplused. Later he said that Peck had done the lion's share of the damage to the Orange. Pittsburgh won, 30–0.

After the Washington and Jefferson game of the same year, an enthusiastic Associated Press sportswriter reported that Peck had "just about outplayed" the entire W.&J. center trio—the center and both guards. Peck and his guards worked in close harmony. He hit so sharply that sometimes he could turn his opponent over to one of the guards while he rushed ahead to attack the secondary. On Pitt's end sweeps, he broke through so fast that he could knock down a man or two and still arrive at the end in time to meet the Panther carrier and run interference for him downfield. There was no stopping him going down under punts; he made as many tackles as the ends. He was accurate in his passing from center to lead the fast-breaking backs in Warner's single- and double-wing attacks. Moreover he had a trick of handling the ball in such a manner that opponents were sometimes lured off side.

Peck was born at Lock Haven, Pennsylvania on May 30, 1891. He came from a large family, and after he had attended the normal school at Lock Haven and been graduated from the Pawling Prep School on the Hudson, he got a job in Pittsburgh. Several years elapsed before he was ready to continue his education. He enrolled at the University of Pittsburgh in the fall of 1913, and majored in economics. Freshmen were then permitted to participate in varsity sports, and Bob made the team as a halfback. Joe Duff, Eddie Hart's old "sidekick" at Princeton, was head coach. Pitt squared accounts with such rivals as Penn State, Cornell, Carlisle, West Virginia, and Lafayette, but they lost to Washington and Jefferson and Bucknell. Navy, unusually strong that year, was held to a scoreless tie. Peck was the unsung blocking back and linebacker. Some accounts class him as only "fair to middling," with injury-prone legs, but in the season review he was one of four players listed as outstanding. The "big wheel" was J. Hubert Wagner, end and captain, who became a successful surgeon.

The next season (1914) Joe Duff made the decision to shift Peck to center. The job seemed made to order for Bob, and he became a star immediately. In the opening game of the season, Pitt defeated a strong Cornell team 9–3. Toward the end of play, Cornell worked the ball to Pitt's 4-yard line, but with Peck backing up the line the Ithacans could go no farther. Against Navy, he blocked a kick, recovered the ball, and ran 20 yards to a touchdown, which gave the Panthers a 13–6 victory. Pitt also defeated other strong rivals such as Pop Warner's Carlisle Indians, 10–3 and Penn State, 13–3. The sole setback was at the hands of Washington and Jefferson, 10–13. Peck put on a whirlwind exhibition against the Presidents, and Pitt fans insisted that he outplayed Burleigh Cruikshank, who appeared on a number of All-America selections. Apparently Frank Menke agreed with them, because he gave Bob a place on his All-America team. Pittsburgh was rated fifth in the East by the *New York Sun,* the highest rating attained by them up to that time.

In 1915 Pittsburgh changed coaches, although Duff had produced excellent teams and had given Peck the basic training to become a great center. The new coach was the famous Pop Warner, who had been secured from Carlisle. Pop polished and developed Peck into a master of his position. Against Carnegie Tech, that year, Peck injured a leg on the opening kickoff, but he kept on going, and it was not until near the end of the first half that Warner realized he was hurt. Bob's ankle was so badly bruised and sprained that it was feared that he would not be able to play against Penn State. The Pittsburgh papers wailed in woe; he was "the heart of the Pittsburgh team," "a tower of strength." His value may be judged from the fact that, with him playing even on a lame leg, the betting odds were 10 to 8 on Pitt; if he did not play, it was even money. He played, and Pitt won, 20–0.

Peck was very popular at college, but that was probably due more to admiration than to affection, because he was a tough customer. A sportswriter, noting that his middle name was Durham and that he was inclined to be loquacious, asked a student why no one thought to call him "Bull." The student answered that no one would dare call him that. Bob was such a hero and natural-born leader that when it came time to elect a captain for the 1916 team, he received the honor by acclamation.

Pittsburgh won all its games in both 1915 and 1916. Penn State, Washington and Jefferson, Pennsylvania, Carnegie Tech, Navy, Allegheny, and Westminster appeared on the schedule each year, and in addition Carlisle was played in 1915 and Syracuse in 1916. Captained by a clever quarterback, "Chalky" Williamson, the 1915 team was generally rated third in the nation, behind Cornell and Harvard, but in the following year everyone gave first place to the Panthers, although Parke H. Davis and Tom Thorp had them share the top spot with Army. That was the first Pitt team to play under the three-year-eligibility rule, so the criticism formerly leveled at the Panthers for playing freshmen no longer applied.

Warner called the 1916 team the greatest he had ever seen. It was loaded with talent. Camp did not believe in going overboard. He placed Peck on his first All-America team, and Pat Herron, end, on the second, but other selectors were more generous. Clarence "Tiny" Thornhill and Tom Seidel, tackles; Andy Hastings and Jimmy DeHart, halfbacks; George McLaren, fullback; and Dale Sies, guard, each appeared on at least one such selection, while Jock Sutherland, guard, and Cliff Carlson, end, secured top rating the following season, along with "Foxy" Miller who had understudied J. Morrow at quarterback in 1916. It was truly an imposing array, and Pop Warner made the most of it.

Peck's selection as All-America center ended an interesting three-year duel waged with John McEwan of Army. They never faced each other in a game, and were rated strictly on their performances against the rest. In 1914, Army won all games and Big John was the All-America choice. The next year Pittsburgh won all its games, and Peck ascended the throne; therefore 1916 was the "rubber" year. Each captained his team and led it through an unbroken string of victories. Of twenty-six All-Eastern teams considered, Peck was on thirteen and McEwan on thirteen, but Camp and the majority of selectors of All-America teams favored the Pittsburgh man, with the Cadet a close second.

Warner called Peck "the best all-around lineman" he had ever seen. In addition to Warner, Shaughnessy, and Jock Sutherland, such critics as Dan Daniel, *New York Tribune*, 1929; Joe Godfrey, *All-Sports Magazine*, 1924; and George F. Rhodes, *Outing Magazine*, 1923, considered Bob the greatest of centers. He was good at other sports, too. He was on the Pittsburgh baseball team as a freshman and sophomore and played "a peppery game at first base." The 1914 team was the best Pitt had ever had up to that time, winning twelve and losing five. Peck was also on the varsity basketball squad as a freshman.

In September, 1917, Peck joined the staff at Culver Military Academy as an instructor in athletics. He coached football, baseball, and basketball. On Sundays he slipped over to Youngstown, Ohio, to play professional football with the Patricians, which also included Stan Cofall and Charley Bachman of Notre Dame and "Tommy" Hughitt of Michigan. Because of the war and the demands of the draft, the team was soon forced to suspend operations. Bob joined the Marines in May, 1918, and was sent to an officers' training camp at Quantico, Virginia. By the time he finished the course and was commissioned a second lieutenant, the war was over and he was relieved from active duty in June, 1919.

The fall of 1919 found him back at Culver. According to the records of Dr. Harry A. March, he played at least one game with the Massillon Tigers, against the Canton Bulldogs on November 16, 1919. Many of his former teammates at Pittsburgh were with the Tigers, among them Pat Herron, Tiny Thornhill, Jock Sutherland, and R. A. Gougler. Gus Dorais of Notre Dame, Shorty

Miller of Penn State, and "Nasty Bob" Nash of Rutgers were other noted stars on the team, but the Bulldogs, with the famous Indian halfbacks Jim Thorpe and Joe Guyon, won the game 3–0, through a 50-yard drop-kick by Thorpe.

At Culver, Peck was named head football coach in 1921 and director of athletics in 1930. His teams were well coached and usually gave a good account of themselves. Among the noted athletes he developed was his successor at Culver, Russell D. Oliver, one of the few men to win three letters in each of three major sports at Michigan. Others were Wendell Osborn, center for Navy; Leo Hoffman, another Michigan football star; and William Breckenridge, who became a major-league baseball pitcher.

Bob was still director of athletics at Culver on June 19, 1932, when he died of a heart attack while playing on the academy golf course.

WILLIAM HENRY LEWIS

(5:11; 177)

The center whom Camp picked for his All-Star team in 1904 was Bill Lewis, a Negro who was born in Berkeley, Virginia, in 1868, shortly after the close of the Civil War. His parents had been slaves, and his father, after being emancipated, became a Baptist preacher. Later in life Bill was elected to the Cambridge City Council in 1899, and to the Massachusetts State Legislature in 1902, and was appointed Assistant United States Attorney of Boston in 1903 and Assistant Attorney General of the United States in 1910.

Prior to enrolling in the Harvard Law School, Lewis played freshman football for one season and varsity for three at Amherst. He made an enviable reputation for himself, and captained the team in his senior year, 1891. He helped the Lord Jeffs to several outstanding achievements, particularly in 1890 when they defeated Cornell and Dartmouth, scored against Harvard, and held Yale to a 0–12 score, and Wesleyan, also a power at that time, to 6–8.

Lewis played at Harvard in 1892 and 1893, the years during which Lorin E. Deland introduced the dangerous and spectacular mass-momentum plays such as the "flying wedge" in place of a kickoff, the "horse's neck," an application of the principles of the flying wedge to scrimmage, and the "turtleback," in which the team massed in a solid oval. The ball was snapped and passed to someone within the oval; then the whole mass began to move around the end. In the wedge plays the offense was in motion toward the opponents before the ball was put in play. Devastating as the plays were, Yale managed to stall them sufficiently to eke out a victory, by an identical score, 6–0, in both 1892 and 1893. In each case it was the only defeat suffered by the Crimson all season. In 1893 Bert Waters, the captain, was incapacitated through his brush with Frank Hinkey in the Yale game and Lewis was elected to captain the Crimson in its last game, with Pennsylvania. Under his leadership Harvard won, 26–4.

Caspar Whitney thought very highly of the Harvard material in 1892, and gave All-America honors to Lewis, Ma Newell, tackle; Bertram Waters, guard; Frank Hallowell, end; and Charles Brewer, halfback. Everett Lake, who had been an All-America halfback the previous year, became governor of Connecticut. The next year, Whitney was not so favorably impressed, and only Lewis, who was then twenty-five years old, made the All-America team.

Lewis was light but strongly constructed, and highly intelligent. He carefully studied the game and his opponents, and never wasted his strength in needless motion. He was cool under pressure, very active, and could outwit a rival. He could block well and he fed the ball accurately and cleanly to his quarterback in the split-second timing required by the "flying" plays. As was customary at the time, he passed the ball with one hand. The other arm was used as a shield in front of his face to discourage heavy-handed individuals from trying to ram his nose down his throat. For many years Lewis took time off from politics and his law practice to serve as line coach and as a member of the football committee at Harvard. In 1898, when Harvard won the championship, he was credited by some with devising a special defense that halted Pennsylvania's dreaded "guards-back." He was easygoing and modest, with a keen sense of dry humor, but as a coach he had the reputation of being a hard driver on the field. When Walter Camp revised his book on *How to Play Football* for Spalding's Athletic Library in 1903, he invited Lewis to contribute a chapter on "Defense." He died on January 1, 1949.

HENRY JUDSON HOOPER

(5:07; 236)

When Walter Camp published his All-Time selections in 1910, he ranked Hooper next to Germany Schulz among the centers. Thus, according to the Campian school of thought, Harry was the greatest of the old-type, pre-1906 centers who reigned in the days when no neutral zone separated the rush lines and when push-and-pull mass play prevailed. That would seem sufficient reason to include him in this collection. Built along the generous lines of a coke oven, Hooper could not be budged on defense. Many of Dartmouth's plays consisted of the ballcarrier following Harry, who waded through the opposition, keeping his feet remarkably well. On tackle-back plays, when the mass hit the line, he ran around to help push. His weight, strength, and leg drive assisted considerably. Considering his squat build, he was remarkably quick. He passed well to the quarterback and kicker, and a wet ball did not bother him. In 1910 Camp said that Hooper went far toward developing the position along modern lines, but how the Maestro arrived at that conclusion neither the writer nor those with whom he consulted could fathom. It would appear that Hooper marked the end of the old era and Schulz the beginning of the new.

When Harry attended Phillips Exeter, he was sought by many of the larger colleges, but he elected to attend Daniel Webster's "little school" in New Hampshire where the football team was coached by Fred G. Folsom. Dartmouth was little (800 students), but the 1903 rush line was the heaviest in the country. From tackle to tackle, it averaged close to 220 pounds. At the end of the season, the Big Green might have been the best team in the nation. It lost but one game, to DeWitt's Princeton champions, 0–17, after outrushing the Tigers 225 yards to 64. In defeating Harvard 11–0, it outrushed the Crimson, 245 yards to 45. It ended the season by slaughtering its time-honored rival, Brown, 62–0. Camp put Hooper on his first All-America team and ranked the team third, behind Princeton and Yale. Sir Walter's chief rival in recording current football history, Caspar Whitney, was far more generous. He gave Dartmouth second place and named Hooper and Captain Myron Witham, quarterback, on his first All-America team, and Joe Gilman, guard; Leigh "Bull" Turner, tackle; and Jimmy Vaughan, halfback, on the second. Ralph Glaze, an end, became an All-American the next year.

No one knows how high Hooper might have rated among the centers of history had he played out a normal span of four years. His tremendous achievement as a freshman suggests that he might have developed into the greatest of them all. Shortly after the season of 1903, his only one in college football, he died from complications arising from an appendectomy. A terror on the field but mild-mannered and soft-spoken off the field, he was idolized by his teammates, many of whom were at his bedside when he died.

AWARD-WINNING CENTERS

Casimir J. Myslinski, *Army*	ROCKNE, 1943
Charles P. Bednarik, *Pennsylvania*	ROCKNE, 1947; MAXWELL, 1948
Robert Pellegrini, *Maryland*	ROCKNE, 1955
Jerry Tubbs, *Oklahoma*	ROCKNE, 1956

5

QUARTERBACKS

CAMP, 1910	Eckersall, *Chicago*
YOST, 1920	Eckersall, *Chicago*
TREVOR, 1927	Eckersall, *Chicago*
GULF, 1933	Eckersall, *Chicago*
SHAUGHNESSY, 1943	Clark, *Colorado College*
A.P., 1951	Eckersall, *Chicago*
RICE, 1954	Baugh, *Texas Christian*
WEYAND, 1955	Baugh, *Texas Christian*
HELMS, TO DATE	Eckersall, *Chicago*
ADDITIONAL	Daly, *Harvard and Army*
	Pfann, *Cornell*

WALTER HERBERT ECKERSALL

(5:07; 142)

"Eckie, Eckie, break your neckie,
Eckersall."

The Michigan rooters joined full-voiced and wholeheartedly in the rousing chorus. That was in 1905. The object of their solicitude was probably the most feared, and also one of the smallest, men in football. But little Eckie could outkick any of the big fellows, and when he ran in the open he was as difficult to catch as a frightened jackrabbit. He was smart and shrewd—and very fast. At college he dropped track in favor of baseball, but at high school he was coholder of the national interscholastic record for the 50-yard dash (5⅗ seconds) and for the 100-yard dash (10 seconds), and he also held the Illinois state interscholastic record for the 220-yard dash (22 seconds). He was born on June 17, 1886, in the south side of Chicago in what was then the "Woodlawn Area." In his freshman year at Hyde Park High School, his speed and fierce tackling earned him a position at end. The next season he was shifted to quarterback, and developed into one of the greatest in history.

Even though Hyde Park boasted of a large number of players of high caliber, including the famous Hammond boys who later starred at Michigan, Eckie captained the team in both his junior and senior years. Each of those teams made a notable record; the one of 1901 was undefeated, and vanquished the University of Chicago, 6–0, on the latter's own field. In that game a long run by Eckersall set up the score, and Tom Hammond carried the ball over. In the following year Chicago edged out the schoolboys 6–5, but Hyde Park won all games with school teams and buried Brooklyn Polytechnical Preparatory School, one of the best in the East, under a 105–0 score. Near the end of that game, Eckersall broke his left collarbone—the only serious injury in his career.

When Eckersall matriculated at Chicago it caused a surprise, because it was supposed he was going to Michigan. He said that he made the decision because the university was near where he lived. At Chicago he came under the coaching of the Old Master, Amos Alonzo Stagg. The Maroon had a capable veteran quarterback in Lee Maxwell who became president of the Crowell Publishing Company. He and Eckersall alternated during the first few games, but by the time of the first conference game, with Indiana, the freshman had the job. He cinched his hold in that game, twice getting away for touchdown runs of three-quarters of the length of the field, and drop-kicking a goal from the 45-yard line. He starred in every subsequent game that year, with his top performance against Wisconsin when he kicked three field goals to score all of Chicago's points in a 15–6 victory. A field goal then counted five points.

In selecting an All-Western team for 1903, Walter Camp gave the nod to Sig Harris of Minnesota, claiming that Eckersall's play in the final game, lost to Michigan, had been disappointing except for his tackling, which he called "phenomenally good." That tackling of Eckie's always aroused Camp's enthusiasm. He once said that the only man he ever saw hit harder was Frank Hinkey, another little fellow. In 1904 Camp was in a quandary whether to choose Vincent Stevenson, who had driven Pennsylvania to the championship, or Eckersall. He took both, putting the Chicagoan at end, and he expressed the wish that Stagg would play him at end on defense.

The season of 1904 was a great one for Eckersall. He broke the morale of a good Texas team by running back the opening kickoff 107 yards to a touchdown. He got loose for 95 yards against Iowa, and he ran back a kickoff 106 yards against Wisconsin. Camp could not have faulted him on his play against Michigan that year. His punting was marvelous and helped hold down the score to 12–22. One of his kicks sailed 75 yards through the air. And to climax the day he scooped up a fumbled ball and scored a touchdown. On defense he closed up so fast that he frequently was able to stop Heston as the Wolverine Thunderbolt was bulling his way through or around the line. Once in the open, Heston jumped clear over his head, but so great was Eckersall's speed and coordination that he ran down his man in twenty yards. Because of Heston's lethal straight arm, Stagg taught Eckersall to let him pass and tackle him from the rear. Considering how fast Heston was, Eckersall was probably the only player in the world who could have got away with it.

Running back kicks had been Eckersall's speciality in 1904. It was drop-kicking that brought him the most headlines the following season. In a morass, with the ball so slippery it could be held only with difficulty, he kicked a field goal from the 23-yard line for the only score of the game with Wisconsin. Chicago won 4–0, that being the first year that the value of a field goal was four points. Eckie got two from near midfield against Purdue, and against Illinois he tallied five to equal the all-time record for a single game. In that contest, he also scored a touchdown for good measure.

On Thanksgiving Day the unbeaten teams of Chicago and Michigan met at Marshall Field, Chicago, to determine the championship of the West. Since Yost took control in 1901, the Wolverines had never tasted defeat—fifty-six consecutive games with only a tie with Minnesota in 1903 to mar a perfect record—2,821 points against 40 by all opponents. The 1905 team had not been scored upon, and was naturally the favorite. The bitter feeling that prevailed at most important games in the West was even more intense than usual. The year before, Michigan had incapacitated four Chicago players in the first twenty minutes of play. For the 1905 game, officials with eastern affiliations were chosen, and Stagg took good care to brief them on the subject of mayhem.

With such a grand fight in prospect, everybody who could get to Chicago and had the two dollars necessary for a ticket wanted to be at the game. The stands were enlarged to accommodate 25,791. The gates were opened at eleven-thirty, and the stands were filled long before the kickoff at a quarter to two. Walter

Camp and Caspar Whitney had come bustling out from their eastern fastnesses to witness the wingding. The first half was a stalemate. Neither Michigan's bruising assault nor Chicago's tricky open plays advanced the ball much beyond midfield. Joe Curtis, huge Michigan tackle, was causing Eckersall trouble when the latter punted. Several times Eckie was able to get the ball away only by means of a clever side swing of his leg. Toward the end of the half, Joe pressed too hard and bumped into Eckersall after the kick was made. Eckie, quick to react, flopped to the ground and lay still. The officials, anxious to prevent a recurrence of the roughhouse of the previous year, banished Curtis for unnecessary roughness—and Eckersall got up and resumed playing. That disqualification was a decided break for Chicago.

Even without its strongest lineman, Michigan kept pushing the attack in the second half. A good Michigan kick followed by a penalty put Chicago back on its 8-yard line. It was second down with 20 yards to go and a strong wind blowing against the Maroon. A fair catch by Michigan would give the talented Tom Hammond a chance to kick a field goal, so Eckersall did not kick; he executed what Stagg, to this day, calls the most daring play he ever witnessed in an important game. Eckersall faked a kick and then raced around Michigan's left end to gain the necessary yardage before being forced out of bounds. Of all his sensational plays, that might well have been his favorite.

Time was runing out when Eckersall punted from midfield. Because of the head wind, he sent the ball low and hard across the goal line. A Michigan substitute caught it and tried to run it out. He had barely run clear of his own goal line when Arthur Badenoch and Captain Mark Catlin hit him and threw him back over the line for a safety, according to the rules then in effect. Chicago now led, but there was still considerable football to be played. Once Johnny Garrels, a hurdler who was to win a silver medal at the Olympic Games in 1908, got loose around end. Eckersall nailed him after a 28-yard gain. Again Tom Hammond broke into the clear, but Eckie brought him down with one of the most vicious tackles of the season. So Chicago won, 2–0, and ended Michigan's long reign. Tearing down the goalposts had not yet been thought of, but the fans tore down the fences around the park. Joy reigned throughout the city, and the celebration continued into the night.

Between them, the two distinguished experts from the East gave the new champions more All-America honors than had ever been conferred on a western team. Naturally Eckersall was the Number One quarterback. Camp picked Catlin for his second team, but Whitney put the captain on his first. Whitney had Hugo Bezdek, fullback, and Bubbles Hill, guard, on his second eleven. Camp also named Bezdek, but on his third team along with Bert Gale, the center. Arthur Badenoch, tackle, and Leo DeTray, halfback, were also highly rated. The champions elected Eckersall their captain for 1906.

After the glorious championship year, the season of 1906 was something of an anticlimax. That was the year when "new football" came into existence with the forward pass authorized and many of the objectionable features of the game curtailed. The Western Conference leaned over backward in the reform movement. Among other things, training tables were abolished and a college was permitted to play only five games a season. After beating Purdue and Indiana, Chicago dropped a game to Minnesota. Stagg had been working on the pass, but a rainy day restricted its use against the Gophers. After that reverse, he really opened up. He had developed a form of "keeper play" for Eckersall in 1903. Now he expanded its scope, and Eckersall could fake to one of the backs and then carry or pass. Chicago crushed Illinois 63–0 and Nebraska 38–5 with Eckie executing some fancy passes, particularly to Walter Steffen. Against Nebraska, in his last college game, Eckersall duplicated his record feat by kicking five field goals. He was again selected for All-America honors by most critics.

Following graduation, Eckersall accepted a position in the

sports department of the *Chicago Tribune*. He also played in a few professional football games during the season of 1907. Except in Ohio, professional football was not held in high esteem, but Chicago promoters assembled a team around Eckersall. The "big" game was against St. Louis, for which he received a high of $300 —and he earned it by scoring all his team's points, three field goals, to win 12–4. Rube Waddell, Connie Mack's eccentric pitcher, played with St. Louis and seemed to feel that his mission was to put Eckie out of business. When the Chicago players became wise to that, they ganged him, and a badly battered Rube was soon forced to the sidelines. Eckersall retired from pro football after 1907, but he played a few seasons with Adrian C. "Cap" Anson's independent professional baseball team, the Chicago Colts. He was a third baseman and a good one, but not quite up to big league standards. When that became apparent, he dropped baseball, too.

In that busy fall of 1907, the *Tribune* sent him to Philadelphia to cover the Carlisle-Pennsylvania game inasmuch as the Indians were later to play Chicago. The head linesman failed to appear, and Eckersall was pressed into service. He liked officiating, and it was not long before he was one of the most sought-after officials in the country. He worked Army-Navy, Army-Notre Dame, and Western Conference championship games. Later, he branched out and refereed boxing bouts. All that time he continued with his work at the *Tribune*, and earned the reputation of being one of the leading authorities on college football. His All-America and All-Western selections were eagerly read by fans everywhere.

He was much attached to his widowed mother, and her death affected him profoundly. His friends soon became alarmed at his failing health. During the football season of 1929, on several occasions, he left a sickbed to fulfill officiating commitments. He continued his work with the newspaper, and as usual wrote the review of the season for the *Official Guide*. On March 24, 1930, he suffered a heart attack and died in his rooms at the Chicago Athletic Association—about a year after his mother's death.

EARL HARRY CLARK

(6:00; 183)

Football buffs were surprised when the All-America selections were published at the end of the season of 1928 and the Associated Press named, at quarterback, Dutch Clark, who was virtually unknown outside his home area. It seems that Frank Frawley and C. L. "Poss" Parsons, veteran Denver sportswriters who knew a superplayer when they saw one, "sold" Clark to Alan J. Gould, sports editor of the Associated Press. It took courage for the latter to name the youngster over Howard Harpster of Carnegie Tech and other well-publicized and highly efficient quarterbacks but it proved a smart choice. A few years later he could smile when Clark made the All-Pro team in his rookie year, and he could laugh out loud as the years rolled by and the fame of his protégé increased.

As late as 1952, Arthur Daley of the *New York Times* doubted if there were was "a greater or more versatile backfield performer than Dutch Clark." Another noted writer, Robert Harron, called him the greatest pro player of all time, fit to challenge Jim Thorpe as football's greatest. Bob Considine felt that no better player ever lived, and Bill Corum thought he was "probably" the best of all time. While Clark was still in college, Ike Armstrong, coach of rival Utah, stated that he was the best he had ever seen. Dutch was a thoroughbred—a clean-living and unassuming gentleman. On "Dutch Clark Day," in Detroit in 1937, the Governor of Michigan, Frank Murphy, wrote of him, "He is a thorough sportsman in every sense of the word."

The "hometown boy who made good" was born at Fowler, Colorado, on October 11, 1906. He was called "Dutch" and the "Flying Dutchman," but his ancestors were English and Danish. At Pueblo High School he won sixteen letters. Although he was an All-State football player and a 10.1-second man on the track, it was at basketball that he first obtained national prominence.

After he was named to the All-America interscholastic basketball team in 1926, the Big Ten colleges commenced rushing him. He started for Michigan but switched to Northwestern. After a short stay he became homesick for the mountains and returned to Colorado, where he matriculated at Colorado College, a small, privately endowed coeducational institution at Colorado Springs.

Dutch led the freshman team in scoring, and the next season (1927) was at tailback on the varsity. William Travis Vande Graaff, former Alabama and West Point tackle, developed a light, fast team that featured a lateral passing attack from single and double wing. He had several very good men; in addition to Clark, G. A. Cecil, guard, and J. R. Vanderberg, quarterback, were All-Conference selectees but the team lacked reserve strength. In the last game of the season, the Tigers met Colorado Aggies for the championship. Clark went 35 yards to a score, but the Aggies won 20–7. That was the closest the Tigers came to the title (which they had last won in 1900) during the years that Clark played.

The 1928 team was called the most spectacular in the conference, but that was because of Dutch. Material was fast running out, and Vande Graaff did not have enough good men to withstand the pressure of the conference powerhouses. The campaign was built around Clark. He played quarterback or fullback, called the signals, and did most of the running, passing, and kicking. Operating usually from a short punt formation, he carried the ball 135 times in eight games and gained 1,349 yards, almost a first down every time he ran. He also completed 44 passes, scored 14 touchdowns, 16 points after touchdown, and a field goal for 103 points to lead conference scorers. His finest run came in a victory over Wyoming when he intercepted a forward pass, completely reversed the field, and ran 40 yards to a score. He usually played safety on defense, but in emergencies backed up the line. It was a tribute to his courage that he was reputed to play best in losing games. His running and passing kept the Tigers close in a loss to Utah, the ultimate conference champion, 21–27. The Utah game was called the most thrilling ever played in Salt Lake City. That was in Clark's All-America year.

Clark's lower legs were rather thin, which made for nimbleness and speed, while his well-muscled thighs gave him driving power. His quick reflexes, body control, and sense of rhythm, made him an elusive runner. His whirling motion made it wellnigh impossible for a tackler to hit him squarely, and when he was thrown he had the knack of falling so that he was not injured. In the pro game such authorities as Red Grange and Bronko Nagurski were to say that he was one of the most difficult men to tackle. His loyal coach, Bully Vande Graaff, insisted that he did not have a single weakness.

Dutch was captain in 1929. He was in for a difficult time, and later admitted that he had not enjoyed playing that season. His innate modesty had something to do with this state of affairs. The acclaim he received from all sides annoyed and embarrassed him, particularly because he realized that, in some sections, it was felt that only a strong publicity campaign had given him his All-America rating. The pressure on him was enormous. The crowds came to see Superman in person, but, alas, Colorado College still lacked sufficient strength to support him well. Opponents mobbed him on every play, yet he escaped injury and played full time in every game. In fact, he took time out only once during his entire four years in college, and that was in the Colorado Aggie game in 1928.

It was a rough, hard season emotionally as well as physically, but it was not without its compensations. Clark piloted his team to the first victory scored over Colorado Aggies in five years. He broke through the middle of the line and gave a magnificent demonstration of weaving and dodging, as he ran 50 yards to a touchdown. Colorado College won, 14–13, with Clark converting after both touchdowns. He was also featured in the late Bob Ripley's "Believe It or Not" series. The caption read, "Captain Clark scored all points for both teams, score Colorado College

3, Denver 2, December 2, 1929." Denver put terrific pressure on the Tigers, but Clark's punting (he averaged 45 yards with 11 kicks) and a fighting line held them off. In the second period, he tried to kick from behind the goal line. The pass was poor, and before he could get the ball away he was smothered for a safety —two points for the opposition. A minute and a half before the end of the game, he drop-kicked a field goal from the 33-yard line for his team's three points. In twenty-two consecutive varsity games that was the only one in which he did not score at least one touchdown.

There is a story behind the Denver victory. According to Juan J. Reid, present dean of men and former athletic director, who played in the game, the referee at first refused to allow the goal, claiming the ball had passed over the left goal post and not over the crossbar. One of the players, John Cogan, was Phi Beta Kappa and a close student of the rules. He tipped off Clark that it was a goal if the ball passed over a side post. Dutch demanded an examination of the rules, and the referee had to reverse himself. On New Year's Day, 1930, Dutch was starting quarterback for the West team in the Shrine game at San Francisco. The East, with Nagurski, Cannon, and other heroes won, 19–7, but Clark drove his team to a touchdown and kicked the conversion.

Clark had poor vision, one eye being seriously defective, and he was obliged to wear glasses off the field, but despite that handicap he was a remarkable all-around athlete. In the Conference, freshmen were permitted to play all varsity sports except football. He was a member of the basketball and track teams for four years. He was All-Conference at basketball four times and captained the team twice, while at track and field he broke the conference hammer-throw mark with a toss of 163 feet 3 inches. In 1930 he placed fourth in that event at the national A.A.U. championships. He played baseball in his senior year— playing on Friday or on Saturday morning and competing in track Saturday afternoon. He pitched and played in the outfield. His high batting average earned him a place in the All-Conference outfield. In addition, Clark was above average at golf, bowling, and pocket billiards and he won a high-school letter at tennis.

After graduation, Clark returned to assist Vande Graaff with the backs. He also was head coach of basketball and baseball and retained the latter positions through the spring of 1933. In the fall of 1931, he signed with the Portsmouth (Ohio) Spartans in the National Professional Football League. In one of his early appearances, Portsmouth defeated the Brooklyn Dodgers 19–0, and rookie Clark scored all 19 points. The next year he led the league in scoring with 39 points and in kicking field goals with three. Both in 1931 and 1932 he was All-League quarterback. Even though he met with such success, he returned to college coaching and handled all sports at Colorado Mines for the academic year, 1933–1934.

The Miners were none too successful, winning one and losing five, and Clark decided to return to the pro ranks. In the meantime, the Portsmouth franchise had been transferred to Detroit. Clark enjoyed four tremendous seasons with the Lions, during which time he was All-League quarterback each year. He narrowly missed individual scoring honors in 1934, but he topped all scorers the next two seasons with 55 points in 1935 and 73 in 1936. During those three years, he completed 72 of 146 passes and gained approximately five yards every time he carried the ball. In 1935 he drove the Lions to the world championship in a playoff won from the New York Giants 26–7. Clark was called the hero of the game. He ran 40 yards to the Lions' second touchdown, but it was his generalship and handling of the team that won him the most praise. George "Potsy" Clark, Detroit coach and no relation to Dutch, said that during the season the latter made almost no mistakes. He instilled such a degree of confidence in the players that they regarded him as infallible.

Clark served as player-coach with the Detroit Lions in 1937 and 1938. Despite the added burden, he made the All-League team in 1937. His 1938 team finished second to the Green Bay Packers for the Western Division championship. That season marked the end of his playing career. The next year he accepted a more remunerative position, as head coach, with the Cleveland Rams, and his release from the Lions specified that he would no longer play. He was with the Rams for four seasons and later coached the Seattle Bombers and assisted with the Los Angeles Rams, the latter having acquired the Cleveland franchise.

During off seasons Dutch returned to Pueblo where he had business interests, but in the fall of 1951 he was again in Detroit, this time as athletic director and head football coach at the University of Detroit. His last team, 1953, tied with Oklahoma A.&M. for the Missouri Valley Conference championship, but inasmuch as the Titans had beaten the Cowpokes 18–14 during the regular season, they were considered best in the conference by most critics. Clark developed such star backs as Bob Burgmeier and Lee Riley; the former led the conference in scoring and the latter in pass receiving. After that season he retired from football and accepted a lucrative position in Detroit, where he is now a successful businessman.

SAMUEL ADRIAN BAUGH

(6:02; 180)

They called him "Slingin' Sammy," and he holds all kinds of passing records, but Dick Seither of the *New Orleans Times-Picayune* claims that the greatest game in Baugh's entire career was one in which he did very little passing because of a heavy rain. That was in the Sugar Bowl on January 1, 1936, when Texas Christian played Louisiana State. Baugh, who as usual played the full game against L.S.U., punted the wet heavy ball fourteen times, averaging 48 yards a kick. His blocking, ballcarrying, and defensive work were classified as superb. He made the longest run of the day, 45 yards, while on several occasions his tackling prevented touchdown runs, and twice he intercepted State passes deep in his own territory. Writing in 1952, Seither said that he considered Baugh's performance "the most phenomenal stand-out in Bowl history."

That game, played before 35,000 drenched and shivering spectators, was a queer one. Baugh attempted to pass from behind his own goal line, but the wet ball slipped out of his hand and fell in the end zone for an automatic safety. Later Baugh jockeyed his team into scoring position, and Taldon Manton, the fullback, place-kicked a field goal from the 26-yard line to give the Horned Frogs the victory by the baseball score 3–2. Baugh had a hand in that score, also; he held the ball for the kick. It is safe to say that, even had Baugh never passed, he would have been considered a truly great back. As it was, his varied accomplishments made him "the most valuable player the Southwest Conference ever produced," to quote Joe Utay, who had been writing about Southwestern sports ever since he captained Texas A.&M. in 1907.

Baugh (pronounced to rhyme with law) was born on a farm near Temple, Texas, on March 17, 1914, the son of a railroad employee. From earliest childhood, Sammy displayed a fondness and aptitude for sports. At the local high school, he started as an end but was shifted to quarterback. In 1931 his family moved to Sweetwater, Texas, where he played on the high-school team for two seasons. He also played baseball, not only at school but with a town team. As a hard-hitting, strong-armed third baseman, he was sought by several colleges, but none seemed interested in his football potentials.

Sammy's success at football provides an inspiration to youngsters ambitious to make the grade in athletics, or for that matter in any other activity. He studied football technique and spent many hours during the off-season practicing sprinting, punting, and throwing the ball at a moving target. Though he increased his speed, he was never so fast as Eckersall or Daly. Rather he was known as a "smart" runner. His punting, of course, was outstanding. By the time he entered T.C.U., in the fall of 1933, his passing had improved to the extent that he won a place in the freshman backfield. Leo "Dutch" Meyer, who coached the freshmen, was also varsity baseball coach and had been instrumental in interesting Sammy in T.C.U. The next year, Meyer moved up to become the varsity football coach and was in a position to continue his efforts with the tall sophomore.

Sammy threw some touchdown passes and earned his letter but was not in the starting lineup in 1934. His hard work and conscientious effort toward self-improvement had begun to pay off, though, and he was a "top hand" in 1935. Improving steadily, week after week, by the time the climactic games of November were reached he was riding a tidal wave of popularity and success. His name was on the lips of every cactus-country fan and in headlines of the newspapers throughout the United States. He "riddled Texas with bullet-like passes"; his "dazzling passes and running dominated the game" against Rice; and his "passing and all-around generalship were the features of the contest" against Santa Clara. The last named was played in San Francisco in December, and Baugh passed to a touchdown, once punted 71 yards, and got off a quick kick that gained 65 yards.

The 1935 meeting of Texas Christian and Southern Methodist, with the conference title and a Rose Bowl bid at stake, proved to be a thriller. Both teams were undefeated and untied. In a wild, wide-open contest, Baugh all but threw his arm off. He pitched strikes but for some unaccountable reason his usually reliable receivers could not hang onto the ball. Even so, he completed 17 of 43 passes for 172 yards and a touchdown and had only one intercepted. With the Mustangs leading 20–14, T.C.U. still had a chance. Baugh passed his team to the 28-yard line, where the ball was lost on a fumble. Later he passed to the 35-yard line as time ran out. S.M.U. went to the Rose Bowl and lost to Stanford 0–7, while T. C. U. was invited to the Sugar Bowl as previously noted. Captain Darrell Lester, the giant center, was on a majority of the All-America teams, and Baugh appeared on such authoritative ones as the United Press and International News Service. Other Frogs meriting All-Southwestern laurels were Walter Roach, end; Tracy Kellow, guard; and James Lawrence, halfback. The Associated Press rated T.C.U. tied for fourth in the nation.

In the middle of the next season, 1936, Baugh sustained a leg injury and was on the bench when Texas A.&M. downed the Horned Frogs. Once again sound, Sammy passed his team to victories over Arkansas, the ultimate conference champion; Baylor, Texas, and Rice. In the Rice game he set up a score with a 23-yard run after taking a lateral pass. S.M.U. was played in a steady rain, reminiscent of the Sugar Bowl game earlier in the year. With passing all but impossible, Baugh's running was the Horned Frogs' chief threat, while his punts, which averaged 44 yards, and his defensive work contributed largely to stopping the Mustangs. The final count was 0–0. With Sammy passing under normal conditions, T.C.U. defeated Santa Clara, at the time the only unbeaten major team in the country, and Marquette, in the initial game of the Cotton Bowl series.

Sammy completed 109 out of 219 passes for 1890 yards and 11 touchdowns that season, and during his three varsity years, 274 out of 599 for 3,439 yards and 39 touchdowns. He was just about a unanimous All-America choice for 1936. Captain Walter Roach, his favorite receiver, also won national acclaim, and William "Cotton" Harrison, a guard, was All-Conference. Three precocious sophomores who later became All-Americans were Charles "Ki" Aldrich, center; I. B. Hale, a 246-pound tackle; and David O'Brien, Baugh's 152-pound understudy. Even though he participated in sports during the entire academic year, Baugh maintained a high scholastic standing.

Upon his graduation, Baugh signed with the football Washington Redskins and the baseball St. Louis Cardinals. After the latter farmed him out to the American Association, he decided to concentrate on the gridiron game. His debut in professional football occurred on September 1, 1937, at Soldier Field, Chicago, before 84,500 fans. It proved to be an auspicious beginning.

Playing with the College All-Stars against the reigning champions, the Green Bay Packers, he threw a 22-yard pass to his old college rival from Louisiana State, Gaynell Tinsley, who caught the ball on the 25-yard line and went on to the only touchdown of the game. After that, Baugh's punts kept the pros well bottled up, and their desperate attempts to pass to Don Hutson and others were checked by the steady defense of Sammy and his mates. The All-Stars won, 6–0.

When Baugh joined the Redskins, in 1937, they were in their first year in Washington, the franchise having been transferred from Boston. The team employed a single-wing formation with Baugh at left halfback. The Redskins met the Chicago Bears, on an ice-covered field, for the national championship. In the first half, Sammy threw a 42-yard pass to Cliff Battles to set up a touchdown, but the Bears led at half time, 14–7. In the second half, Sammy, limping from the force of the Bears' assault, unlimbered his arm. He threw a touchdown pass of 55 yards to Wayne Millner, another of 29 yards to the same player, who ran 48 yards to the end zone, and, finally, a 35-yarder to Ed Justice for another counter. Then, to make victory sweeter, he overhauled and downed a Bear player when the latter had a clear field before him. The Redskins won, 28–21. During the season, Baugh gained over 200 yards carrying the ball, but he became so valuable as a passer that he was not encouraged to run with it in later years.

The Redskins finished second in the Eastern Division the next year and again qualified for the championship play-off in 1940, but that is one that Washington fans prefer not to think about. The Bears won 73–0, although, curiously, the Redskins made eighteen first downs against seventeen for the Bears. After dropping to third place in 1941, the Redskins again faced the Bears in 1942. That time Fortune smiled on Washington as Baugh's quick kicks against the wind and a 23-yard scoring pass featured their triumph, 14–6. Again it was Bears versus Redskins in 1943! Sammy passed for two touchdowns, but after he left the game with a concussion, the Redskins were through and the Bears went on to win 41–21. The next time the Redskins were in the play-off was in 1945 when they lost to the Cleveland Rams, 14–15. Two of Baugh's ribs had been torn loose in front, and he played a quarter of the game with them taped up. That was the last world championship game Baugh played in. He continued to be one of the league's brightest stars for several more years, and retired after the 1952 season.

Baugh had played on two world and three division champion teams and had been named to the All-League team, by various agencies, eight times, 1937, 1940, 1941, 1942, 1943, 1945, 1947, and 1948. He held so many league records that it is difficult to keep up with them. Some have been broken, but the majority have withstood the efforts of later generations. Here are his marks: Most passes completed, career, 1,709; one season, 210 (1947). Most passes attempted, career, 3,016; one season, 354 (1947). Most yardage gained on passes, career, 22,085; one season, 2,938 (1947); one game, 446 on 17 passes against Boston (1948). Fewest interceptions, one season, 4 out of 182 attempts (1945). Most touchdown passes, career, 187; one game, 6 against Brooklyn (1943). Best passing efficiency (500 or more attempts), 56.7; one season, 70.3 (1945), 128 completions in 182 attempts. Most punts, game, 14 against Philadelphia (1939). Best punting average, one season, 51.4 yards with 35 punts (1940). Most seasons active player in league, 16. Most years leading passer, 6 (1937, 1940, 1943, 1945, 1947, and 1949). A few personal records: most passes completed, one game, 29 against Los Angeles (1949); most touchdown passes, one season, 25 (1947); most consecutive games throwing touchdown passes, 10 (2 in 1942 and 8 in 1943). In addition he intercepted 11 enemy passes in 10 games in 1943.

And Sammy holds or held other records for championship play-off games: Most championship games, 5 (1937, 1940, 1942, 1943, and 1945). Most passes completed, 42; attempted, 81; yardage gained, 632; touchdown passes, 6. For one game, passes completed, 18; attempted, 33; yardage gained, 335; touchdown passes, 3—all were made against the Chicago Bears, 1937. Most punts, all games, 14. Longest punt, 85 yards against Chicago Bears, 1942.

Baugh bought a 2,000-acre ranch near Rotan, Texas, and upon his retirement from league play was ready to settle down. On the side, he assisted his friend Murray Evans with the coaching at Hardin-Simmonds University at Abilene, Texas. When Evans resigned at the end of the 1954 season, Sammy, to the surprise of many, accepted the job. He labored with the Cowboys for five seasons. His greatest achievement was in 1958, when his team finished unbeaten in the Border Conference and took the title. A postseason game, in the Sun Bowl at El Paso, was dropped to Wyoming by the close score of 6–14. One of his best players was Sammy Oates, a deaf mute, who made the All-Conference team at end as a freshman. In 1960 and 1961, Baugh was head coach of the New York Titans in the newly organized American Football League. His teams placed second in the Eastern Division in 1960 and third the following year.

Baugh has come down in history as the most talented and perfect of all passers. Steve Owen called him the greatest, and Mel Hein thought that he came as close as anyone could to being a "one-man team." Sammy was calm, and he thought fast and clearly under pressure. With a strong arm and powerful wrists he could throw long distances, but his most effective pass was one over the middle of the line. He threw with speed and accuracy, with no lost motion, and he was clever in faking a pass in one direction and throwing in another. It was remarkable how quickly and effectively he adapted himself from his previous style of quarterback play to that required by the T-formation. Most players have found this transition quite difficult. Though he smiled a lot and was a friendly man, in a game he was a cold-blooded, hard-driving, and thoroughly tough "hombre."

CHARLES DUDLEY DALY

(5:09½; 154)

Pat Kennedy, President Kennedy's grandfather, and Charlie Daly's father, Tim, were contemporaries; each operated a prosperous saloon in Boston and sent a son to Harvard. Daly's coach at Harvard was W. Cameron Forbes, who later distinguished himself as Governor General of the Philippines and as Ambassador to Japan. President Kennedy's maternal grandfather, Congressman John F. "Honey Fitz" Fitzgerald, gave Charlie an appointment to West Point, where he played on a team managed by Douglas MacArthur. In later years he coached Dwight D. Eisenhower, Omar N. Bradley, James A. Van Fleet, and many others who became famous soldiers. In his own line, Daly was as famous as any of them. When he played, he was the greatest backfield man yet to appear on an American gridiron and he became almost equally successful as a coach. Camp placed him on his All-Star team in 1904. In selecting the best quarterback of all time, in 1928, John Heisman said it was a toss-up between Eckersall and Daly. He gave the nod to the former "merely because he was a bit heavier." The "joker" was that Daly was twelve pounds heavier than Eckie and over two inches taller.

Alert, exuding self-confidence, and bubbling with nervous energy, Charlie somehow gave the impression of being smaller than he was. On and off the field, his sharp black eyes constantly darted around, sizing up the situation. Paradoxical as it may seem, he was a reserved, sensitive man not given to talk—unless with friends, when he was apt to prove voluble. To those who knew him well, he was a delightful companion, but others thought him aloof.

Daly was born at Roxbury, Massachusetts, on October 31, 1880, and attended Dwight School and Boston Latin prior to entering Harvard in the fall of 1897. That season he was a substitute quarterback on the freshman team, but the next year, in a surprise move, Coach Forbes placed him on the varsity. How well he succeeded may be judged from an appraisal made by Walter Camp at the end of the season. He wrote, "The man who would try to improve upon Daly as a quarterback would either not know Daly or else be ignorant of the requirements of the position." The 1898 team progressed steadily through its schedule. Army, Dartmouth, Carlisle, Pennsylvania, and Brown were among major teams defeated, and the season ended with a handsome 17–0 victory over Yale—Harvard's first triumph over the Blue since 1890. Harvard was rated first in the nation. Camp and Whitney both placed Daly, Captain Ben Dibblee, halfback, and Jack Hallowell, end, on their first All-America teams. Whitney also named Walter Boal, a guard. Both agreed on Percy Haughton, tackle, and Leicester Warren, halfback, for the second array. Again Whitney proved the more liberal by giving second-team berths to Malcolm Donald, tackle; William Burden, guard; and William Reid, fullback.

In generalship and getting the most out of a team, Daly probably never had a peer. Coach Forbes told the writer in 1953 that Daly's play calling was chiefly responsible for the 1898 victory over Pennsylvania when he ran the Quakers' great guards weary by mixing power drives with wide sweeps. He was probably as fast as Eckersall, and developed a stop-go technique, based on a change of pace, that made him "the most alert tackle-dodging runner in the history of the game." He did not always sidestep. When a tackler came at him very low, he hurdled; when rather high, he dived under him. Percy Haughton, who did the punting in 1898, could get off his kicks in 1⅝ seconds from the snapback, and required little protection, so the speedy Daly was sent downfield with the ends. Charlie's speed stood him in good stead in track sports. In the spring of 1899, he won the running broad-jump in the dual meet with Yale, and placed third in the Intercollegiates and second in the Harvard-Yale versus Oxford-Cambridge dual meet held in London.

In 1899, after Haughton had graduated, Daly did most of

the punting. In a Pennsylvania game, on three occasions, his center heaved the ball over his head. Each time, Daly ran back, retrieved the ball, dodged the onrushing Quakers, and got off a good kick. His coolness in such cases was proverbial. In a Carlisle game, in 1900, he drop-kicked a field goal from the 35-yard line with, as the papers reported, "Indians all around him." His defensive work was extraordinary. He once told James A. Farley, former Postmaster General, that to the best of his recollection the only tackle he ever missed was in 1901 when he played with Army against Harvard. Camp criticized him for letting Chadwick get away in the Yale game of 1900, but at that stage Daly was too badly crippled to do much of anything.

Ben Dibblee took over the coaching duties in 1899. The Crimson continued rolling up a string of impressive victories, and finished the season unbeaten. Yale was outplayed by a wide margin, but the game ended a 0–0 tie. Daly, who was hailed as the hero of the game both offensively and defensively, was again everybody's All-America choice, and was elected captain for his last year. The Crimson had not been beaten since Charlie Daly began quarterbacking them, and they approached the Yale game of 1900 with a string of 32 consecutive defeatless games. Daly had never been injured in a game, but shortly before the meeting with Yale he wrenched a knee in practice. He was in bed a week and was in no condition to play; but because he was captain he started the game, but had to retire early in the second half. Gordon Brown's formidable Eli team won 28–0. Daly was named on seven of the eight All-America and All-Eastern teams that were published. The lone critic to pass him by was Walter Camp, who dropped him to the second team in favor of Yale's Bill Fincke.

Daly's playing career did not terminate on that low note. The next season (1901) found him a "plebe" at West Point. Army played all members of the traditional "Big Four." Harvard, champion that year, gave the Cadets their sole reverse, 0–6. Yale was tied 5–5 through Daly's 35-yard dropkick, while his conversion earned a 6–6 draw with Princeton. Pennsylvania was smashed, 24–0. Navy, which had beaten Army the previous season, had another very strong team, but Army had Daly. In addition to handling the team flawlessly and punting well (in one half he averaged over 40 yards against the wind), he drop-kicked a 35-yard field goal, ran back a kickoff 98 yards to a touchdown, and kicked goal for all of Army's points in an 11–5 victory. And he saved the game by overhauling Fred McNair after the latter had run back a punt 65 yards. President Theodore Roosevelt, who saw the game, told the West Point superintendent, "Tell Daly, I said it was a great day for the Irish." The black-haired little Irishman was again a unanimous choice for the All-America team. Charles Patterson wrote in *Outing* that "Daly's work was the best of his career."

The criticism of his continuing to play after his experience at Harvard nettled Daly, and he decided to quit in 1902 but was persuaded to play against Navy. After a couple of tune-up games, he piloted the team to a 22–8 victory. Understandably because of his limited playing, Camp placed him no higher than on the third All-America team, but at least one selection, that of the *New York Tribune*, had him on the first team. Paul Bunker, who was destined to die in a Japanese prisoner-of-war camp, appeared on Camp's team as a halfback and on Whitney's as a tackle. The latter also had Captain Robert "King" Boyers, center, on his first team, and Edward Farnsworth, tackle, on the second, while Camp liked Henry Torney, fullback, for his third team. That was the team that Douglas MacArthur managed. It was considered Army's best to that date, and was rated third nationally by Whitney.

Daly definitely retired from playing after the 1902 Navy game, but he helped with the coaching during his two remaining years at the Military Academy and also in 1905. He resigned from the Army in 1906, was with a Boston brokerage firm for a few years, and in 1910 became Fire Commissioner of Boston. He joined the coaching staff at Harvard in 1907, and continued when Percy Haughton took command the following season. In 1913 a special act of Congress restored him to the Regular Army as a first lieutenant, and he was promptly detailed as head coach at West Point.

Army sorely needed him. During the previous seven seasons, the Cadets had downed Navy but once, and had not scored on their arch rivals since 1908. Daly whipped a team into shape. After suffering its sole reverse at the hands of the Dorais-Rockne Notre Dame team, Army won the "big one" from a heavily favored Navy team 22–9. During Daly's four years as coach, Navy was beaten each year and his teams broke even with Notre Dame, winning two and losing two. In 1914 and 1916 Army won all games. The 1914 team was rated first in the nation by the Helms Athletic Foundation, and the 1916 team was given a share of the title, with Pittsburgh, by Parke H. Davis and Tom Thorp. During those four years, Daly developed the following who were rated All-American by Walter Camp: Louis Merillat, end; John McEwan, center; Elmer Oliphant, back; Alexander "Babe" Weyand, tackle; and Lawrence "Cowboy" Meacham, guard.

When World War I came, Daly went on active duty, rose to the grade of colonel commanding a regiment of field artillery, and also served on the General Staff in Washington. At West Point, football had been discontinued in 1918, and early graduation had stripped the Corps of most of its seasoned players. That was the discouraging situation confronting Daly when he was again detailed as coach in 1919. Starting from scratch, it took him four years to maneuver Army into its former position. In 1922 he again produced an unbeaten team. It took a thriller from Navy, 17–14, and tied both Yale and Notre Dame. His Walter Camp All-Americans for that period (1919–1922) were: Edgar Garbisch, center; George Smythe, quarterback; Walter French, back; Earl "Red" Blaik, end; and Waldamar "Fritz" Breidster, guard.

Daly had been under terrific strain, and felt that he could

stand the pace no longer. With a winning team, he resigned as coach. In 1933 he was retired from the army for physical disability, and made his home in Pacific Grove, California, where he took up painting as a hobby. On February 12, 1959, he died as the result of a heart attack, and was buried at West Point with full military honors.

GEORGE ROBERTS PFANN

(5:09½; 172)

In 1924 Knute Rockne hailed Pfann as the best quarterback since the introduction of the forward pass in 1906, and he placed him with Thorpe, Grange, and his own beloved Gipp in an All-Star backfield. About the same time, Walter Trumbull rated the Cornellian second only to Eckersall, while W. B. Hanna, another New York newspaperman, went even farther and called Pfann the greatest quarterback of all time. In 1938 George Trevor named Pfann on an All-Time, All-Eastern eleven. Pfann led the Big Red teams during the Golden Age of Cornell football. Each of the three teams he played on won eight games, and they rolled up a total of 1,051 points against 81 by opponents.

In 1923 Walter Camp called Pfann as good a field general as any playing, and said he was the cleverest pass receiver he had ever seen. But Pfann's chief claim to fame was his power running. Like Oliphant, he had heavy, powerful legs, and because of his low-slung center of gravity it was extremely difficult to knock him off his feet. He traveled so low it was said that he "ran on his knees." He was a determined runner who would twist and bore for additional yardage with opponents draped all over him. With such a build and a reasonable amount of speed, he was naturally a first-class blocker. In every way, he fit perfectly into the single-wing tackle smashing that constituted Coach Gilmour (Gloomy Gil) Dobie's chief offensive weapon.

The first of Pfann's perfect teams functioned in 1921 with Eddie Kaw as the big gun. In the muck and rain of Franklin Field, Kaw tallied five touchdowns against Pennsylvania. The Quakers were laying for him the next year, when he captained the team, but they were not prepared for Pfann. When they stopped Kaw, Pfann took up the burden and gained five or more yards at a clip, principally off tackle. It took three or four men to stop him, and on a gallop around end he shook off five tacklers and straight-armed two more. Cornell won 9–0 with squatty, hard-running George setting up the scores.

Pfann was captain in 1923, and that time Pennsylvania was laying for him. Every time he got his hands on the ball, Quakers swarmed all over him, but they still could not keep him bottled up. In a hard-fought 14–7 victory, he scored both of his team's touchdowns, one after taking a 30-yard pass from Bob Patterson and running 10 yards and the other by crashing off tackle from the five-yard line. One of the Philadelphia papers wrote that Penn had been "Pfann-ed." Previous to the big game, Cornell had defeated Columbia, Dartmouth, and Colgate.

Among the All-Americans or near All-Americans who played with Pfann during those three happy years were Eddie Kaw, Charles Cassidy, and Floyd Ramsey, backs; David Munns, end; and the tackles so essential to the success of the Dobie system: Wilson Dodge, Leonard Hanson, Frank Sundstrom, and Frank Kearney.

Pfann, who also starred at defense on the Cornell lacrosse team, was a brilliant student and won a Rhodes scholarship. At Oxford he was a lacrosse "Blue." He brought his winning ways with him and helped Oxford down Cambridge 7–6 in 1927 and 10–3 in 1928. From 1931 to 1935 inclusive he coached football at Swarthmore College, but the famous old Quaker institution that had produced many strong teams was then in the process of deemphasizing the sport, and his teams did only "as well as could be expected." Pfann became an attorney and is now counsel for the Cooperative Grange League Federation, with offices in Ithaca, New York.

AWARD-WINNING QUARTERBACKS

David R. O'Brien, *T.C.U.*	HEISMAN, MAXWELL, CAMP, 1938
Paul V. Governali, *Columbia*	MAXWELL, 1942
Angelo B. Bertelli, *Notre Dame*	HEISMAN, CAMP, 1943
Leslie Horvath, *Ohio State*	HEISMAN, 1944
John C. Lujack, *Notre Dame*	HEISMAN, MAXWELL, CAMP, 1947
Vito Parilli, *Kentucky*	CAMP, 1950
Ralph V. Guglielmi, *Notre Dame*	CAMP, 1954
Paul Hornung, *Notre Dame*	HEISMAN, CAMP, 1956
Randy Duncan, *Iowa*	CAMP, 1958
Richard Lucas, *Penn State*	MAXWELL, 1959

6

HALFBACKS

CAMP, 1910	Weekes, *Columbia*	Heston, *Michigan*
YOST, 1920	Thorpe, *Carlisle*	Heston, *Michigan*
TREVOR, 1927	Thorpe, *Carlisle*	Heston, *Michigan*
GULF, 1933	Thorpe, *Carlisle*	Grange, *Illinois*
SHAUGHNESSY, 1943	Thorpe, *Carlisle*	Grange, *Illinois*
A.P., 1951	Thorpe, *Carlisle*	Grange, *Illinois*
RICE, 1954	Thorpe, *Carlisle*	Grange, *Illinois*
WEYAND, 1955	Thorpe, *Carlisle*	Grange, *Illinois*
HELMS, TO DATE	Thorpe, *Carlisle*	Grange, *Illinois*
ADDITIONAL	McClung, *Yale*	Kelly, *Princeton*
	Strong, *N.Y.U.*	White, *Colorado*

HAROLD HATHAWAY WEEKES

(5:10½; 178)

Back when the nineteenth century was about to give way to
the twentieth and the winning political ticket was McKinley and
Roosevelt, the prize football combination was Weekes and Morley. Those talented players complemented each other so beautifully that it was impossible to determine which was the more
valuable. Weekes was shy and self-effacing, in contrast to the
dominating Morley, who was four years older and possessed the
added glamour of coming from the "wilds" of New Mexico where
he had been reared on a ranch. Morley was the first to be selected
for Walter Camp's All-America team, in 1900, with Weekes gaining the honor the following year. Knute Rockne once expressed
the opinion that Morley rated next to Heston as the best halfback
of the pre-forward-pass age, but when Camp announced his
All-time team in 1910, he included Weekes, so it is Weekes who
qualifies for this gallery of immortals, but his partner should
not be forgotten.

Weekes was a New York boy, born at Oyster Bay on April 2,
1880, into an old Long Island family. He was a freshman when
Columbia resumed playing football in the fall of 1899 under the
coaching of George Foster Sanford, former Yale center. Columbia's wonderful graduate schools attracted much talent, men who
had played at other colleges. Bill Morley, mature and confident,
who had previously attended Pennsylvania Military College
and the University of Michigan, was at home in such fast company and made the team at right halfback, but the slim, nineteen-
year-old freshman seemed lost in the scuffle. Although Weekes
had played well in the backfield at Morristown School in New
Jersey, Sanford started him with the scrubs as an end. Later,
Harold was used as a substitute halfback. Sanford soon realized
that he had something special, and kept the freshman under
wraps until the Yale game, when he started him at left halfback.

Columbia and Yale fought through a scoreless first half. Late in the second half, Morley recovered a fumble on Yale's 2½-yard line. Columbia pounded the line and Morley went over, but the referee claimed that the advance had been made after he blew his whistle, and he refused to allow the touchdown. With the Columbia rooters on their feet chanting, "Robber, robber!" Morley again plowed into the line, but he fumbled. Yale recovered the ball and promptly punted it out of danger. Columbia now had possession on Yale's 45-yard line. The ball was given to Harold Weekes. He streaked through a hole off tackle and sped all the way to a touchdown. Columbia won, 5–0. Charles Halsted Mapes, noted author and a Columbia graduate, told about the game in one of his books. He ended the story with the poignant plea, "God! Why has life so few such moments."

More glory was expected when the team faced the Carlisle Indians on Thanksgiving Day. That was Pop Warner's first year at Carlisle. Against Columbia, he introduced a crouching start for the backs and a formation in which all the linemen took position on the same side of the center. The game was turned into a rout. Both Morley and Weekes, who labored heroically on defense, had to be withdrawn because of injury and fatigue. The Indians won, 45–0. It had been a particularly trying day for Weekes. Columbia had a hurdle play in which he was pushed over the low-charging lines. In perfectly legal procedure, for that time, the Indians hit the ballcarrier on the face with the heel of the hand. Holding the ball with both arms to prevent its being stolen, Weekes had no way of protecting himself, yet he never faltered in his attempts to get over the line. It was a fine if unrewarding exhibition of courage. Camp honored Weekes with a position on his third All-America team.

Morley was captain in 1900. With a veteran team, Columbia played all members of the "Big Four." After dropping games to Harvard and Pennsylvania, the Blue and White again faced Yale. That Eli team, captained by F. Gordon Brown, a four-time All-America guard, was destined to clobber Princeton 29–5 and

Harvard 28–0 and win the national championship. Columbia held Yale to a 5–12 score, and it was Weekes who tallied the touchdown for the New Yorkers. Behind magnificent blocking by Morley and Wright, he skirted an end, jumped over the head of a back who dived for his legs, dodged another, and outran the others to cover 55 yards.

Mindful of Weekes' unique qualifications and the manner in which Carlisle had stopped the hurdle play, Sanford came out with a "flying hurdle." When the ball was snapped, the center and guards, with arms and legs locked, did not charge. The tackles turned slightly in order to protect the play from the flanks. The quarterback took the ball from the center and fed it to Weekes, who dashed up from a position five yards to the rear. Using the back of Edward "Bessie" Bruce, the center, as a springboard, Weekes leaped into space. The other two backs and the ends, who ran back from their position on line, joined in pushing him up and over. His run and jump and the push of four strong men sometimes caused him to rise almost six feet off the ground as he sailed over the locked lines. He drew up his knees, and anyone who got in his way was apt to have his face kicked in. That was the unique and dangerous play that Columbia unveiled against Princeton.

On a 90-yard march against the Tigers, Weekes did most of the damage with the flying hurdle. Bill Morley was pushed through center for a touchdown. Fortunately, Bruce kicked the extra point, because Princeton later scored but failed to convert, and Columbia took the game 6–5. Much the same Indian team that had massacred Columbia the previous season was beaten 17–6 on Thanksgiving Day. When Camp rated the teams he gave Columbia Princeton's place in the "Big Four" of 1900. Nine All-American and All-Eastern teams for this year were seen. Morley and Weekes each appeared on five, but Camp favored Morley, with Weekes and Charles "Jack" Wright, the 245-pound guard on the second team, Henry Van Hoevenberg end on the third, and Jerry Sykes quarterback on the honorable-mention list.

William Raymond Morley was the best defensive back and the best interferer in the game, very effective for short, sharp smashes at the line and a good punter and drop-kicker. Muscular, active, intuitive, and self-reliant, he richly deserved All-America rating, but after Weekes' own performance during the season the latter must have wondered what it took to get into Camp's good book. As a matter of fact, Camp and others spelled it out. They granted that Weekes was a brilliant halfback, but they felt that he relied too much on Morley. So it was in the nature of a break for Weekes when Sanford shifted Morley, who had returned for additional graduate work in 1901, to quarterback. With Bill unable to get out to head the interference, and with the other great blocker, Jack Wright, graduated, Weekes was obliged to go more on his own, and he succeeded well enough to satisfy Camp, who gave him a first-team berth on the All-America team while dropping Morley to the third.

Columbia's most important victory in 1901 was over Pennsylvania, 10–0. Weekes, who was used to run the ends, gained 230 yards and scored both touchdowns; one after a 75-yard run and the other after traveling 18 yards. Moreover, he did some magnificent tackling in the open. Sanford placed too much reliance on the flying hurdle in the games with Yale and Harvard. Both had much-superior manpower, and Weekes was seldom able to get a good takeoff. Morley showed to better advantage against Yale. He outpunted the Blue and scored with a dropkick from the 20-yard line. In a loss to Syracuse, Weekes hurdled to Columbia's touchdown but was injured. Despite a weak leg he set up the winning touchdown against Navy by gaining 65 yards in three end sweeps, and in the season's final game he scored two touchdowns in a 40–12 victory over Carlisle.

Weekes was elected captain for 1902. A graduate coaching system was installed, and Morley was chosen to succeed Sanford. Thus the Weekes-Morley combination continued another year. In early games, Weekes ran wild. He scored six touchdowns on runs of from 35 to 75 yards against Fordham, and made the longest run of his career, 107 yards, in returning a kickoff against Hamilton. It was a different story in the important games. Morley, too, relied heavily on the flying hurdle. In the Princeton game, Dana Kafer a Tiger halfback, hurdled with Weekes, and they crashed into each other over the embattled lines. Both were injured. Kafer's broken shoulder kept him out of the Yale game and might have cost Princeton the championship. Weekes was never quite up to par after that day, although he gamely played out the season. Camp did not include him in his All-America listings, but Caspar Whitney, who had always ignored Weekes while giving top billing to Morley, relented and gave Weekes a place on his second All-America team.

Weekes was one of the fastest men on the field, and many times tackled opponents from behind after they were in the clear. Although never an Intercollegiate sprint champion, he won many points in dual meets. He had a nice change of pace and was able to put on an extra burst of speed, which tended to make him the finest end-runner the country had yet produced. In the open he employed a peculiar shuffle to avoid tacklers. John Heisman said he "slithered sideways like a fiddler crab." Unlike many light-footed runners, he was difficult to bring down, and frequently dragged a tackler a few yards. In his 80-yard run against Dartmouth in 1899, he was hit three times, but each time he broke loose. In the spring of 1901 he took the strength tests conducted by Dr. Dudley A. Sargent of Harvard and finished fourth among the strong men of the colleges of America—just two-tenths of a point out of third place. In the tests for back and legs, he placed first. At the beginning of a game he was apt to be tense and sometimes fumbled, but in general he handled the ball well. He was a sure tackler and a fairly good punter and blocker.

After a season as head coach at Kansas (in 1903) during which the Jayhawkers defeated Oklahoma, Kansas State, Colorado, Missouri and others, but lost to Nebraska, Weekes settled down in Wall Street and became a wealthy stockbroker.

He died in a New York hospital, after a long illness, on July 26, 1950. Weekes survived his partner by almost a score of years. Morley was a mining engineer in his native New Mexico, and died on May 27, 1932.

WILLIAM MARTIN HESTON

(5:08; 184)

"Heston's name never dies," Frank Menke once assured us, but such a future seemed very remote indeed when, in the spring of 1901, a twenty-three-year-old teacher sat behind his desk in the crossroads schoolhouse at Wolf Creek, Oregon, feeling that he was now safely launched on his life's work. An amazing series of circumstances—and coincidences—make Heston's story read like fiction.

The story starts in Galesburg, Illinois, where, on a neighboring farm, Heston was born on September 9, 1878. His father, very poor with a large family, decided to seek greener pastures farther west. He moved his family to Iowa and then to Kansas, and when his Civil War pension came through, continued on to Grants Pass, Oregon, where his wife's family lived. Here, young Martin, as he was then called, herded cattle. During the three months a year that he could be spared from farm work, he went to school, a three-mile walk each way. He doggedly kept at it, but it was not until 1898, when he was twenty, that he gained admittance to the San Jose Normal School in California. He earned his way at school by working as a hotel janitor, field hand, and paper boy, and at various other chores. At high school his only extra-curricular activity had been singing in the boys' choir. He had never seen a football until his arrival at San Jose, but he was strong and willing and he was given a place on the team, as a guard.

Now, further to link together our chain of events, let us go back to Illinois—to Champaign, Illinois. George Huff, Director of Athletics at the University of Illinois, had a visitor—a tall, well-muscled young man named Fielding H. Yost, who was looking for a coaching job. It is strange that a job was not looking for him. After playing at West Virginia and Lafayette in 1896, he coached Ohio Wesleyan to a tie with Michigan and victory over Ohio State in 1897. His 1898 Nebraska team won the championship of the Western (Missouri Valley) Conference, and then he moved to Kansas and won it there, too. His Jayhawkers won ten straight. Mr. Huff was properly impressed by the earnest young fellow with the engaging grin, but because there were no vacancies at Illinois, Yost moved on to California. In 1900 he performed the "hat trick." He coached Stanford to a victory over California, the Stanford freshmen to victory over the Bear cubs, and Lowell High School to the state interscholastic championship. Then came another call.

At San Jose, in 1900, Heston was captain of the eleven that was slated to play Chico State for the normal school championship. It was a rematch because the teams had already played a draw. Heston, with the approval of the coach and players, approached Yost for assistance. He must have been most persuasive, because Yost agreed to coach for expenses only. Heston was moved to left halfback. His playing, coupled with the wizardry of Yost's coaching, gave San Jose the victory and the championship. Heston would now have some pleasant memories when he returned to Oregon and began teaching.

Another quick shift of scenes. Michigan's athletic director, Charles Baird, was in trouble. The Michigan coach had resigned, and there was difficulty locating a suitable replacement at that late date. By chance he discussed his trouble with Director Huff of Illinois. The latter thought of Yost, and recommended him. What if he were tied up by contract, as were most coaches? But Yost was again out of a job. California and Stanford had agreed to rely upon graduate coaching after the 1900 season. When

Yost, now a free agent, received a "feeler" from Baird, he dispatched a box crammed full of scrapbooks, clippings, and other papers testifying as to his prowess as a coach. One glance at that record and Yost was hired.

The new coach's thoughts turned to the serious youngster with the persuasive tongue at San Jose, and he wrote suggesting that Heston come to Michigan and study law. The latter was reluctant to give up teaching, and even after Yost persuaded him that it would be to his advantage to make the move, he lacked funds with which to pay for the long journey to Ann Arbor. Yost could offer no financial inducements. At that stage, Fate again intervened, producing a stranger from Toledo, Ohio, a minister of the Gospel who had come out on a round-trip ticket but had decided to remain in California. He sold Heston the return ticket for $25.00. All summer, Heston had driven a fruit truck in San Francisco, and he had a little money, not much but enough to get started. While at Michigan he worked as a bookkeeper and later sold advertising space in a magazine.

Yost was delighted to see his protégé, but he tried not to let it show. Heston did not start in the early games. Against Albion, Michigan's opening opponent, he went in for a short time and instantly stole the show. While on defense, he hurled himself through a gap in the Albion line, intercepted a lateral pass, and ran to a score. Such bizarre doings aroused the enthusiasm of the students. In the second game, against Case, he played longer— long enough to score four touchdowns. The next game was against a conference rival, Indiana. When Heston did not start, the students rose in their wrath and demanded that he play. Yost took about three minutes to make up his mind. He sent Heston in at left halfback, and kept him there for four years.

The team was largely a veteran one. Playing their last year were such stars as Neil Snow, end on defense and fullback on offense; Captain Hugh White and Bruce Shorts, tackles; and Ebin Wilson, guard. Other newcomers, in addition to Heston, were Dan E. McGugin, guard, and George "Dad" Gregory, center. McGugin became the famous Vanderbilt coach and married a sister of Yost's wife. Gregory, Heston's roommate was a droll fellow with the finest mop of hair on the campus. He commenced calling Heston "Willie," and the nickname has stuck through the years. Because of his florid complexion, Heston had been called "Rosie" in high school, and at San Jose he was known as "Judas" because of his favorite swearword, "Judas Priest." He was not the only one of that crew to acquire a lasting nickname. Yost was a driver, and his incessant demand that the players "hurry up" caused Detroit newspapermen to dub him "Hurry Up" Yost, a name that also stuck.

Yost's driving methods paid off. His players moved with military precision, and executed plays faster than any other team in the nation. Harrison "Boss" Weeks, the quarterback, would start calling signals while the men were still on the ground from the previous play. There was a sequence in which four or five plays were run off without bothering with signals. Speed, endurance! The Wolverines had both, and wore down all opposition. Running from the old T, they also had a wing shift and operated from both a balanced and an unbalanced line. Four conference rivals were easily disposed of: Northwestern, Indiana, Iowa, and Chicago. Pop Warner's Carlisle Indians were humbled 22–0, and a breathtaking score of 128–0 was rolled up against Buffalo, which had earlier defeated Foster Sanford's Columbia team. Michigan did not play Wisconsin, which also won all conference games. Officially, the two teams shared the title.

The Tournament of Roses Association, in an attempt to introduce variety into the program of the annual festival, invited Michigan to send its team to Pasadena to play Stanford. The resulting contest was the first of what is now called the Rose Bowl games. It was eight below zero when the team left Ann Arbor, and the game was played with the temperature at 85 degrees, but the Wolverines seemed as indifferent to the weather as to human elements. Without using a substitute, they blasted Stanford 49–0.

Neil Snow scored five touchdowns. Heston, although frequently used as a decoy and blocker, gained 170 yards in 18 carries.

At last the season was over. In eleven games, Michigan had scored 550 points, their opponents none. That was the first of Yost's famous point-a-minute teams. The next year, in eleven games, the Wolverines piled up 644 points but had twelve scored against them; 1903 saw a 565–6 record posted in twelve games, while in 1904 the count was 567–22 in ten games. Many of those contests were not of full length. West Virginia was beaten 130–0 in thirty-six minutes of play in 1904. Yost claimed that Heston scored 100 touchdowns during his career, but Willie told the writer that he kept careful check and it was *only* ninety-three. That accounted for 465 points—555 by modern values. Each year that Heston played, Michigan was rated at or near the top of the colleges of the country by some competent critic, and during that period the Maize and Blue was never defeated, with just one tie marring the record.

That drawn game occurred in 1903. Boss Weeks had captained the 1902 team to victories over Wisconsin, Minnesota, Chicago, Notre Dame, and all other opponents. Of that champion team, only Captain Curtis Redden, end; Joe Maddock, tackle; Dad Gregory, center; and the halfbacks, Willie Heston and Herbert Graver, returned for further action. Around that nucleous, Yost built another unbeaten combination. The critical game turned out to be with Minnesota. Dr. Henry L. Williams coached the Gophers. His assistant for the line, Pudge Heffelfinger, introduced the double line of defense that kept Heston from running wild. In the second half, Willie got under way and set up a touchdown by gaining 57 yards. All reports agree that he then scored, but Willie insists that it was Joe Maddock who took the ball over. Tom Hammond converted, but Minnesota later evened the count 6–6. A half-century later Heston still recalled vividly that Heffelfinger strode up and down the sidelines shouting to the Minnesota players: "Kill Heston! You can't win with Heston in there!"

Michigan won all other games that year, and, with Heston as captain, made a clean sweep in 1904, in which Minnesota was not played. During those wonderful years, Heston was the force that kept the Wolverines rolling. In the climactic games with Chicago in 1903, Michigan gained 260 yards, of which Heston accounted for 237. The next year, against the Maroon, he ground out 240 yards in 38 rushes. Walter Camp, who was somewhat dilatory in recognizing western talent, placed Heston on his third All-America team in 1901 and 1902, but elevated him to the first team in the remaining two years. Camp believed that Heston's strongest play was a smash off tackle, but others thought he showed to the best advantage when he put down his head and butted his way up the middle. He was such a fast starter that he generated terrific power almost immediately after taking off. Yet when the thickset, heavily muscled Willie lit out for an end, it was a revealing sight. He could run the hundred in 10⅕ seconds, and even the conservative Camp admitted he could dodge with the best in the East.

Keene Fitzpatrick, the Michigan trainer, is authority for the statement that Heston could beat Archie Hahn, Michigan Olympic sprint champion, at 40 yards. Heston usually ran close to the ground, with high knee action. It appeared as though his knees might crack his chin. He could straight-arm with either arm with speed and power. And he had another way of getting by a would-be tackler. In a game with Chicago, while running in the open, he leaped clear over Eckersall's head. Willie was never injured in college play and he never quit; he fought for the very last inch, and such continuous pressure frequently enabled him to tear loose after it seemed as though he were stopped. He was also a wonderful defensive player. On one occasion, with a flying tackle, he caught and held Eckersall by an ankle with one hand.

Heston took a brief fling at coaching and professional football. Coming up from poverty, he drove a hard bargain. Drake University paid him $1,200 in 1905, the highest salary any Michigan man had ever received for coaching. Drake won four and lost four, and his contract was not renewed. At the end of the season he played one game with the Canton Bulldogs against the Massillon Tigers for a record sum of $600 and expenses. Owing to lack of practice and condition, his offensive work was not up to his high standard, but he did very well on defense. He coached North Carolina State in 1906 to ties with such southern powers as Virginia, Clemson, and Washington and Lee. Again he topped off the season with a pro game against the Massillon Tigers. That time, as captain of a team of college all-stars, he injured his leg early in the contest. After that he retired from football and plunged with his usual vigor into the practice of law.

In 1911, Heston served as assistant prosecuting attorney for Wayne County, and in 1916 he was elected to the Recorders Court bench, from which he resigned in 1923 to devote full time to his private practice and real-estate business. Now the Wolverine Thunderbolt, in his eighties, keeps physically fit by taking brisk mile walks every day. He spends his time between homes on the Gulf of Mexico at Anna Marie Island, Florida, and on Manistee Lake in northern Michigan. Both his sons followed him to the football field at Michigan. They, too, were halfbacks, but neither could match "the Old Man."

JAMES FRANCIS THORPE

(6:01; 183)

"Jim Thorpe!" shouted the conductor as the train eased into the station at the town of some 3,000 inhabitants in the Pennsylvania coal regions.

"This place used to be called Mauch Chunk," explained a passenger to his neighbor. "It was renamed after the famous Indian athlete." And Carlisle, in the southern part of the state, unveiled a bronze tablet in the center of the city to commemorate the fact that it was there, at the Indian school (now the Army War College), that Thorpe became a sports legend. Even while he lived, Warner Brothers made a feature motion picture of his life story. In 1953 notice of his passing rated Column One, Page One, of the *New York Times*. President Eisenhower and other distinguished citizens wrote or wired their condolences to his widow. Los Angeles and Carlisle vied for the privilege of providing a final resting place for him. An offer was made to enshrine him in the National Indian Hall of Fame at Anadarko, Oklahoma, but he was buried among his people, the Thunderbird Clan of the Sac and Fox Nation, at Shawnee, Oklahoma, near where he was born.

In 1950 the Associated Press polled 391 sportswriters and broadcasters to determine the best in various branches of athletics for the first half of the twentieth century. The race for football honors narrowed down to Thorpe and Grange. Jim won with 170 points to Grange's 138. Bronko Nagurski was third with 38 points. Another poll was for the greatest male athlete in all sports, amateur or professional. Again Jim's name led all the rest. He got 875 points, with his closest rivals Babe Ruth, 539; Jack Dempsey, 246; Ty Cobb, 148; and Bobby Jones, 88.

Thorpe has long been a legend. No feat on the athletic field seemed beyond his prodigious powers. It is unnecessary to enumerate his strong points as a football player. Gil Dobie, the gloomy one, summed it up by saying, "I doubt if there was any one who could do all things as well as Thorpe." Jim ranked at the top or very close to it among the players of all time in every phase of backfield play, except possibly forward passing, which was in its infancy while he was at Carlisle. And, at that, he was one of the best passers and receivers of his day.

Thorpe's sole weakness, and a serious one, was that he was lazy. The shock of combat filled him with joy. When the play was rough and the opposition strong, he was in his element. Then he

shone with rare brilliance. "An unbelievable competitor," said
Bill Langford, one of the game's leading referees. But training
and practice irked Jim, and he avoided them whenever he could
get away with it. Even in games he loafed when he saw no need
of exerting himself. The most horrible example of that unfortunate tendency occurred in the game with Pennsylvania in 1912.
Well into the last quarter, Carlisle was leading, thanks to a 75-
yard touchdown run by Jim. Pennsylvania began passing. Jim
saw one coming in his general direction, but it looked wild and
he watched in tolerant amusement while an earnest young Quaker
end named Lon Jourdet gave it the "old college try." But Jourdet
made a "circus catch" and scored a touchdown and Pennsylvania
went on to win. Pop Warner was furious. Jim lamely said, "I
didn't think he could get it." Incidents like that caused Pop to
claim that Ernie Nevers, his fullback at Stanford, was a better
player, but after Jim's death Pop broke down and admitted that
Thorpe was the greatest of all time. But every lapse Jim made
owing to laziness or carelessness, he atoned for with a dozen or
more superman achievements.

Jim was not a full-blooded Indian; his father was half-Irish,
and his mother, quarter-French. He was also supposed to have
some Dutch and Welsh blood in his veins. His great-grandfather
was Black Hawk, the famous war chief of the Sac and Fox against
whom a young captain of volunteers named Abraham Lincoln
campaigned in 1832, although Lincoln admitted that the only
bloody fights he engaged in were with mosquitoes. Jim was born
on May 28, 1888, in a one-room cabin on the banks of the North
Canadian River, about ten miles north of Shawnee in what was
then called Indian Territory. His mother saw the bright sunlit
path leading to the cabin and, following the Indian custom of
naming a newborn child after the first sight that met the mother's
eyes, she called him Wa-Tho-Huch, which means "Bright Path."
Jim had a twin brother, Charles, who died before reaching man-
hood. Working and playing on the farm, and accompanying his
father on long hunting trips, helped Jim develop the speed,

strength, stamina, coordination, and intuitiveness that were to make him famous.

After a brief stay at Haskell Indian Institute at Lawrence, Kansas, where as a little boy he saw his first football, Jim returned home. In 1904 he went to the Industrial School for Indians at Carlisle where Pop Warner presided as football and track coach. Jim, who was assigned to the tailor shop, soon began playing football, first with the trade-school team (as a guard) and later with the "Hotshots," the scrubs. By 1907 he had worked his way up to the varsity as a substitute halfback. The following year he made the big team and distinguished himself by kicking three field goals against Penn State and running 45 yards to a touchdown that led to a draw with Pennsylvania, the only game not won by the latter all season. Walter Camp took notice, and gave Jim a berth on the third All-America team.

Jim's five-year term at the Indian school expired in the spring of 1909. Warner always maintained that he thought Jim had returned to Oklahoma, and it was there that he located him in the summer of 1911 and persuaded him to return to Carlisle to train for the Olympic Games. Jim came back and was the sensation of the football season. The Indians' principal game resulted in a victory over Percy Haughton's Harvard team at Cambridge, 18–15. Jim, with a heavily bandaged and badly swollen ankle, place-kicked four field goals, from the 22-, 15-, 34-, and 38-yard lines. He also kicked goal after touchdown. During the 70-yard advance to that score, Jim did his full share of ballcarrying. At the very end of the game, he was replaced by Sousa, but Warner explained to the press that it was not because of injury; he merely wanted to rest Jim's weak ankle. The following Christmas, the big All-American played Santa Claus at a party for Indian children.

Thorpe, by that time an Olympic hero, captained the redmen in 1912. It was during that season that Warner introduced his "doube wingback," or B formation, according to what Thorpe told the author. There seemed to be some confusion about that inasmuch as Warner contradicted himself in his writings. In 1954 I wrote to him, asking if it were true that this celebrated formation was first used in the Army game in 1912. Pop was then dying, which I did not know. B. H. Winkelman, his long-time friend and associate, replied that my assumption was correct. Warner left it up to the Indians as to who should be the first victim of the new formation. They promptly answered, "The Soldiers"—Army having taken Harvard's place on their schedule. The Cadets had one of their usual heavy, rugged teams with a new halfback named Dwight Eisenhower beginning to attract attention.

According to Bill Stern (and Warner confirmed it), Pop, who looked something like an Indian and had developed some of their mannerisms, appealed to his braves before the game in this fashion: "These men playing against you today are soldiers. They are the Long Knives. You are Indians. Tonight we will know whether or not you are warriors."

Despite that passionate charge, the Indians got off slowly, and Army scored an early touchdown. The Cadets played a seven-man line, backed by Eisenhower with another back, Charles Benedict, coming up fast to assist him on line smashes. On one occasion when Jim broke through, Ike and Benedict hit him simultaneously, one high, one low, and laid him out with a damaged left shoulder. When Referee J. A. Evans announced that the authorized two-minute time-out period had elapsed, Thorpe was not ready to resume playing. Leland Devore, Army's captain and All-America tackle, said, "Nell's Bells, Mr. Referee, we don't stand on technicalities at West Point; give him all the time he wants." Jim revived quickly after that. The *New York Times* mentioned that the "long count" lasted only three minutes. Nothing annoys an Indian more than being patronized by a white man. When he got back in action, Jim was fired up, and vented his wrath on that Army team, paying particular attention to Devore. Jim told me that this was his finest game, and Warner agreed with him. The *Howitzer*, a cadet publication, stated, "The running of Thorpe was by far the most wonderful and spectacular ever seen on our field." And most of the stars of the storied "Big Three" for twenty years had appeared on that field.

While Jim was working such havoc, he kept his eyes on the Army linebacker. I asked him if he remembered playing against Eisenhower. He nodded, and then added, "Good linebacker." Once, when Ike and Benedict seemed to have him cornered and dived for him, he stopped short. They crashed head on, and Thorpe continued on his way. Both were taken out. That was the extent of Eisenhower's injury. It was not in that game but in the one the following week against Tufts that he received the knee injury that, when aggravated by a riding-hall accident, forced Ike to stop playing. He started both the Carlisle and Tufts games, so it would seem that, until he was hurt, he was a regular and not a substitute, as has frequently been implied. He was only a "yearling," a sophomore.

Thorpe played such an extraordinary game that it seems an insult to his memory to attempt to embelish his deeds. The Indians won 27–6. Jim's playing set up every score, but for reasons unknown his signal was not called when the ball was close to the goal line. Alex Arcasa got three touchdowns, and Joe Bergie, the fourth. Jim scored three points, the result of kicking goals after touchdown. His touchdown run that was not allowed was a 45-yard runback of a punt. The ball was called back, and Carlisle penalized. When Army kicked again, Jeff Keyes, Army's star back, kicked away from Thorpe, so the latter had no opportunity for a repeat performance. Another yarn has it that, at one stage, Thorpe completed six consecutive forward passes to Arcasa. Carlisle completed only four all day, and Jim caught one of them. It was thrown by Gus Welch. Jim leaped about two feet off the ground, twisted in the air, and snared the ball far above the heads of the defenders. He was indeed a superman that day. The cadets in the stands, although sadly humbled, gave Thorpe a rousing ovation.

After that victory, the overconfident, careless redskins went to

Philadelphia and lost to four-times-beaten Pennsylvania, but they regained prestige on Thanksgiving Day against Brown, a team that had beaten Pennsylvania 30–7. It was to be Jim's last game in school, and in a snowstorm he put on another great show. He scored three touchdowns, kicked two goals, and set up the other scores. Carlisle won, 32–0. After that performance, Referee Mike Thompson called Thorpe "the greatest football player— ever." During the season, the Indians had scored 505 points against 114 in 14 games. Jim alone tallied 25 touchdowns, 33 goals after touchdown, and five field goals for a total of 198 points. Again, as in 1911, Walter Camp placed him on the All-America team.

It is debatable whether Thorpe was better at football than in track and field sports. His amazing exploits at the Olympic Games at Stockholm in 1912 were expunged from the records, but they will always be remembered in the athletic lore of our country. Against the greatest all-around athletes in the world, he won four of the five events in the pentathlon. In the other event, the javelin throw, in which he placed third, the United States was not even entered in the individual championship, since the event had first appeared in A.A.U. competition only three years before. In the decathlon, Thorpe accumulated 8,412.96 points, almost 700 more than the second-place man. It was quite fitting that King Gustavus of Sweden, in awarding him his trophies, uttered the historic remark, "You, sir, are the greatest athlete in the world." President William Howard Taft sent him a personal letter of congratulation.

In January, 1913, while Jim's football feats still provided much food for discussion, the storm broke. The *Worcester* (Massachusetts) *Telegram* announced that Jim had played professional baseball with the Rocky Mount and Fayetteville clubs, in North Carolina, during the summers of 1909 and 1910 while he was absent from Carlisle. Jim played under his own name and collected about $15.00 a week—hardly more than expense money. But it made him a professional, and his prizes were returned to the Swedish Olympic Committee for redistribution. The act aroused a storm of indignation against the A.A.U., and efforts were made, and continued up to the time of his death, to restore his trophies and records. It might be noted that the more elaborate trophies that he won were permanent challenge trophies kept at the International Olympic Headquarters at Lausanne, Switzerland, and were never his personal property. Jim explained to the author, in 1952: "I was just a dumb Indian kid. How was I to know playing baseball for money made me a professional in football and track?"

John McGraw promptly signed the big Indian to a three-year contract with the New York Giants at $5,000 a year—good money for playing baseball in those days. McGraw ruled with an iron hand, and easygoing, fun-loving Jim, indifferent to training regulations and slothful at practice, aroused all the fire in his nature. He rode the Indian hard and refused to allow him to play regularly. At Carlisle, Jim had been nicknamed "Libbling," which literally means "horsing around." That trait infuriated the hard-boiled little manager, especially after Jess Tesreau, one of his better pitchers, injured a shoulder in a friendly clubhouse wrestling match with Jim. McGraw kept Jim on the Giants' roster until 1919, although he was lent to Cincinnati during part of 1917 and farmed out to Milwaukee, then in the American Association, in other years. He was sold to the Boston Braves in 1919, and McGraw let it be known that Jim could not hit a curve ball. At Boston, Thorpe played in 60 games. Every pitcher knew of his alleged weakness, yet he batted .327. He was too much of a "hell-raiser," so, despite his showing, he was shipped to the minors, where he lingered for four seasons before quitting baseball.

During most of those years, Jim also played professional football. In 1915 he helped revive the Canton Bulldogs, and played at $500 a game. Except for the season of 1921 with Cleveland, he remained with Canton until 1923, when he organized his own team, the Oorang Indians, from former Indian college players. It was with the Bulldogs that he enjoyed his greatest years—unfortunately before professional records were kept. Claims, which I have been unable to verify, have been made that in a game he punted 90 yards in the air, and in another place-kicked a field goal from 75 yards out. By 1924 he was with the Rock Island Independents, and the following season received a bid from the New York Football Giants. At the age of thirty-six years he could still play, but his disdain for training rules caused his release after three weeks. He finished the season with Rock Island, played some with St. Petersburg, Florida, the following winter, and was back with Canton in the fall of 1927. Seemingly indestructible as he was, he could not last forever: Portsmouth Ohio, in 1928; Hammond, Indiana, in 1929; and he was finished as "big-time" player after fifteen years in the pro game.

All games were fun for Thorpe. Endowed with a magnificent physique, he reached the pinnacle of athletic fame with such ease that he never took life seriously. That was an unfortunate attitude. With his playing days over, at forty-one, he had nothing productive to which to turn. He was so bighearted and gullible that the money he had made was gone. He had also succumbed to the curse of his race—the white man's firewater. For a time he was able to capitalize on his athletic reputation, and lectured on sports, managed independent baseball teams, took bit parts in the movies, and so on. At one time he was digging ditches at $4 a day. Funds were raised to assist him, but he never seemed able to get back on his feet financially. He was such a likable fellow that no one censured him for his failings; rather he aroused sympathy because it was felt that he had been a victim of bad breaks and exploitation.

In 1945 he married Patricia Askew of Louisville, Kentucky. She provided what he needed, a firm but understanding manager. They organized a small band of Indian dancers and singers, with a speech by Jim as a feature of the show. A number of night-club bookings were secured, but soon misfortune struck again. Jim had a cancerous growth removed from his lip, and was not allowed to talk. On March 28, 1953, that strange life of glory and tragedy came to a sudden end. Old Jim, apparently in good health, died of a heart attack in his trailer near Lomita, California.

I heard one of Jim's speeches. Whoever arranged it did a good job. In his usual modest manner, Jim was still able to enumerate his athletic achievements.

"I thank the Associated Press for naming me the outstanding athlete of the first half of the twentieth century."

"I thank Walter Camp for twice picking me for his All-America football team."

"I thank Grantland Rice for putting me on his All-Time All-America football team."

"I thank the King of Sweden for calling me the greatest athlete in the world."

"I thank"—"I thank"—on and on he went. Jim had lots to be thankful for, but, in the end, his luck ran out.

HAROLD EDWARD GRANGE

(5:11; 175)

Red Grange was the most widely publicized college player of all time. When he took his prestige and talents into the professional field, he gave new life to a floundering sport and started it on the road to its present state of affluence. And after all the years, his face is as familiar to millions of football followers as it ever was in the days of his youth. Every Saturday, during the season, his likeness is flashed on TV screens throughout the nation while he comments on one of the leading games. Red has succeeded in other endeavors, but football has been his life work.

Bob Zuppke, the Illinois coach, called the gaunt redhead a "soundless rocket," and claimed that he came closer to perfection than any other player he had ever seen. Red was the greatest broken-field runner in history. He was not too difficult to down when tackled, but the trick was to get a hand on him. Blinding speed, intuition, and peripheral vision by which he could see to the sides as well as to the front were combined with an ability to dodge, weave, cut, twist, glide, and change pace perhaps never seen before or since. At times he seemed to flit through a mass of tacklers like a wraith. After a few games Number 77 was known from ocean to ocean as the "Galloping Ghost." His enduring fame rests largely on his running, but he was proficient at all the duties of a halfback.

Red was born on June 13, 1903, at Forksville, a small community in the Pennsylvania lumber country north of Williamsport. His 200-pound father was said to be the toughest man in the camps, so, naturally, he was a foreman. When Red was five his mother died, and the family moved to Wheaton, Illinois, where there were relatives. They were very poor. After Red was graduated from grammar school he secured a job on an ice truck, and kept it for eight summers. The long hours of hard work developed his physique, improved his stamina, and served to give him another nickname, the "Wheaton Iceman." At Wheaton High School he began as an end but was moved to left halfback his sophomore year. He won his letter at football, basketball, baseball, and track in each of the four years at school. In his senior year, at the championship track meet of the seven-school conference to which Wheaton belonged, he won both dashes, both hurdles, and both jumps. Later he said he preferred baseball, and felt he was best at basketball. At college, he never went out for basketball or track, but he was a pitcher and outfielder on the baseball team.

When Grange went to Illinois, he was quite certain that he lacked the size and ability to play conference football, but friends who were aware of his success in high school persuaded him to try out for the freshman team. A series of surprises was in store for him: he made the squad, he made the team, and at the end of the season he was elected captain. That year he formed a partnership with Earl Britton that was to endure through his college career. Britton could block as well as Grange could run, and they formed a perfect pair. Grange's natural modesty was always in evidence. He meant it when he said that his runs were made possible only because of the blockers, and his insistence that they receive their share of credit won the admiration of the forgotten men up front—even hard-boiled old pros—and they blocked for him harder than ever. Grange also approached perfection in his adherence to coaching instructions and training regulations. Like Ty Cobb at baseball, he wanted to be the best, and he was willing to work and make sacrifices to attain his goal.

In 1923 the redheaded sophomore was on the big team. He claimed to have been nervous at the beginning of the first game, with Nebraska—as anyone might have been facing the formidable Cornhuskers who were to give a Notre Dame team its sole setback of the season. Red overcame his nervousness in the way he knew best—by gaining ground. In 39 minutes of play, he scored all of his team's three touchdowns; one of them came after he carried a punt back 65 yards. In a tough game with Chicago, he intercepted a pass and ran 43 yards to the three-yard line, whence he plunged to the winning touchdown. He also ran back an intercepted pass 92 yards against Northwestern, and scored the winning touchdowns in the games with Iowa, Ohio State, and Wisconsin. Illinois and Michigan each won all conference games, and shared the championship. Grange, who topped the conference scorers with 72 points, was a unanimous All-America choice. Captain Jim McMillen, a guard who became professional wrestling champion of the world, and Frank Rokusek, an end who lost his life in World War II, also appeared on some honor rolls.

Grange was a sensation as a sophomore, but he was even better the next season. He had worked hard to become an accomplished passer and had perfected a cutback with which to vary the pattern of his end sweeps. The game with Michigan had been eagerly awaited ever since the close of the previous season. Already, in 1924, Illinois had downed Nebraska and Butler, while the Wolverines had beaten Michigan State and Miami (Ohio) to run their unbeaten string to twenty games. George Little was the Michigan coach, but Fielding Yost, the athletic director, still had much to say. As Little ruefully remarked, "When we win, it's Yost's team; when we lose, it's Little's." It was warm on the day of the game, and Zuppke started a new fad by having his players remove their stockings. Michigan suspected trickery, and would not allow the game to start until they had inspected the Illinois shanks.

With the pressure on, Red enjoyed one of his best days. On the opening kickoff, he carried the ball back 95 yards to a touchdown. He scored from scrimmage on runs of 67, 56, and 45 yards. Four touchdowns within 12 minutes! After that he needed a rest, and he did not get back into the game until the third quarter, when he got his fifth touchdown on a 12-yard burst through the line. Before the game was over he threw a 23-yard scoring pass to Marion Leonard. That game marks Grange's all-time high for advancing the ball—480 yards; 402 in 21 rushes and 78 on six passes. Illinois won 39–14, making all its scores while Grange was in the game.

Illinois was still unconquered when Chicago was encountered. Stagg had a heavy, strong team and decided that the only way to stop Grange was to keep the ball away from him. Chicago played "possession football," and succeeded admirably. Well into the second period, the Maroon had scored two touchdowns and Illinois had the ball for but one play—a punt from behind the goal line. Then the Illini received a kickoff and Grange got busy making up for lost time. He gained 69 yards in eight plays, the last being a touchdown drive from the four-yard line. Chicago recevied and scored another touchdown. It was again Illinois' turn, and Red went over from the five-yard line after gaining 40 yards in nine runs and grabbing two passes for 44 yards. By that time the boys were getting tired, but Red got away once more, for 80 yards and a touchdown. The game ended in a 21–21 tie. Some consider it to have been Grange's greatest performance. Stagg said that "virtually single-handed" he had carried his outplayed team to a draw. That game gave Red his second highest yardage count—311 from runs and 150 from passes. On most, if not all, of his gains against Chicago, Grange ran to his left—to dispose of a rather persistent later tradition that he ran well only to his right.

Chicago took too much out of the Illini, and the following Saturday a game was dropped to a fired-up Minnesota team that had not won a conference game. Red got a touchdown on a short run and then injured a shoulder. He had to be taken out, and did not play in the last game on the schedule, a victory over Ohio State. The defeat by Minnesota cost Illinois the conference championship, which went to Chicago, unbeaten although tied three times. Again Grange was a unanimous All-American. That was the last season that Walter Camp published his selection, as he died the following March. He called Red "a marvel."

Grange was captain in 1925. His green team, lacking an adequate quarterback, lost three of its first four games. In a defeat by Iowa, Grange ran back the opening kickoff 85 yards for a touchdown. In the fourth game, lost to Michigan by a field goal, Grange played quarterback. That made the difference, and his team won all remaining games. It was as a quarterback that he was selected on most All-America teams that season.

Red's greatest exhibition that year was against Pennsylvania the week after the Michigan game. Eastern fans had heard so many Grange stories that they were highly skeptical. Some of them were sorry that, on a muddy field, he would probably not be able to do his best. In addition, Pennsylvania had a strong unbeaten team that had already downed Chicago, Yale, and Brown. It was raining, but 65,000 spectators crowded the stands at Franklin Field. Illinois employed a single-wing formation with an unbalanced line, and Grange usually ran to the strong side, but early in the game he slipped through the weak side and went 55 yards to score without a Quaker touching him. Later he ran back a kickoff 59 yards to set up a touchdown by Earl Britton. In the third period, he ran 15 yards around an end for another score, and in the fourth he scored again on Bob Zuppke's famous "flea flicker" play. Grange knelt as though to hold the ball for Britton to place-kick. It was snapped to the fullback, who passed it to Chuck Kassel, who had turned around from his position at right end, and Kassel lateral-passed it to Grange, who was heading for the wide open spaces, and ran 25 yards through the startled Quakers. Illinois' 24–2 victory increased the prestige of western football and the personal fame of Red Grange. He had gained 363 yards in 36 carries. Illinois then went on to whip Chicago, Wabash, and Ohio State. Against the Buckeyes, Red gained 235 yards to bring his three-year total to 4,280— 3,637 by rushing and 643 by passing. He scored 31 touchdowns. Damon Runyon wrote, "There is only one Mr. Harold 'Red' Grange."

Following his last college game, Red created a sensation by announcing that he was leaving college in order to play with the Chicago Bears. Professional football was not in good standing, and received limited coverage by the press. Although there were a number of good pro teams, in most places the public was indifferent. College authorities, in particular, were opposed to the game, and Zuppke had begged Grange not to take the step. Curiously, the co-owners of the Bears, George Halas and Ed Sternaman, were two of his former players. The promoter of the deal was Charles "Cash-and-Carry" Pyle. The offer of big money dangling before his eyes was too much for Grange, and he reached an understanding with Pyle, who in turn negotiated with the Bear owners. For weeks rumors had circulated that Red contemplated such a move, but, as he later explained, he did not accept money or sign a contract until after the Ohio State game, so he felt justified in assuring the Illinois authorities that he was still an amateur while representing the university.

The "Illinois Flash" made his debut in the pro ranks against the Chicago Cardinals on Thanksgiving Day, 1925, after only three days of practice with his new associates. The game ended in a scoreless tie, with Red saving it by intercepting a pass on his own five-yard line. Pyle and his associates lost no time in "making hay" while Red's name was still hot. In seventeen days the Bears played ten games, but Grange, after the emotional and physical strain of a long college season, was unable to go the route. The Bears won five straight. In the seventh game Red injured an arm rather badly and had to be taken out. For the first time he heard a crowd booing him. The same thing happened in the next game. He was obliged to sit out the two remaining games, and as a result thousands of dollars had to be refunded to disgruntled ticket purchasers. The Bears lost the last four games. The season was not over yet. After an eight-day rest, they moved out on a 7,000-mile winter tour that took them to Florida and to the Pacific Coast. Red's arm had healed sufficiently for him to appear in all games. Wherever he played, attendance records for professional football were broken. The tremendous and favorable publicity accorded all those Grange games is still being felt at the box offices. For his first season, it is understood that he received approximately $125,000, and he turned down a lucrative contract to endorse a brand of cigarettes because he never smoked.

Failing to break into the Bear organization, Pyle organized a league of his own and put a team in New York—the Yankees, who played at Yankee Stadium. Grange had a half-interest in the club. The first season was fairly successful, but in an early game the following fall Grange tore a tendon in his leg. He was out for four weeks, back for a while, and then out again for almost two weeks. He was in no condition to play, but because all game contracts called for him to participate, and without him the club suffered heavy financial loss, he played out the few remaining games. Believing that his playing days were over, he did not renew his three-year contract with Pyle, and relinquished his share in the Yankees. Pyle continued for another season, but with no Grange, attendance fell off to such an extent that he dropped the franchise.

Red in the meantime was developing his other interests. In the summer of 1926, he made a football movie, *One Minute to Play,* which was well received. The next summer he appeared in an automobile picture, *Racing Romeo,* which was not a success. Beginning in the fall of 1928, he did a football skit on a six-month vaudeville tour, and during the summer of 1929 he starred in a "talkie" called *The Galloping Ghost.* That did quite well, too.

In the fall of 1929, Grange was back with the Chicago Bears. Though he was never again able to "cut" as he formerly had, and so was not his old self, his leg had responded to treatment and rest, and he alternated at halfback with Paddy Driscoll. For the next three years, Red held down the left-halfback post. All-League teams were selected in 1931 and 1932, and he was named each year. In 1932, when he captained the Bears, they won the world championship by beating Portsmouth. Red took a pass from Bronko Nagurski in the end zone for the only touch-down of the game. His legs began going bad on him again, and he was a part-timer in 1933 when the Bears retained the championship by taking a play-off game from the New York Giants. With the score 23–21, he tackled a Giant in the open just as the game ended. To make the feat more difficult, Red had to tackle him around the arms so that he could not lateral pass to a team-mate who was coming up fast. Red was not able to engage in the play-off in 1934, won by the Giants, but in the last game in which he ever played, on January 27, 1935, at Hollywood, California, he led the Bears to a victory over the champions.

Red helped to coach the Bears for nearly three seasons. Late in the fall of 1937, he gave up coaching to devote his time to business. After serving as sales manager of a soft-drink company, he opened his own insurance brokerage, which is still in operation. In the meantime he had built up a heavy schedule of radio and TV assignments and speaking engagements. He was elected to the Board of Trustees of the University of Illinois in 1950, and seems to have well merited the title that Bob Zuppke conferred upon him, "Outstanding Citizen."

(THOMAS) LEE McCLUNG

(5:10; 167)

Camp's All-Star halfbacks in 1904 were McClung of Yale and Kelly of Princeton. "Bum" McClung, who came from Knoxville, Tennessee, played on the varsity for four years, and the team he captained (1891) was considered the strongest yet developed in America. With such superstars as Heffelfinger, Hinkey, and McClung it had to be good, and the other players measured up to standard. Those making Caspar Whitney's first or alternate All-America teams at one time or another were: John "Josh" Hartwell, end and captain of the crew and later prominent New York physician; Wallace Winter and Hamilton Wallis, tackles; Stanford Morison, guard; Francis Barbour, quarterback; and the backs Laurence Bliss and Vance McCormick. The last-named became a newspaper publisher and a power in Democratic national political circles. The only man in the starting lineup who failed to win recognition from Whitney was George Foster Sanford, the freshman center who played only that season and later became a wealthy insurance broker and a successful football coach. Sanford, a bellicose individual, is supposed to have announced on the first day of practice that he was Yale's center and would knock the block off anyone who disagreed with him. He got the job.

It was not only superior material that made that team so outstanding. Walter Camp, assisted by McClung, who was a resourceful, intelligent leader, perfected teamwork to an extent hitherto unknown. Players usually took it easy on offense when a play was not in their vicinity, but under the new system an assignment was found for every man on every play. It marked a tremendous advance in football technique and tactics. In thirteen games, that team rolled up 488 points and was not scored upon. It defeated Harvard 10–0 before 25,000 at Hampden Park, Springfield, and Princeton 19–0 before 40,000 at Manhattan Field, New York.

McClung was not particularly fast, but he was a shifty, calculating runner who could dodge, pivot, and change direction to either side without sacrificing speed. For him, Camp brought out the "crisscross," later called the "naked reverse," but McClung himself devised the "cutback" in which he started for an end and then cut back over tackle. He hit the line for Yale's single touchdown against Harvard in both 1889 and 1890, and his 40-yard run set up a score against the Crimson in 1891. Against Princeton, in 1890, he registered four touchdowns and four conversions. He scored approximately 500 points during his four years of playing, a record that has never been approached at Yale. It is no wonder that the Yale students paraphrased a popular song, "Hold the Fort," and rendered it "Hold the ball, Mc-Clung is coming."

"Bum" was also a baseball player of ability. He played in the outfield in 1889 and was at first base the following two seasons. Yale won the college baseball championship in 1889 and 1890. In his senior year, he was voted the most popular man in his class.

Following graduation, McClung traveled for a year, and then, in the fall of 1892, became University of California's first professional football coach. His team tied Stanford, coached by Walter Camp, 10–10. After engaging in railway work for a number of years, he became Treasurer of Yale University in 1904. In 1909 he was made Treasurer of the United States, and held the office until he resigned in 1912. He served as a member of the board of directors of several corporations, and for a time was on the National Council of the Boy Scouts of America. He was only forty-four, in 1914, when he contracted typhoid fever and died in a hospital in London, England.

ADDISON WILEY KELLY

(5:09; 170)

"King" Kelly came close to being another in the long line of Yale football immortals. Yale had a wealth of material, and when the club-footed Kelly reported for practice at New Haven, he received such scant consideration that he quit in a rage and matriculated at Yale's archenemy—Princeton. Apparently he was handled more diplomatically there, because he seemed satisfied even though he was not heard of as a freshman and was only a substitute as a sophomore. That was in 1895. He got in the game against Yale in the second half with the Blue leading 12–0, and it looked as though his chance had come. With Kelly powering the ball through the line, Princeton advanced once to the five-yard line and again to the 20-yard line, but could not score either time. Eventually a drive started at midfield carried over the goal line. Later the Tigers blocked a kick for another score, but Yale, thanks largely to the brilliant running of Captain Brinck Thorne, also scored two touchdowns. The game ended 20–10, and Kelly had to wait another year for revenge.

Though having a deformed foot, Kelly was fast enough to slip around an end for 10 or 15 yards, but he was not a breakaway runner. His forte was hitting the line, and in that role he was the best of his time. In 1896 Princeton revived the old "revolving tandem" on tackle, and it whirled Kelly for so many gains against Yale that the game turned into a rout. Even he must have been satisfied with the 24–6 score. Caspar Whitney said of his performance, "Such determined, irresistible line-bucking as his has rarely been seen and certainly never surpassed."

The Tiger team, unbeaten (although tied by Lafayette) and rated first in the nation, was one of Princeton's best of all time. In addition to Kelly, the backs were Fred Smith, quarter; Billy Bannard, half; and Johnnie Baird, full. The captain was Garry Cochran, an end whose muscular arms started the revolving tandem in motion. At tackles were Bill Church and Arthur "Doc" Hillebrand, while the center was Robert Gailey, who became a missionary in China. All those men were on some reputable critic's first or second All-America team.

The next year (1897) Kelly was injured and did not start against Yale. But he insisted upon going into the game. Herbert Reed says that he gave "one of the greatest exhibitions of a born runner, of a football genius." Carrying the ball almost every time, he plunged through the line or slid off tackle for 55 yards, only to have Princeton lose the ball (and the game) on a fumble. In previous years Caspar Whitney had picked the annual All-America team for *Harper's Weekly*, but in 1897 he was out of the country, and Walter Camp assumed the task. Camp placed both Kelly and Cochran, who was again captain, on the first team.

Kelly played first base on the Princeton baseball team for four years, and in his last season (1898) was selected by *Outing* for their All-Eastern team. Princeton had champion teams in 1896 and 1897. In 1900 "King" succeeded Garry Cochran as football coach at California. Cochran's teams had beaten Stanford both years he coached, but Kelly had the misfortune of having Fielding H. Yost as his opposite number, and Stanford took the annual game 5–0. Kelly returned east and became a stockbroker. In 1925 he was made a member of the firm of J. P. Benkard and Company in New York City. He died in 1942, at the age of sixty-six.

E(LMER) KENNETH STRONG

(6:01; 201 in college, 210 as a pro)

Grantland Rice's earliest selections for all-time halfbacks were Thorpe and Heston. In his next evaluation he replaced Heston by Strong, but in 1952 Strong yielded the place to Red Grange, whom Rice had placed at quarterback in 1939. Ken Strong came close to being at the very top of both college and professional players. Walter Steffen, long-time successful coach at Carnegie Tech, and a judge on the Illinois Superior Court, who had been an All-America quarterback at Chicago, claimed, in 1928, that Strong was the best back he ever saw—better than either Thorpe or Heston. Ten years later, Jerry Lewis, a sportswriter, expressed the belief that Ken was the greatest football player since Red Grange. Obviously, Rice was not the only expert who thought highly of the big boy from West Haven, Connecticut.

At New York University Strong came under the inspiring leadership of John F. "Chick" Meehan, who employed a showy "military shift" to confuse opponents and please the public. Strong's heavily muscled legs generated tremendous power, but he was also a very fast and elusive runner in the open. Not only was he one of the leading forward passers in the game; he was equally proficient as a receiver. A tough defensive player, he was rated among the best blockers in college; he was a 60-yard punter and a deadly place-kicker who never lost his poise or nerve and whose stamina was remarkable. As a sophomore he made the team as a blocking back, and did not get his name in the headlines until he became a ballcarrier the next season.

New York University fielded a talented team in Ken's senior year, 1928. It lost to Lou Little's Georgetown Hoyas, 2–7, and defeated Niagara, West Virginia Wesleyan, Fordham, Rutgers, Colgate, Alfred, and Missouri. In the important intersectional

victory over the Missouri Tigers, 27–6, Strong scored three touchdowns, one after a 77-yard run, and passed 30 yards for the
fourth one. On November 24th the Violets played unbeaten
Carnegie Tech, conqueror of Georgetown as well as of Notre
Dame, Pittsburgh, and Washington and Jefferson. Against the
Tartans, Strong experienced his greatest day in college football.
He ran 40 yards to one touchdown, hit the line for another, and
passed for two more. N.Y.U. won 27–13, and was considered by
some critics as the best in the East. During the season, Ken scored
22 touchdowns and 28 conversions for 160 points to lead the
nation in scoring. He was on 16 of the 18 All-America selections
that the writer examined. Alfred Lassman and Leonard Grant,
tackles, and the ends Robert Barrabee and Jere Nemeck also
came in for much praise.

In the pro game, Strong played with the Stapletons of Staten
Island from 1929–1932; New York Giants, 1933–1935; New York
Yankees, 1936–1937; and with the New York Giants in 1939 and
Jersey City Giants in 1940. In 1938 he was barred from organized
football because of having jumped to the outlaw Yankees. From
1943 to 1948 he was again with the New York Giants, but was
used almost solely as a place-kicker. While he played with them,
the Giants were world champions in 1934 and division title hold-
ers in 1933, 1935, and 1944. Ken held several scoring records:
36 points (4 touchdowns, 9 conversions, and 1 field goal) in five
championship play-off games; 64 points for a single season in 1933
and 17 points for a single game. That last occurred in the play-off
victory over the Chicago Bears in 1934, in the famous "basketball-
shoes game" when he scored two touchdowns, one after a 41-yard
run; two extra points, and a field goal from the 38-yard line. In
total number of points scored during a career, he was second only
to Don Hutson, with 496: 35 touchdowns, 169 conversions, and
39 field goals. In 1944, he led the league by kicking six field
goals. In 1931, when Jack Reardon of New York, a league official,
started the practice of selecting All-Pro teams, he gave a place to
Strong, who was then with Stapleton. Ken again made the honor

team, as a Giant, in 1934, after having been on the second team in 1933. Ken Strong Day was celebrated at the Polo Grounds on December 24, 1946.

At college, Strong was also a standout baseball player. As center fielder and clean-up batter, he was a member of the N.Y.U. team for three years, and his 450-foot home run is still the longest ever hit on Ohio Field. The Violet team of 1928 was one of the best college baseball teams in the country, with 15 victories against 3 defeats. Ken was signed by the New York Yankees but was sold to the Detroit Tigers for $40,000 and five players. Farmed out to Toronto, he batted .342. He was about to be recalled by Detroit when, while trying to make a difficult catch, he crashed into the wall at the Buffalo park and injured a wrist. The accident and a subsequent botched operation terminated what probably would have been a brilliant baseball career. Strong is now a sales representative of Mason Burrows, Incorporated, in New York.

BYRON RAYMOND WHITE

(6:01; 187)

Dwight D. Eisenhower, the old West Point halfback, and many other great football players have risen high in the Federal Government, but no other All-American has gone so far as "Whizzer" White, now an Associate Justice of the U.S. Supreme Court. Largely because of that achievement he is included in these sketches, although, like Ken Strong, his credentials both in college and in professional football are ample.

White was born at Fort Collins, Colorado, on June 9, 1917, and entered the University of Colorado from Wellington where he had starred in high-school athletics. For three seasons he was the varsity quarterback, and his progress may be judged by the season notes. In 1935, his sophomore year, little was said of him; the next year he was considered a "topnotch back," and in his last season he was called "renowned." In 1936, when he ran back kickoffs 102 yards against Denver and 90 against Utah, he led the conference scorers with 54 points and was named for the All-Conference team.

But 1937 was the glory year. Under Coach Bernard F. Oakes, the Buffaloes won all eight regular-season games, opening with a 14–6 victory over Missouri and climaxing it by crushing Denver 34–7 on Thanksgiving Day before 28,157 people, the largest crowd ever to witness a sports event in that region. As conference champion, Colorado was invited to the Cotton Bowl to play Rice, Southwest Conference titleholder. During the first quarter of that game, White passed to Tony Antonio for a touchdown, intercepted a pass, and ran 50 yards to another and kicked both conversions, while his punting and defensive work held the Owls in check. In the second quarter his overmatched team crumbled, and Rice took the game 28–14.

Whizzer had broken Dutch Clark's conference scoring record with 103 points; and, including the bowl game, he tallied 122 points to top major college scorers. He led the colleges, large and small, in three departments: longest runback of a punt, 97 yards against Utah; longest punt without roll, 84 yards against Missouri; and most points after touchdown (including bowl game), 25. In 181 carries, he gained 1,121 yards.

Whizzer was on just about everybody's All-America team. *Liberty Magazine*'s poll revealed that every man who played against Colorado voted for him. *Liberty* also placed his teammates G. Moore, center, and E. Cheney, halfback, on its All-Conference team. In addition to being a fast and elusive runner and a superb kicker and passer, White blocked and tackled well above average. Tall, agile, with fast reflexes, he also played on the basketball team, and in his senior year (1938), when Colorado lost a play-off to Denver for the division championship, he was selected as a guard on the All-Conference team. At the end of his junior year he was made a Phi Beta Kappa, and he went on to earn a Rhodes scholarship.

He was anxious to get on with his studies at Oxford, but the Pittsburgh management was even more anxious to have him play pro football. The offer of $15,000 a season was too good to ignore, and he signed with them for 1938. He repaid their confidence by leading the league in ground gained, 567 yards in 152 carries, and won a place on the second All-Pro team. He then went to Oxford, but England's plunge into World War II caused him to abandon his studies at the end of a year and return to the United States, where he enrolled in the Yale University Law School. He was graduated first in his class, and was called by the Professor of Law as "probably the best all-around student I have ever had."

The seasons of 1940 and 1941 found him back in pro football, with the Detroit Lions. In 1940 he again was the league's chief ground gainer, with 514 yards in 146 attempts, and that time he was on the first All-Pro team. Arthur Daley of the *New York Times* stated, in 1950, that White was the best, or "perilously close" to the best, football player he ever saw.

White was appointed to the Naval Reserve in May, 1942, and assigned to intelligence duties. He was serving on the staff of the commander, Destroyer Squadron 23, when the squadron won the Presidential Unit Citation "for extraordinary heroism in action against enemy Japanese forces during the Solomon Island Campaign from November 1, 1943, to February 23, 1944." Whizzer personally received a Bronze Star Medal because "his outstanding courage and efficiency contributed materially to the destruction of the enemy forces."

On May 21, 1944, he reported as Air Combat Intelligence Officer on the staff of Vice Admiral Marc A. Mitscher, Commander, Fast Carrier Task Forces, Pacific Fleet. He was on the flagship *Bunker Hill* when it was severely damaged by enemy Kamikaze planes that plummeted to her deck off Okinawa on May 11, 1945. White's "performance of duty was distinguished by resourcefulness, skill and courage and was at all times in keeping with the highest tradition of the naval service." He received a commendation ribbon. He became a lieutenant and had a tour of duty in the office of the Chief of Naval Operations in Washington prior to his release from service.

White practiced law in Denver except for the period when he served as clerk to Chief Justice Fred M. Vinson of the Supreme Court of the United States. He became active in politics, and in 1960 promoted a "Citizens for Kennedy" organization throughout the nation. There was no surprise when he received the important post of Deputy Attorney General in the new Kennedy Administration. In 1962, President Kennedy named White as an Associate Justice of the U.S. Supreme Court, saying that he had excelled in everything he had attempted in peace and war.

❖ ❖ ❖

AWARD-WINNING HALFBACKS

Jay J. Berwanger, *Chicago*	HEISMAN (INITIAL), 1935
Clinton E. Frank, *Yale*	HEISMAN, MAXWELL (INITIAL), 1937
Nile C. Kinnick, *Iowa*	HEISMAN, MAXWELL, CAMP, 1939
Thomas D. Harmon, *Michigan*	HEISMAN, MAXWELL, CAMP, 1940
Bruce Smith, *Minnesota*	HEISMAN, 1941
William M. Dudley, *Virginia*	MAXWELL, CAMP, 1941
Frank Sinkwich, *Georgia*	HEISMAN, CAMP, 1942
Robert H. Odell, *Pennsylvania*	MAXWELL, 1943
Glenn W. Davis, *Army*	MAXWELL, CAMP, 1944; HEISMAN, 1946
Charles Trippi, *Georgia*	MAXWELL, CAMP, 1946
E. Doak Walker, *S.M.U.*	HEISMAN, 1948
Charles Justice, *North Carolina*	CAMP, 1948

AWARD-WINNING HALFBACKS *(continued)*

Victor Janowicz, *Ohio State*	HEISMAN, 1950
Francis Bagnell, *Pennsylvania*	MAXWELL, 1950
Richard Kazmaier, *Princeton*	HEISMAN, MAXWELL, CAMP, 1951
William Vessels, *Oklahoma*	HEISMAN, 1952
John J. Lattner, *Notre Dame*	MAXWELL, 1952; HEISMAN, MAXWELL, 1953
Donald McAuliffe, *Michigan State*	CAMP, 1952
Howard Cassady, *Ohio State*	HEISMAN, MAXWELL, CAMP, 1955
Thomas McDonald, *Oklahoma*	MAXWELL, 1956
Peter M. Dawkins, *Army*	HEISMAN, MAXWELL, 1958
William Cannon, *Louisiana State*	HEISMAN, CAMP, 1959
Joseph Bellino, *Navy*	HEISMAN, MAXWELL, CAMP, 1960
Ernie Davis, *Syracuse*	HEISMAN, CAMP, 1961

7

FULLBACKS

CAMP, 1910	Coy, *Yale*
YOST, 1920	Oliphant, *Army*
TREVOR, 1927	Mahan, *Harvard*
GULF, 1933	Coy, *Yale*
SHAUGHNESSY, 1943	Gipp, *Notre Dame*
A.P., 1951	Nevers, *Stanford*
RICE, 1954	Nagurski, *Minnesota*
WEYAND, 1955	Blanchard, *Army*
HELMS, TO DATE	Davis, *Army*
ADDITIONAL	Butterworth, *Yale*
	Kimbrough, *Texas A.&M.*

NOTE: Oliphant, Mahan, Gipp, and Davis were essentially halfbacks. Each one was selected as a third back to round out a trio, with Thorpe and Heston in the case of Oliphant and Mahan, and Thorpe and Grange for Gipp and Davis.

EDWARD HARRIS COY

(6:00; 195)

Big, blond, stub-nosed, Ted Coy's appearance and achievements made him the all-time glamour boy of football. Tim Cohane, the Yale historian, felt that Burt L. Standish (Gilbert Patten) must have had someone like Ted in mind when he began writing his Frank Merriwell stories a decade before Ted found his way to the campus at New Haven. A graduate of Hotchkiss School, where his father had been headmaster, it was natural for Coy to seek his education at Yale where his brother, Sherman "Shirt" Coy, had received some All-America recognition while playing right end on Gordon Brown's championship team in 1900. The season of 1906, when Ted Coy entered Yale, was the one in which numerous reforms went into effect, among them a three-year eligibility rule for which Harvard and Princeton could be grateful. Coy had to be content with playing left tackle and captaining the freshman team which defeated the Harvard cubs 28–10 and Princeton freshmen 14–0.

In 1910 Walter Camp wrote that no other player had ever presented such a remarkable combination of qualities, and the coach of rival Princeton, Bill Roper, claimed Coy was the best he had ever seen. In 1938 George Trevor ranked Coy, as a line plunger, second only to Bronko Nagurski, whose reputation as a fullback rested chiefly upon his professional performances. Coy loved to hit a line or run over a tackler, but he was also shifty, and used a jabbing straight-arm. He ran higher than most backs using high knee action—again and again those knees were compared to pistons. Herbert Reed said he was "all corners." Though abnormally muscled, he moved freely and gracefully. His punting was exceptionally good, but he also excelled in drop-kicking, forward passing, blocking and tackling, and to those skills he added an unquenchable fighting spirit, almost unlimited stamina, and seeming immunity to injury.

Coy, who was born at Andover, Massachusetts, on May 24, 1888, was nineteen years old when he took his place behind the Blue line in the fall of 1907. He speedily proved his right to be there, making spectacular runs of 105 yards against Springfield, 80 yards against Villanova, and 60 yards against Holy Cross. Against Army his 70-yard run which would have broken a score-less tie was nullified by a penalty. That tie was the only blot on the Yale escutcheon when it lined up against Princeton. The Tigers had a strong team that had given the Carlisle Indians their sole reverse of the season, but Yale ruled a favorite. Princeton dominated the first half and left the field at intermission with a comfortable 10–0 lead. It was in the second half that the spot-light was focused on Coy.

Between the halves, Yale's captain, Lucius Horatio "Ray" Biglow, summoned Foster Sanford, the old Blue who had brought Columbia into football prominence. Sanford was a great coach, particularly in line play, but Walter Camp did not approve of some of his ideas, and at that game he sat in the stands. At Big-low's request he came to the dressing room, rallied the appar-ently beaten team, and sent it back on the field ready to win. But the revitalizing process took well over the allotted time, and as a result of that incident a rule was passed penalizing a team for not appearing on the field on time.

The turning point of the game came early in the half when Tad Jones, the Eli quarterback, ran back a punt 40 yards. Coy's interference was reminiscent of the days of Heffelfinger. He bowled over three different opponents before Jones was hauled down on the 32-yard line. A few plays put the ball on the 22-yard line, and then Jones called on Coy. Of those twenty-two yards, Coy accounted for all except two. Six minutes after the opening of the second half he was over for a touchdown. Biglow's goal brought the count to 6–10. Princeton kicked off, and Coy, carry-ing the ball on almost every play, hit the line and rounded the ends in a march of almost the length of the field. He got over the goal line, but the ball was brought back and Yale penalized.

Shortly afterward, Yale was again in range. A pass from Tad Jones to Clarence Alcott put the ball on the 10-yard line. From there it was Coy all the way. Biglow's goal made the final score 12–10. Near the end of play, Coy almost got away again after running back a kick 30 yards.

The following week, Coy pounded out two more touchdowns against Harvard. The feature of that game was a 30-yard run by Jack Wendell, Crimson halfback, late in the game. On a double-pass play, he circled an end and broke into the clear. Only Coy stood between him and the goal, but that was enough. Ted dropped him on the five-yard line. Harvard had not scored on Yale since 1901, and was determined to make it now; but the Yale line, with the massive Coy crouching behind it, held, and the Elis took the ball on the one-foot line. When Coy got off one of his booming punts, further danger was averted. Yale was rated first in the nation in 1907. For his All-America team, Walter Camp named Biglow, Jones, and Alcott. He thought that Coy needed more experience, and he placed him second to Jim Mc-Cormick, the Princeton captain. However, Caspar Whitney, whose selections were then rated practically on a par with Camp's, and other noted critics had Coy on the first team.

Ted took up in 1908 where he had left off the previous season. The headlines read, "Coy plunged to touchdown," score Yale 5, Syracuse 0; "Coy plunged to touchdown," score Yale 6, Army 0; "Coy kicked field goal," score Yale 10, Brown 10. Walter Camp was again advisory coach. His attitude toward Coy, at that time, is not understandable. There was a shortage of ends, and with the approach of the game with Princeton, Camp persuaded Captain Bob Burch and Field Coach Ray Biglow to shift Coy to end. That move set the stage for one of the most dramatic games ever played. Yale was unbeaten. Princeton had lost to Dartmouth and been held to scoreless ties by Lafayette, Syracuse, and Army. The Elis were heavy favorites, but the Tigers refused to concede anything. On a miserable rainy afternoon, the mediocre Princeton team proceeded to outplay Yale during the first half, and led 6–0.

Foster Sanford was again in evidence in the dressing room between halves, but that time his interest centered principally on one man. Burch had been injured, and Coy was appointed acting captain. Sanford took him aside and begged him to shift himself back to fullback. As captain, Coy was supreme on the field, but Camp had told him to remain at end, and apparently he did not want to defy the old man. The second half promised to be a repetition of the first. It was almost half over, and the Yale stands were chanting "Put Coy at fullback." Coy responded, and moved himself into the backfield. The cold rain had increased in volume; large areas of the field were churned into thick mud, and darkness was settling when Coy began to carry the ball. In an unbroken series of straight hard smashes at a line that knew he was coming, he covered 45 yards to a touchdown. Henry Hobbs converted to tie the score.

Time was running out and the stands were in an uproar when Yale got possession on Princeton's 38-yard line. "Give me the ball!" screamed Coy in his high-pitched voice. He tore through the Tiger line like a locomotive. On the 16-yard line, Princeton's gallant little captain, Eddie Dillon, dived at Coy's churning legs. Coy was stopped, but Dillon was carried from the field. Then two more vicious smashes, and Coy was over. In another stunning finish, he had led the Blue to victory, 11–6. But that was the climax. The next Saturday, Percy Haughton's powerful and superbly coached Harvard team contained the Elis, and won, 4–0. It was the only loss that Coy would suffer in his varsity career of twenty-nine games. Camp joined the vast majority that year, and picked Coy for his All-America team.

Ted was captain in 1909, and there was no further thought of playing him anywhere but at fullback. With a veteran team, the future looked bright at New Haven. Then, two weeks before the opening game, the fans were shocked to learn that Coy had undergone an appendectomy. He sat out the first four games. It was not intended to use him in the fifth, against Army. In the second half, with Yale leading by a touchdown, the Cadets began to drive Yale back, and Coy was permitted to go in with instructions only to kick and pass. He revitalized the team. Once it looked as though he were going to disobey orders. He started on an end sweep. Army closed up fast, and Coy, while running at top speed, punted 70 yards. His 30-yard pass to Henry Vaughan scored the winning touchdown. Other old rivals were disposed of: Brown 23–0 and Princeton 17–0. To keep his record intact, he cracked the Princeton line for a touchdown—and he also kicked a field goal against the Tigers.

As the season neared its end, it was obvious that the meeting of Yale and Harvard would again be for the championship. The two powerhouses outclassed all other teams in the country. For Ted it would be a rubber game; he had helped win in 1907 and Harvard had returned the compliment in 1908. This time, though, he was not to do much ballcarrying, but he could still kick. After all, wasn't he supposed to be the reincarnation of Frank Merriwell? Against Harvard, Coy was the difference between a stalemate and a victory. The game was largely a repetition of the one of the previous year, with two formidable lines fighting each other to a standstill. Dan I. Sultan, who became one of the leading generals in World War II, was assistant line coach at West Point when I played. In order to whet our appetites for "Navies," he would tell us about that 1909 Yale-Harvard game, which he had witnessed. He claimed the line play was the best he had ever seen. In fact, it was magnificent: "Every face was dripping blood."

Coy kicked frequently, and gained an average of ten yards an exchange. His tremendous punts were well covered by the ends. The ball swirling down from a great height proved difficult for the Harvard backs to handle. His drop-kicks, off the instep rather than off the toe, were also very high, and the officials experienced difficulty judging whether or not the ball had passed over the crossbar. Coy tried four times for field goals, and succeeded twice. The value of a field goal had been reduced to three points that year, but Harvard was also forced to a safety to bring the score to 8–0.

Coy's team closed the season of ten games, unbeaten, untied, and unscored upon to take its place among the great elevens of history. The line averaged 209 pounds from tackle to tackle. Coy, Carroll Cooney, center; Hamlin Andrus, guard; Henry Hobbs, tackle; John Reed Kilpatrick, end; and Stephen Philbin, halfback, won places on Camp's first All-America team. The following were named for first-team honors by at least one or another critic whose selection was published in the annual *Guide:* Arthur Howe, quarterback (picked by Camp in 1911); William Goebel, guard (picked by Camp in 1908); Theodore Lilley, tackle; and Walter Logan and Henry Vaughan, ends. Fred Daly, halfback, was elected captain for the next year. Yale had giants in those days.

Coy was a quiet, good-natured, likable sort, a thorough sportsman and a good leader. He did not restrict his athletic activities to football. He won his letter at baseball, as a first baseman, and at track in which he picked up points in the dual meets and placed third in the shot-put in the Intercollegiate championships in 1910. Against Princeton, in 1909, he won the shot-put and hammer throw and was third in the highjump. Between seasons he found time to sing in the glee club and engage in other club affairs.

After graduation, Coy was appointed head coach of the 1910 football team. He did not meet with the success of his playing days, and to all practical purposes was supplanted by Tom Shevlin toward the end of the season. During World War I he was a special investigator for the Department of Justice. He engaged in several occupations, and was affiliated with a New York insurance company of which his old coach, G. Foster Sanford, was a partner when he was stricken with a heart attack. Pneumonia set in, and two days later, on September 8, 1935, he died.

EDWARD WILLIAM MAHAN

(5:11½; 171)

The characteristic that stands out preeminently in Eddie Mahan's makeup, aside from his competitive instinct, was his modesty. His gentle, unselfish nature, ready wit, and keen sense of humor made him a popular man. He was no prude; in fact he was considered quite lively as a young man. At parties, after refreshments, he was apt to break into song with such touching ditties as the one about throwing overhauls in Mrs. Murphy's chowder, or he might render with great emotion the poem about the wake when they put the beer on the corpse. But when the subject was Eddie Mahan, he froze. At dinners and other affairs in his honor he has been known flatly to refuse to comment on his athletic exploits. Attempts by Harvard to keep abreast of his career after graduation are usually met with the laconic reply, "Nothing of note." B. G. Waters, III, of the Harvard publicity office, admits that his files contain remarkably little information concerning Mahan "other than the superlatives of the sports-writers." But those superlatives are sufficient evidence of his worth.

Mahan came from that spawning ground for athletes, Natick, Massachusetts. Mike Murphy, Keene Fitzpatrick, and Pooch Donovan, famous athletes who became even more famous as trainers, hailed from Natick, and while Mahan ruled the gridiron in 1915, another product of his hometown who was destined to do great things for Harvard football, Eddie Casey, was the star of the freshman team. Mahan was born on January 19, 1892, and he grew up to turn the town upside down with his deeds as a local high-school football player. In appreciation of his contribution to their happiness, the townspeople presented him with a handsome gold watch when he finished school.

From Natick, Mahan went to Phillips Academy at Andover. It is interesting to note what John J. Hallahan, the Boston sportswriter, said about the young Mahan after the 1910 season. He wrote, "He could carry the ball well, punt a long distance and with an accuracy that was expert; tackle like a fiend and drop-kick like an artist." What could Hallahan add to that the next year when Eddie again sparked his Andover mates to a decisive victory over Exeter? He simply wrote that Eddie "was more in evidence than ever before." In the 1911 game with Exeter, Eddie attempted a field goal. The ball fell short, struck the ground twice, and then bounced over the crossbar. Referee Mike Thompson refused to allow the goal. His decision, based on the spirit rather than on the letter of the rules, seemed to have been somewhat arbitrary because, in a duplication of the freak play on the same day, the goal was allowed and enabled Princeton to defeat Dartmouth.

Mahan was sought by many colleges, but he chose Harvard, where his fellow townsman, Pooch Donovan, was trainer. He captained the freshman team, and the game with the Yale cubs is a perfect example of his courage and leadership. Yale led at half-time, 14–0. Then Mahan ran 30 yards to a touchdown, and passed a like distance into the end zone for another. Harvard had failed at both attempts to convert and Yale increased the lead with a field goal; but Eddie, undaunted, sparked a 40-yard drive that ended with him cracking the line for a score. His team won, 18–17, and finished the season with a perfect record. Charley Brickley was the reigning star of the varsity, but already there was talk that the tall freshman would eclipse him.

The next season (1913) Eddie moved up into an all-star backfield. He was a sensation in the early games, but a spider bite became infected and he missed a game with Cornell and did not start against Princeton. The Tigers showed far more class than expected, and pushed the Crimson around considerably during the first period. When Mahan went in, the tide turned. Princeton had to modify its defense somewhat in order to guard against Mahan's end sweeps, but even so, he got away for a 52-yard run, dodging through the mud and shaking off several tacklers before being downed. Brickley won that game with a dropkick, 3–0. Against Brown, Mahan's forward pass to Tack Hardwick for a touchdown, and against Yale his long high punts, came in for much acclaim. Harvard beat the Elis 15–5. Walter Camp placed Mahan on his All-America team, and for each of three years he was an almost unanimous choice.

Plagued with injuries in 1914, Mahan missed the ties with Brown and Penn State and the "squeeze" victories over Michigan, Washington and Jefferson, and Tufts. He got back in time for the meeting with Princeton, in which he kicked two field goals and averaged 45 yards with his punts, as Harvard won, 20–0. In the dedication game in Yale's magnificent new bowl, Harvard gave the Elis an unmerciful beating, 36–0. Eddie passed to Hardwick for a touchdown, set up two more with his passes, and another with his running, and kicked a 20-yard field goal. He also ran back a punt 45 yards, and while Fred Bradlee was benched Eddie did most of the line plunging. People marveled at his stamina, and Camp labeled him the best backfield man in the country "by all odds."

No critic admitted that Mahan, elected captain for 1915, had a weakness, but evaluating his strong points was more difficult. Camp thought his greatest strength lay in end running, especially from short kick formation, and in running back kicks. Grantland Rice agreed with Camp concerning Mahan's open-field running, and also lauded his ability to pick an opening. In the open he was deceptive, similar in style to Don Hutson in later years. Instead of dodging, he twisted his torso as though his body were going one way and his feet another. As he explained to Hardwick, "I give them a leg and then take it away." He could spin out of a tackler's grasp or reverse his field, had a fine change of pace and a deadly straight-arm. Most impressive was the way he could change direction, even at sharp angles, without losing speed. Until the coming of Red Grange, his equal as a broken-field runner had not been seen.

Although unsurpassed as a ballcarrier, he was so versatile

that his punting, drop-kicking, forward passing, and defensive work were all classed as magnificent. Because of his eagerness to learn, he was easy to coach. He studied every feature of play and overlooked nothing that might improve his work. He even insisted upon flat shoelaces in his punting shoe. He practiced sprinting under the direction of Pooch Donovan. Cool, seldom nervous or worried, he had a keen football sense. Brickley said that "no defense could be built against him." When James N. Young, former associate editor of *Collier's*, asked Jim Thorpe whom he considered the greatest back (next to himself), the Indian unhesitatingly named Eddie Mahan. General Joseph J. "Red" O'Hare, former player, coach, and official, felt that Mahan was superior to Thorpe because of better teamwork and greater intelligence. John Heisman and Big Bill Edwards also rated him with the best.

Mahan's senior year was usually considered to have been his best, although it was during that season that he suffered the only defeat of his collegiate career. Prior to meeting Cornell, Harvard had won four games to bring its undefeated string to 33. Victories had been scored over Colby, Massachusetts, Carlisle, and Virginia. Mahan set up two touchdowns against the Indians, one on a pass play and the other on a long run after at least six Indians had hit him. Against a powerful Virginia team, which had already beaten Yale, Harvard was unable to tally a touchdown, but Eddie won the game 9–0 with field goals from the 13-, 41-, and 25-yard lines. Unaccountably, he experienced an "off day" against Cornell, and Harvard lost. He was guilty of several fumbles, and while he made a few nice gains, he was pretty much held in check by the tough Cornell defense. Eddie took his failure in that game much to heart, and years later he said it was the one game that he could never forget. Possibly it was to counteract that reaction that Percy Haughton, never given to lavish praise, took occasion to proclaim Mahan as "the greatest football player God ever made!"

Mahan was back in stride the following week against Penn

State, which had tied Harvard in 1914. His brilliant play helped Harvard to beat the rugged Pennsylvanians 13–0. In what he was to characterize as the hardest game in which he ever played, Harvard defeated Princeton 10–6, and the game was not over until the final whistle sounded. Mahan's 25-yard run put Harvard in position for Dick King to score a touchdown. Eddie converted and also kicked a field goal from the 42-yard line. He scouted Yale the following Saturday when Harvard defeated Brown, the other team that had tied the Crimson the previous year.

It was expected that the game with Yale would be close; Harvard ruled a slight favorite at 5 to 4. The game resulted in what was called "the New Haven wreck"—the Elis were mangled 41–0, with Eddie scoring 29 of the points. Harvard's first touchdown was scored by Dick Harte, who scooped up a loose ball when a Yale back fumbled one of Mahan's skyscraping punts. The last was made by Dick King, after running 57 yards. In between those scores, Mahan crossed the Yale goal line four times. He also made good with five conversions. He had atoned for his spotty performance against Cornell, but that defeat could not be erased and the unbeaten Ithacans were given first place in the nation, with Harvard second. Camp placed Mahan, King, and Joe Gilman, tackle, on his All-America team; Don Watson, quarterback, on the second, and Harrie Dadmun, guard, on the third.

Mahan was also a brilliant baseball player. He pitched Harvard to a victory over Yale in both his sophomore and junior years. Illness prevented his appearance, except as a pinch hitter, against the Blue in his senior year. He was unbeaten against Princeton, defeating the Tigers all three years. In 1915 and 1916 Harvard was champion of the so-called "Big Three." It was in 1916 that Eddie pitched the Crimson to a 1–0 victory over the world-champion Boston Red Sox. Pitching and playing left field that year, he batted .350, fielded .956, and was selected, as a pitcher, by Edward B. Moss on his All-Eastern team for the Spalding publications.

After graduation, Mahan joined Andy Smith, at California,

as backfield coach, but the war cut short his stay on the Coast. Eddie craved action, and enlisted in the Marines in July, 1917. A year later he won a commission at officers' training camp and was assigned to the 13th Regiment, commanded by the celebrated "Fighting Quaker" Smedley D. Butler. He served in France from September, 1918, to September, 1919, and was awarded a letter of commendation acknowledging services "of the highest efficiency" rendered at Brest. He was honorably discharged as a first lieutenant in October, 1919. Although he saw no combat, Eddie saw plenty of action on the gridiron during the war period. In 1917, while at League Island, Philadelphia, he captained the football team and was selected on the All-United States Service Eleven by Paul Purman, sports editor of the Newspaper Enterprise Association. The following season he played with the Saint-Nazaire Marines, coached by Eddie Hart. The 89th Division, ultimate champion, won a bitterly contested game from the Marines 13–0. Mahan was selected for the All-A.E.F. team.

Following the war, Mahan went into banking business in New York, occassionally breaking away to do some coaching. In 1924 and 1925 he was baseball and backfield coach at Harvard, and also took a whirl at backfield coaching at Boston College. One war was not enough for him. World War II found him back in uniform, this time in Navy blue. He was on active duty from January, 1941, to November, 1945, became a commander, and served as assistant commandant for logistics of the 14th Naval District at Pearl Harbor. Since then he has been kept busy by his duties with the Massachusetts State Conservation Department.

"Character in big letters is what Eddie has always had," says his Harvard teammate and captain, Walter H. Trumbull.

ELMER QUILLEN OLIPHANT

(5:07; 174)

A noted educator remarked that Oliphant was the most likable egotist he had ever known. Ollie is such a remarkable fellow
that no one could be blamed for swallowing the fantastic stories
he relates about himself. With him nothing seems impossible. He
was a chunky little towhead with relatively short limbs and the
torso of a heavyweight. His round, pink face and disarming smile
made him appear quite boyish, and his manner was that of a
naïve, friendly, overgrown kid. Underneath smouldered a fierce,
uncompromising determination that brooked no interference.

Ollie was born in Bloomfield, Indiana, on July 9, 1893. After
being graduated from Linton (Indiana) High School, where he
was an All-State end, he played some summer baseball. The great
Hans Wagner inquired if he would be interested in a tryout with
the Pittsburgh Pirates. Ollie told him that he planned on going
to Purdue. "Get your education," said Wagner, "I always wished
I had one." Too bad that old Hans is no longer around to give
that advice to schoolboys who sign pro contracts and spend the
best years of their lives in obscure bush leagues!

Apparently Purdue did not believe in overdoing aid to athletes. While working his way through college, Ollie held down
such jobs as waiting on tables, handling laundry, firing furnaces,
and clerking in a shoe store. During summer vacations he worked
for a coal company in Dugger, Indiana. His work consisted of
firing boilers early in the morning and again in the evening and,
in between, mining coal underground. No wonder he developed
the strength and endurance of a bull!

Ollie played end with the freshman team, but when he was a
sophomore he was changed into a halfback by Coach Andy
Smith. It was a wise move, because the next year (1912) Purdue
rose to fourth place in the conference, with Ollie blazing the way.
Lambert G. Sullivan of the *Chicago Daily News* placed him on

his All-Western team. In 1913 the saying "Stagg fears Purdue," which had amused the West for fifteen years, became a reality. Stagg later said that Oliphant was the bugaboo with which he frightened his players into a tackling frenzy. Oliphant played up to expectations, but Chicago took the game 6–0, and the championship. In a 7–7 tie with Wisconsin, according to the *Lafayette Courier,* Ollie swung wide around an end, ran through two Badger tacklers, dodged another, and shook off two more to cross the goal after a 32-yard run. Harry Grayson of the NEA service said the Badgers saw "pink Oliphants" in their dreams. Walter Camp gave All-America honorable mention to Ollie, Captain George Glossop, center, and Harry Routh, guard.

At Purdue, Oliphant won nine letters—three at football and two each at baseball, basketball, and track, At basketball he had the reputation of being a fast, rough floor player who broke up more plays than anyone else in the conference. In 1913 he was on the second All-Conference team, but the next year he was not only named for the first team but was also rated All-American by the Helms Athletic Foundation. He caught for the baseball team in 1913, but after being elected captain for 1914 he was moved to left field and won a place on the All-Conference team. During the spring he competed with the track team when baseball permitted. When a ball game and track meet were being contested on neighboring fields, as at Purdue, he would move over to win a track event between innings.

Oliphant's first season at West Point (1914) was one of frustration. Plebes were then allowed to play with the varsity, but he failed to win a letter. Why was this great back allowed to sit on the bench with tears rolling down his cheeks, vainly hoping for a chance to play against Navy? Perhaps it was for disciplinary reasons. Ollie's cockiness annoyed some of the older players, especially the captain and quarterback, Vernon Prichard. Also, he had several grandstand tricks of which Coach Charlie Daly did not approve, and it was the opinion of some that he was not a team player. Daly tersely said that Oliphant was not needed, and in a way he was correct. Army won all its games and was rated first by Helms. Navy was beaten 20–0, but there were many who felt that, had "the plebe" played, the score would have been doubled. As it was, Ollie had a hand in the victory over Notre Dame, 20–7, and he had a field day against Maine, when he played quarterback. He ran back a punt 70 yards to a touchdown, turned an end for another 70-yard touchdown run, plunged 5 for another, and passed 30 for a fourth.

To almost everyone's surprise, Ollie was tried at end in 1915. After being wasted in three games, one a loss and another a tie, he was moved back where he belonged just in time for the engagement with a big, rough Georgetown team. In that game he plunged to a touchdown, converted and kicked a field goal from the 35-yard line for ten points. Army won, 10–0. Oliphant was always relaxed. Before the Navy game in 1915, the players, suited and taped, were waiting in the locker room for the word to go. Silence reigned while the men communed with their souls. Suddenly Ollie was heard soliloquizing, "They tell me President Wilson, Admiral Dewey, and about 45,000 people are out there." More silence, and then, softly: "And my girl is out there. Boy, am I going to play a game today!" Army won, 14–0. Oliphant plunged to a touchdown. He broke off tackle, and in a stirring zigzag run went 30 yards to the second touchdown. And he kicked the conversions. After the game, Coach Daly said, "Oliphant, you're a great player, and I'm a poor coach for not recognizing it sooner." Ollie grinned and replied, "Aw, that's all right, Lieutenant." It should be noted that during that long period of frustration, he never complained, but worked hard trying to do what Daly expected of him.

Walter Camp put Ollie on his second All-America team, and later stated that a recheck of the records indicated that Ollie should have been on the first team. After that, there was no doubt that Oliphant was an All-American. For the next two years he was a practically unanimous choice. The few who omitted him explained they did so because of his previous experience at

Purdue. In 1916 he scored 112 points in nine games, and in his final year, 125 in eight games.

The 1916 team, captained by John McEwan, won all its games and was rated by some critics on a par with Pittsburgh for the national title. That year, against Notre Dame, Oliphant kicked two field goals, and his brilliant passing and running helped give Army a 30–10 victory. In the Navy game he ran back the opening kickoff 82 yards. The man who tackled him on the seven-yard line had to leave the game. Ollie then plunged to a touchdown. Later he place-kicked a field goal, and again came through with some clever passing and running. Red Blaik said, quite recently, that Navy feared Oliphant more than any Army player in history. The Midshipmen were out to get him, and he received a savage working over. Bleeding and battered but still smiling, he played the full 60 minutes at top speed. After that game, Camp said that, while Oliphant played, Navy would have to be 25 percent stronger than Army in other respects in order to win.

Navy was not played in 1917 when Ollie captained the team and Geoffrey Keyes was coach. The season closed against Boston College with Oliphant scoring two touchdowns, the second with less than a minute of play remaining, to win 14–7. His team won eight, and lost only to Notre Dame, 2–7. Ollie almost saved that game with possibly his most heroic performance. Carrying the ball on 11 of 13 plays, he fought his way for 64 yards in a 66-yard advance. On the 19-yard line Army tried a pass, but George Gipp broke it up, and that ended Army's chances.

Ollie ran close to the ground, and a man trying to tackle him low was quite likely to bounce off one of his knees. If he came in high, he would probably encounter a jolting straight-arm. Because of Ollie's squat build and a sort of weaving motion that he employed when tackled, it was difficult to stop him and almost impossible to throw him hard. In 1938 George Trevor ranked him among the ten greatest linebuckers in history. He was not a blind plunger. If the hole was blocked, he could slide off and find another place to get through. He was a smart, alert runner, and despite his short legs he could travel fast. He was reliable on defense and a good blocker.

In other sports Ollie was as spectacular as on the gridiron. Because no cadet had ever won his letter in more than three sports, when Ollie made it four the Army Athletic Association passed a special rule allowing him to place a gold star on the crossbar of the A. At baseball, he caught in 1915 and played left field in 1917 and 1918. Because of scholastic difficulties, he did not play in 1916. In 1915 Army, under Coach Sammy Strang Nicklin with Bob Neyland as the top pitcher, won 18 out of 21 games, and defeated Navy 6–5. Ollie, who batted .311, was chosen by Edward B. Moss for his All-Eastern team. The other two years, Ollie really kept his bat warm, averaging .424 in 1917 and .421 in 1918. He captained the team in 1918. Navy was not played during the two war years, nor were All-Eastern teams selected.

Oliphant turned out for basketball in 1915. Some adjustments were necessary after football season, and during that period the Cadets lost two of five games. With Ollie playing regularly, they lost no more. The team's 11–2 record caused the Army Athletic Association to vote major A's to its members. Ollie retained his place on the Helms All-America team. He played again in 1916 but then switched to ice hockey, which, like basketball, was then a minor sport. He played in only one game in 1917, but in the following year made the team at "point" and won a monogram. He had one other A coming—at track, which was then conducted on an interclass basis. To win a letter a cadet had to break an Academy record. Ollie set his sights on George Patton's 220-yard-hurdle record. Because he played baseball in free time, he got up before reveille to practice, and he succeeded in lowering the record to 25 seconds on a grass track. His great disappointment was that he failed to win the heavyweight boxing championship. He tried for it twice, but was outpointed each time. In his senior year he was superintendent of the Sunday school for children on the post.

Ollie selected the cavalry as his branch of service, and remained in the army for about four years. In 1920 and 1921, while on duty at West Point, he played some pro football with the Buffalo All-Americans. In 1921, when General MacArthur made track an intercollegiate sport, he appointed Ollie coach, and the latter led the team through two unbeaten seasons. After the track season of 1922 he resigned, served two years as director of athletics at Union College, and then joined the Metropolitan Life Insurance Company and eventually became head of the group-insurance department and one of the highest-salaried men in the company.

Ollie was far from a brilliant student; he rose to the top in the business world by working harder than his associates. At West Point he was low in his classes, but he soldiered so faithfully that he was made a senior cadet captain, in command of a company. It shocked him when, at a meeting of the Touchdown Club of New York, the question was propounded, "Which would you rather be, a Phi Beta Kappa or an All-American?"

"What a foolish question!" he roared, "Look at me; I was never a Phi Beta Kappa."

GEORGE GIPP

(6:02; 180)

George Trevor, whose colorful prose enlivened the sports pages of the old *New York Sun* for many years, described Gipp as "blazing fiercely like a meteor not long destined to dazzle earthly eyes." In his senior year, 1920, Gipp accomplished deeds that set the whole country agog, and then, with his fame at its height, he was gone.

Gipp was born on February 18, 1895, at Laurium, Michigan, in the Lake Superior iron-ore country. His father was a Congre-

gational minister. George never showed the burning ambition
that characterizes many successful men. Confident of his ability
to get along, he adopted an indifferent attitude toward life in
general. After he was graduated from high school in nearby
Calumet, he was content to drive a taxicab and play sandlot baseball—and other games. Three years after his graduation, he accepted a baseball scholarship at Notre Dame. During the first
two years he earned his board and lodging by waiting on tables.
For spending money, he gambled at cards and billiards with
local and visiting sharps in South Bend. He would never play
for money with other students.

Such an unorthodox background developed a poised, confident individualist who was daring, ingenious, and cunning. He
was a modest, pleasant fellow who lived quietly, had no close
friends, and took little interest in the society of girls. Although
he arrived at Notre Dame as a baseball player, he never played
there after his freshman year. During summer vacations he
played independent ball—perhaps not "for free"—and he did
well enough to attract the attention of big-league scouts. When
his football days were over, he was offered a contract by the
Chicago White Sox, but then it was too late.

Walter Camp wrote that Gipp "could do anything that any
backfield man could ever be required to do and do it in a wellnigh superlative fashion." Nature had been so lavish in equipping
him that he reached the top and remained there without serious
training. Like Jim Thorpe, he played at sports, rather than
worked at them, although, unlike the big Indian, he was always
in good condition and ready to do his best, possibly (as it was
rumored) because he frequently had a sizable wager on the outcome of a game. Knowing full well that his team had to have
him in order to win the big ones, he conserved his energy and
saved himself as much as possible. He was known to step out of
bounds in order to avoid being tackled. He saw no percentage in
risking injury by fighting for that extra yard; he played for
larger stakes.

Originally Gipp did not care for football, and made no attempt to play at high school. At Notre Dame, in the fall of 1916, when every able-bodied student was expected to turn out for football, he dutifully reported for practice with the Brownson Hall group, but he dropped out at the first opportunity. Knute Rockne, then assistant coach, chanced to see him kicking a football for exercise. Gipp's fluid action and powerful kicks interested Rockne, who urged him to try for the freshman team. He experienced no trouble in making it. In a game with Western State Normal, the signal was given for a punt. Standing on his own 38-yard line, instead of punting, George drop-kicked a field goal—62 yards, the second longest on record.

That dropkick has often been cited to show the daring instinct that frequently prompted his actions. Another example occurred in the game with Army in 1920. He was called upon to kick from behind his own goal line. As the teams lined up, he tipped off Roger Kiley, an end, and then instead of kicking threw a pass. All-American Kiley, one of the finest receivers of his time, muffed the ball on the 45-yard line. Arthur "Dutch" Bergman, who played with Gipp and coached Sammy Baugh, maintained that, until the coming of Baugh, Gipp was the best long passer that the game had seen. Rockne, who was never accused of being conservative, was sometimes awed by Gipp's audacious moves.

Audacity was not the only trait of Gipp's that grayed Rockne's meager supply of hair. Gipp had the temperament of an artist, and the coach had to make allowances for his idiosyncrasies. Rockne was young then, and humored his "prima donna" in a way he probably would not have done in later years. Rockne's first major headache came in September, 1917. Gipp quit school, and "Rock" had to follow him to Wisconsin in order to persuade him to return. For cutting too many classes, with the resulting poor grades, Gipp was slated to be dropped from school. He claimed that he had been sick part of the term. With Rockne's intercession, he was granted a special examination to determine his fitness to continue the course. He was a smart boy, and with a little concentration was able to pass. That crisis was hardly over when, in the fall of 1920, Gipp relinquished the football captaincy and transferred to the University of Michigan. He spent several days at Ann Arbor before he was pressured into returning to Notre Dame. For all the trouble Gipp caused him, Rockne had a great affection for the eccentric young man.

In his sophomore year (1917) Gipp stepped into the starting backfield. Notre Dame won six, tied Wisconsin, and lost to Nebraska. Against Army, Gipp's runs and passes gained most of the yardage in a 70-yard drive to a touchdown. Notre Dame was leading 7–2 with the game almost over when Army tried a fourth-down pass over the goal line. Authorities differ, but Rockne said it was Gipp who batted down the ball. He went on to say that no forward pass was ever completed in Gipp's territory. In the game with Morningside, Gipp broke a leg, and that finished his first varsity season.

With the nation at war, Notre Dame's celebrated coach, Jesse C. Harper, left for military service, and Knute Rockne took over for 1918. Notre Dame won three, tied two, and lost one—to the Michigan Aggies. That being a war year, it did not count against eligibility, and Gipp, who played as a member of the Student Army Training Corps, still had two more years of competition. He switched from Arts to Law.

Rockne produced his first all-victorious team in 1919. It won nine straight. As usual, Army was the chief target. The Cadets were ahead 9–0, with the first half almost over, when Gipp, on successive passes, moved the ball 75 yards to the ten-yard line. Two smashes at the stubborn Cadet line yielded only three yards. Gipp realized that time was about gone. At the teams lined up, he called to the center to give him the ball. Before Army or some of his teammates knew what was happening, he threw himself over the goal line. Notre Dame's second and winning touchdown was set up by a long pass from Gipp to Eddie Anderson. The Hoosiers, as they were then still called, won, 12–9. Walter Eckersall placed Gipp on his All-Western team. Other headliners were Captain Leonard "Pete" Bahan, halfback; Frank Coughlin, tackle; Maurice "Clipper" Smith and Heartley "Hunk" Anderson, guards; Ed "Slip" Madigan, center; Joe Brandy, quarterback; and Eddie Anderson, end. All except Bahan and Madigan returned the next year, when Coughlin captained the team.

The season of 1920 was the one that establshed Gipp as an immortal. He ran 95 yards against Purdue and 70 against Nebraska, but his greatest show was against Army. Before that game he entertained the spectators by drop-kicking field goals from the 50-yard line. In the game the only goals he kicked were after touchdowns, three out of four attempts, but he did everything else. Although he starred during the first half, Army led at intermission 17–14, thanks largely to the brilliance of little Walter French. In the second half, Gipp took over. He scored no touchdown, but he passed and ran to submerge the Cadets under a 27–17 score. Sportswriters were dumbfounded. Not since the days of Jim Thorpe had they seen such a magnificent all-around performance. He gained 124 yards from scrimmage, 96 on passes, and 112 running back kicks—a total of 332 yards against a strong Army team that was especially primed to stop him. He had to be good that day. According to Grantland Rice, he had $500 riding on the game.

Following Army came Purdue and then Indiana. Gipp dislocated a shoulder early in the first half and was taken out. Indiana was leading, with the game going into its final minutes. A Notre Dame drive seemed about to bog down on the five-yard line. Gipp begged to go in, and Rockne yielded. The first time Gipp was stopped, but on the second attempt, bad shoulder and all, he bored through to give his team the victory, 13–10. Because of his injury and what was thought to be a cold, he sat on the bench at the last game, with Northwestern. It was played at Evanston on a bitterly cold, windy day. Rockne allowed Gipp to suit up in case he might need him for emergency kicking or passing. Notre Dame had the game well in hand and was about to make another clean sweep of its schedule, but when the crowds yelled for Gipp, Rockne allowed him to go for a few plays—one a 45-yard pass to Norman Barry for a touchdown.

Gipp returned to South Bend with a fever. Unknown to him, he had, during the season, developed a streptococcus infection in his throat. Pneumonia set in. Specialists succeeded in arresting it, but his resistance was so lowered that he no longer had the strength to fight off the throat infection. He was received into the Catholic Church, and the consolation of religion helped him to face death.

"It's tough to go," someone said.

"What's tough about it? I'm not afraid," he replied weakly.

With the Notre Dame student body kneeling in the snow, praying for him, he died on December 14, 1920. At Laurium, where he was buried, and at Calumet, where he had attended school, all business houses closed during the time of his funeral. Later, the people of Laurium dedicated a park and a monument to his memory.

But the spirit of Gipp did not die. Eight years after Gipp's death, Rockne summoned it to help win another game—from the old rival, Army, of course. It was in 1928, and football fans still relish the story. Notre Dame had already lost twice, while Army, sparked by Red Cagle, was unbeaten. No score during the first half. During the intermission, Rockne, his voice hoarse, told the players about the passing of George Gipp, and he added something they had never heard. The dying hero had asked a favor: some time when Notre Dame was being beaten would Rockne ask the boys "to win just one for the Gipper"? Rockne had promised, he told the team, and a moment later Gipp died at peace. "This is the game," Rockne then told the players. In the second half they outscored a superior Army team, and won, 12–6. As Jack Chevigny, who was later to die a hero's death at Iwo Jima, scored one of the touchdowns, he shouted, "That's one for the Gipper!"

Rockne was noted for his ability to play upon the emotions

of his men. His ingenuity in concocting reasons to fire them into action was boundless. There is a great difference of opinion as to the authenticity of the deathbed scene. To a considerable extent it is now discounted. But whether Gipp actually uttered the words attributed to him or whether they were supplied by Rockne's imagination, the fact remains that it was the spirit of "the Gipper" that inspired Notre Dame to victory.

"A most peculiar kind of saint," said Francis Wallace.

ERNEST ALONZO NEVERS

(6:01; 205)

His friends called him "Big Dog." Handsome, yellow-haired Ernie Nevers was so quiet and friendly that he reminded people of a big old shaggy Newfoundland dog. But a Newfoundland dog can become aroused and forget his manners, and because of his size and strength he makes a formidable foe. The same was the case with Ernie Nevers. Don E. Liebendorfer, Sports Publicity Director at Stanford, said that in action he was "a driving, relentless animal who swept aside all that stood in his way."

If you enjoy the crash of combat, if your heart pumps just a bit faster when big men abandon fancy work and apply sheer brute strength, then Ernie Nevers is your man. In hitting a line he displayed the decisiveness of a heavy army tank. With abnormally muscled thighs and speed off the mark, he was at full tilt in two strides, blasting through the line or bowling over a tackle. He possessed little dodging ability and was not an elusive runner, but was fast enough to go to the outside if necessary. Reputedly he never fumbled, and he had almost unbelievable endurance, so much so that he frequently played a full game despite the beating he took in plunging and linebacking.

Nevers was called a coach's dream player. Faithful in training, he was always in prime condition, and he threw himself completely into every play. He never loafed or took it easy, which was the chief reason Pop Warner rated him above Jim Thorpe. Warner called Ernie a player without a weakness, and Babe Hollingberry, Washington State coach, believed he was the greatest player of all time. Nevers was in the middle of the rough line play during most of a game, and he hit as hard on defense as he did on offense. But he was never accused of foul play or of any kind of unsportsmanlike conduct. Although he was in athletics the year around, he was an excellent student. On the field he proved to be an intelligent, calm, confident leader who worked unselfishly for the team and whose determination and fight set an example for his teammates. With instantaneous reactions and coordination, he was also outstanding as a blocker, passer, and punter. Small wonder that the authorities at Stanford retired his "No. 1" after he wore it for the last time.

Ernie was born at Willow Grove, Minnesota, on June 11, 1903, and prepped at Superior (Wisconsin) High School. He played end and halfback on the Stanford freshman team in the fall of 1922. They took an unholy beating from the California first-year men, 54-0, and the future did not look rosy at Palo Alto, especially since the varsity had been beaten five times. That was the year Pop Warner signed to coach Stanford, but as his contract at Pittsburgh still had two years to run, he sent his chief assistant, Andy Kerr, west to install his wing attack. Stanford had been in a long losing streak, and Kerr, in his first year, was not able to stem the tide; but the next season (1923), when Nevers as a sophomore was shifted to fullback, conditions improved. The Indians lost only twice, close ones to Southern California, 7-14, and to California, 0-9. Ernie played such a conspicuous part in that revival that Walter Camp picked him for his third All-America team.

In 1924, when Warner personally assumed to coaching responsibilty, Nevers rose from despair to glory. He broke an ankle in a preseason scrimmage and was not able to play in six games.

He got in against Montana and broke the other ankle. That benched him for the "big one" against California. The Bears and the Indians approached their meeting unbeaten, although the former had been held even by Washington, 7–7. That was to be the last of Andy Smith's "wonder teams" that had begun with Brick Muller five years earlier. The teams played at the California Memorial Stadium before 77,000 with another 24,000 seeing the game from neighboring "Tightwad Hill." It was a dramatic game, with Stanford coming from behind in the closing minutes to score two touchdowns to even the score at 20–20. Walter Camp, who was present, said for sustained interest he never saw a game like it, and in 1948 Warner still considered it his greatest thrill in football. Ernie Nevers was just a spectator.

Stanford took the conference championship on a percentage basis, and was matched with Knute Rockne's famous Four Horsemen team in the Rose Bowl. The game was a "natural," as it brought together what were probably the best two teams in the nation. Nevers played in that game, all sixty minutes of it, with his legs so heavily bandaged as almost to shut off circulation. To deaden the pain, he was given shots of novocaine. And what a game he played!

Notre Dame was leading 20–3 and was again on the move when Nevers intercepted a pass and carried the ball to Notre Dame's 29-yard line. On short smashes he powered the ball to the eight-yard line. With the Irish massed to halt Nevers, Ed Walker flipped the ball to Ted Shipkey in the end zone. In the last quarter, Stanford worked its way down to Notre Dame's 26-yard line, and Nevers gained 20 yards in five terrific charges. It was first down and six yards to a touchdown. In three plays Nevers fought his way through the packed defense to reach the one-yard line. Once more he hit the line, and this time it yielded. Instinctively, Walter Eckersall, the head linesman, threw his arms in the air to indicate a touchdown, but it was not his decision to make. The referee, Ed Thorp, ruled that the ball was eight inches short of the promised land. That decision has been the subject of controversy ever since. Later, when Stanford was passing in desperation, Elmer Layden, who had already accounted for two Notre Dame touchdowns, intercepted a pass and ran for another.

During the game, Stanford had gained 298 yards and 17 first downs to Notre Dame's 179 yards and 7 first downs. Moreover, Stanford completed 11 passes and Notre Dame only 3, but the scoreboard read: Notre Dame 27, Stanford 10, and the Irish were the national champions. In 34 plays, Nevers had gained 114 yards; he backed up the line on defense and averaged slightly over 42 yards with his punts. The question on everybody's lips was, What would he have accomplished had he had two sound legs to carry him? The All-America teams had been selected long before the New Year's Day game, and because of his injured status Nevers had been omitted. Stanford was represented by Captain Jim Lawson, an end, who was placed on the first team by the Christy Walsh All-America Board, and on the second by Walter Camp. Murray Cuddeback, back, and H. H. Shipkey, tackle, were other highly rated Indians.

Nevers captained the Stanford team in 1925. Warner was still the coach, but much of the material of the previous years had been graduated, and the championship game was lost to George "Wildcat" Wilson and his Washington Huskies, 13–0. California was beaten for the first time in eight years, 27–14, with Nevers handling the ball on all except three of the offensive plays. Other rivals were disposed of: Southern California, 13–9; U.C.L.A., 82–0; Oregon, 35–13; Oregon State, 26–10; Santa Clara, 20–3; and Occidental, 28–0. Walter Camp had died between seasons, but Nevers appeared on almost every important All-America selection.

Ernie's debut in professional football occurred shortly after the close of the college season. He was signed to captain the Jacksonville All-Stars in a game with Red Grange and the Chicago Bears at Jacksonville, Florida, on January 2, 1926. In that game, in addition to gaining considerable yardage, he intercepted two passes and twice tackled Grange when the Redhead seemed headed for a touchdown. The following fall he went with the Duluth Eskimos. This team was in financial difficulty and had to depend largely on road games to remain solvent. In September, 1926, the squad left Duluth on a five-month barnstorming trip during the course of which it traveled 17,000 miles, from coast to coast, and played 29 games, once taking part in five within a period of seven days. Nevers missed a total of twenty-seven minutes in all those games.

Nevers remained with the Eskimos until 1928, then served as player-coach with the Chicago Cardinals for the next three years. In the first of those years, the Cardinals defeated the Chicago Bears 40–6, with Nevers scoring every point for his team, the result of six touchdowns and four conversions. It broke the pro records both for most points and for most touchdowns in a single game. The Cardinals alternated two sets of halfbacks, but Ernie played with both. The first time an All-Pro team was selected was in 1931, and even though Bronk Nagurski was tearing lines apart with the Bears, Nevers was chosen as fullback. It was a happy ending, because he retired from playing after that season, although he returned to the Cardinals as coach in 1939. None of his teams won a championship. In 1936 he had coached Lafayette College, but the Leopards won only one game out of nine.

Nevers' athletic prowess was not confined to football. At Stanford he was a pitcher and long-ball hitter on the baseball field, and he also starred at basketball. Baseball occupied his attention in the spring, but in his first year, when the California freshmen were playing baseball and track on adjacent fields, he stepped off the diamond in his baseball uniform and, without practice or warm-up, threw the discus just once, and placed third.

Because of his early defection to the pro ranks, he played baseball and basketball only two varsity years at Stanford, 1924 and 1925. During those seasons he pitched the Indians to four victories in five games with California. His performance against the Bears in 1925 was most unusual. In the opening game of the series he was off form and was beaten by the convincing score of 27–5. Such an enthusiastic reception from the heavy-hitting Californians would have discouraged even the most confident. Undaunted, Ernie took this shellacking in stride and went out to pitch his team to victory in the two remaining games. He broke up the second game of the series with a home run as Stanford won, 4–3. His contribution in the deciding game was even more spectacular. Stanford won 8–4 with Ernie hitting a four run homer. He was given a contract by the St. Louis Browns of the American League, then managed by George Sisler. He pitched in 45 games for the Browns during the seasons of 1926, 1927, and 1928 and then played in the Pacific Coast League for several more seasons.

Ernie was not quite so overwhelming on the basketball court; but he was a handy man to have on the team, and his turning pro just before the 1927 season was described as "a real blow" to Stanford's basketball hopes. When he lowered his head, hunched his big shoulders, and started dribbling the ball, he was once again a fullback in action. Opponents found it wise not to get too close to him, especially as, in those days, offensive fouls were exceedingly rare. He was rough, but he never fouled out of a game. Playing dirty was not part of his nature. Andy Kerr coached the two teams he played on. They compiled good records, but neither was able to beat California for the division championship.

Today, Ernie is in public-relations work in San Francisco. His generosity is still in evidence, as he devotes much time to the Recreation Center for the Handicapped in that city. As fond of sports as ever, he has served for years on the committee of the Bing Crosby Pro-Amateur golf tournament. He makes his home in Tiburon, California.

FELIX ANTHONY BLANCHARD

(6:00; 208)

and

GLENN WOODWARD DAVIS

(5:09; 170)

These two extraordinary young men when teamed together were rated by Grantland Rice "as the two best combination backs that football has ever known." Blanchard and Davis are their names, the legendary "B and D," as Joe Williams dubbed them; Mr. Inside (Blanchard) and Mr. Outside (Davis), as George Trevor put it. During the three years that they played together under Red Blaik, Army was unbeaten and was rated first in the nation each year by the Helms Athletic Foundation. When it came to All-America rating, those boys might have missed a vote or two in the first year together, but after that they were unanimous choices. Cold figures state their efficiency. In 625 rushes they gained 5,169 yards and scored 89 touchdowns. That is an average of 8.3 yards every time one of them carried the ball, and they scored a touchdown for every 7.3 rushes.

Davis was the first of the famous duo to arrive at West Point. His twin brother, Ralph, preceded him into the world by a few minutes, hence the nickname "Junior," which Glenn still carries. The twins were born at Claremont, a suburb of Los Angeles, on the day after Christmas, 1924. At Bonita High School, in La Verne, Glenn earned thirteen letters—four at baseball and three each at football, basketball, and track. In his senior year he scored 236 points, and it was argued that he was already superior to any back in the Pacific Coast Conference. John de la Vega of the *Los Angeles Times* wrote, "Davis is the best athlete ever developed in southern California." Both boys secured appointments to West Point. Ralph was a good substitute end, although he never lettered. His fame resulted from winning the ICAAAA outdoor shot-put championship in 1945. Neither was a good student. Ralph managed to hang on, and was graduated with his class—third from the bottom; but "academics" proved too much for Glenn. He was deficient in mathematics at the midyear examinations and was turned back to join the class that would enter the following summer.

But before Glenn left the Point, he made his mark. In 1943 Blaik installed the T formation in place of his time-honored single wing. Army did quite well despite growing pains and the inability of seniors to practice regularly because of an accelerated training program. Two games were lost, to Notre Dame, national champion, and to Navy, beaten only by the Irish. Davis played fullback and was the key man in the Army attack. Against Columbia he got away for an 82-yard run, and he ran back a punt 75 yards against Yale. In ten games he gained 1,028 yards in 144 attempts, and he appeared on several All-Eastern teams. All-America honors evaded him that year, but they did go to the Army captain and center, Casimir Myslinski, and to Francis Merritt, a tackle.

Davis was back at West Point in 1944, and one of his new classmates was Doc Blanchard. The new boy had a colorful background. His father, a 240-pounder of Louisiana-French extraction, had played at Tulane under Clark Shaughnessy in 1915 and 1916. After playing at Wake Forest for a while, he decided to finish studying for a degree in medicine, and returned to Tulane in 1920. He again played football, that time under the name G. Beaulieu, and in due course earned his degree and opened an office in Bishopville, South Carolina. There his son was born on December 11, 1924. The boy's first nickname was "Bubba." Later he was called "Little Doc." After playing at the local high school, he enrolled at St. Stanislaus College, a prep school at Bay Saint Louis, Mississippi, which his father had once attended. Like Davis, Little Doc became a sensation, was picked for the All-Gulf Coast team, and twice played in the "Toy Bowl" game at New Orleans. Many colleges made overtures to him, but he selected North Carolina, where his cousin, Jim Tatum, was coach. It was near his home, and his father was by now in failing health.

Blanchard performed prodigiously with the freshman team. With the war started, he tried to enroll in the Navy unit at the University but was rejected because of slightly impaired vision in one eye and for being overweight, so he enlisted in the Army. He was serving with chemical troops at Clovis, New Mexico, when he received a West Point appointment. Dr. Blanchard lived just long enough to know that his boy had been accepted for admission to the Military Academy. Father and son had been very close. At West Point, Doc would say that sometimes he seemed to feel his father on the field patting him on the back and urging him to hit hard.

Blanchard and Davis were not the only gifted players to arrive at West Point that summer of 1944. With the war raging around the world, some of the finest football talent in the country gravitated to the two national service academies. With freshmen authorized to play, Blaik had so much superlative material that he was able to field two complete units, one composed chiefly of plebes and quarterbacked by the team captain, Tom Lombardo, who was to lose his life in Korea, and the other led by Edgar "Doug" Kenna. It was a year of retribution. Army had not downed Notre Dame since 1931 or scored on the Irish since 1938. That year they won, 59–0. Pennsylvania, unbeaten by the Cadets in the four previous meetings, was slaughtered 62–7. Navy-subsidized Duke, which became winner of the Southern Conference title and victor in the Sugar Bowl, was conquered 27–7. Others to fall were North Carolina, 46–0; Brown, 59–7; Pittsburgh, 69–7; U.S. Coast Guard Academy, 76–0; and Villanova, 83–0. The wise ones were not unduly impressed; they pointed out that the civilian college teams were below par because of the war. That was true, although Notre Dame, Pennsylvania, and Duke had teams strong enough to have beaten Army teams of previous years. There was no question concerning Navy. It was considered, by some, the strongest team in Naval Academy history. The Midshipmen had beaten Army five straight years. The 1944 meeting, at Baltimore, was for the national championship.

The 66,639 spectators who purchased $58,637,000 worth of war bonds for the privilege of buying tickets got their money's worth. Going into the last quarter, Army led 9–7. Navy pushed deep into Army territory, but Davis, who now played left halfback, intercepted a pass and ran it back 13 yards. Then Blanchard was turned loose. Army went 52 yards in nine plays, and Doc carried seven times to account for 48 yards and the touchdown. Navy stormed back, but the game was put out of reach when the Cadets executed the "California Special." Davis took the ball on a pitchout from Lombardo and ran 52 yards along the sideline to score. The final count was 23–7.

Blaik claimed that this was his greatest squad. From the Lombardo team, Blanchard, Davis, George "Barney" Poole, end, and DeWitt "Tex" Coulter, tackle, appeared on first All-America teams, while from the other group Joe Stanowicz and Jack Green, guards, and Doug Kenna, quarterback, were first-team selections, with Bob St. Onge, center, on the Associated Press third team. Lombardo and many of the others were named to honorable-mention lists. The Army team broke numerous modern NCAA records: total offense, 7.74 yards per play; rushing offense, 7:05 yards per play; number of passes intercepted, 36; points scored, 504; touchdowns, 74; and conversions, 56. Davis broke records by averaging 11.5 yards per play by rushing and by scoring 20 touchdowns. His 120 points also led the nation that year. Dick Walterhouse cracked a NCAA record by kicking 47 conversions; he made good on all three attempts in the Navy game. In addition, Blanchard averaged 56.1 yards on 45 kickoffs. Davis received the Maxwell, Helms, and *Los Angeles Times* trophies as the Player of the Year and the Washington Touchdown Club's Walter Camp trophy as the Back of the Year.

In 1945 Blaik did not have quite the depth of the previous year, so he concentrated on one team. He called it the best *eleven* he ever coached. It was captained by Jack Green. George Trevor, Pudge Heffelfinger, and others expressed the opinion that the Army backfield was the strongest that had ever played. The veteran coach, Ray Morrison, wrote that "Army precision, speed and power were awesome and may never have been matched in college football." The team rolled over a strong service team from Louisville, 32–0; Wake Forest, 54–0; Michigan, 28–7; Duke, 48–13; Villanova, 54–0; Notre Dame, 48–0; and Pennsylvania, 61–0. Again everything hinged on the game with Navy.

President Harry S. Truman was among the 102,000 spectators who witnessed the game at Philadelphia's Municipal Stadium. Army began moving early. Blanchard smashed over from close in for the first touchdown and broke through for 16 yards to get the second. The next trip to the end zone was made by Davis after a 49-yard run. In the second half, Blanchard intercepted a pass and went 52 yards to a score, and Davis slipped off tackle for a 33-yard touchdown run. The final score was 32–13.

That was Doc Blanchard's big season; he took practically all national honors in sight: Heisman and Maxwell trophies as the outstanding player and the Walter Camp trophy as the outstanding back. In addition, the A.A.U. voted him the Sullivan Medal awarded to the amateur athlete who, by performance, example, and influence, did the most to advance the cause of good sportsmanship. It was the first time in the 16-year history of the medal that it had gone to a football player. "B," "D," Green, Coulter, Al Nemetz, tackle, and Hank Foldberg, end, were on first All-America teams; Young Arnold Tucker, quarterback, on second, while third-team selections included Barney Poole, end, and Thomas "Shorty" McWilliams, who had been an All-America halfback at Mississippi State before entering West Point. Again the champions broke records, some made only the year before. In total offense, the team averaged 462.7 yards per game and 7.92 per play. The average net gain per game by rushing was 359.8 yards and per play 7.64. Davis also boosted his figures for total offense net gain per play to 11.74, and for rushing only, to 11.51. Blanchard topped Army scorers with 19 touchdowns, one more than Davis scored. Walterhouse, with 43, did not quite come up to his conversion record.

Despite the honors lavished upon them and the arguments as to which was the more valuable player, neither Doc nor Junior took himself too seriously. There was no room for jealousy, because each was supremely confident in himself, highly respected the other, and was willing to sacrifice himself for the good of the team. They were good friends and popular with the other cadets. Both loved the game, were keen competitors, calm under pressure, and possessed a rare amount of football sense and intuition plus the ability to relax. Blanchard was the better student, and probably would have stood much higher in his class had he not been so lazy. He studied just enough to get by. Doc also ranked higher in military aptitude, and was appointed a cadet-lieutenant in his senior year. But again his carefree attitude hurt him. He skipped a lecture, thinking there would be no check of attendance. He was mistaken, and as a result lost his chevrons and some privileges and had to walk punishment tours for two months. Junior did well, too, in obtaining military rank. He was a cadet sergeant major.

Even in the heat of action, Davis was always ready to smile a boyish smile that must have infuriated opponents who were trying to rough him. His classmates called it "the prize-winning smile." It expressed himself—a frank, unspoiled, good-natured youngster who acted in all naturalness. Blanchard was a happy-go-lucky boy who enjoyed a good joke and was always fooling around the locker room, but he was shy with strangers and so modest that he kept no scrapbooks, clippings, or pictures and didn't want to talk about himself. For relaxation he read Westerns. He liked to ride horseback and swim, and he served as an acolyte at the Catholic Chapel. In a game he was not a "happy warrior," as was Davis. When aroused, his lips would set in a tight line and his face darken. That must have been when Old Doc was telling him to hit hard.

Here are a few things said about Doc during the height of his career. Hy Turkin, sportswriter, remarked, "Steve Owen gives the palm to Blanchard even over Bronko Nagurski." Ray Morrison, famous coach, stated, "Many experts insist [Blanchard] is the greatest fullback of all time." Ed McKeever, Notre Dame coach, called him "Superman in the flesh," and Jack Lavelle, Notre Dame and New York Giant scout, maintained he was "the best football player I've ever seen." Fritz Crisler, Michigan coach, claimed that he "has just as much power as Nagurski, and he's faster," while Gilmour Dobie, another veteran coach, felt that only Jim Thorpe excelled Blanchard as an all-around back.

Doc had a big torso and abnormally powerful thighs and calves. He packed terrific power, yet he was shifty and fast, and in the open used a graceful sidestep that confused tacklers. He got off so fast from a standing start that Davis was probably the only man on the squad who could beat him in a sprint. He won the 100-yard dash at an Army-Cornell track meet in 1945, in ten seconds even. He was a wonderful kickoff man who frequently made the tackle himself, a strong punter who got the ball away very fast, and one of the best pass receivers of his time. He could also pass well, and in blocking and tackling was in the top grade. Leo Novak, track coach, told a story that illustrates Blanchard's natural ability. When he began putting the shot, after the football season of 1944, he could not get it out much over thirty feet. It seems incredible, but the following March (1945) he won the indoor ICAAAA championship with a put of 48 feet 3½ inches. He placed second to Ralph Davis in the outdoor Intercollegiates, but heaved the ball 51 feet 10¾ inches in the dual meet with Navy. He won the event against Navy for three straight years and also captured the heptagonal title in 1946.

As to Davis, he too was the subject of "raves." Lou Little called him the best running back in football history, and Grantland Rice said he was one of the finest. Red Blaik insists that "there could not have been a greater, more dangerous halfback in the entire history of the game," and Ray Morrison thought that "with the possible exception of Buddy Young of Illinois, Davis is the fastest man in football uniform of the last decade, perhaps of all time." Just how fast Davis was may be judged from some of his efforts when the stop watch was running. In 1947 he equaled the indoor ICAAAA championship record for the 60-yard dash, 6.2 seconds. He gave up basketball for track that winter, after having played on the court squad for two seasons, winning his letter and assisting in the defeat of Navy in 1946. In the spring of 1947, after the Army-Navy baseball game, he was driven to the stadium, arriving just in time to change into track clothes. He won the 100-yard dash in 9.7 and the 220 in 20.9, the fastest time in the East that season, and his points helped Army to its first victory over Navy at track in five years. All this was accomplished with no practice except during the previous winter.

During the summer of 1948, Davis broke the profesional football record by running from goal line to goal line, 100 yards on grass, in full football uniform, in 10.8 seconds. Not only did he possess blinding speed; he was also deceptively strong. When he entered the Military Academy, the record for the physical-efficiency test was 865 out of a possible 1,000. Davis raised the mark to 962½. He was alert and steady, and it was uncanny the way he could feint, dodge, sidestep, and change direction at top speed. Men going after him got their legs so tangled that they fell down without getting within ten yards of him. He was a natural blocker and tackler, and he developed into a superior passer and receiver.

With Doc and Junior returning as co-captains, it looked like another superteam for Army in 1946, but times were changing —and fast. With the war over, the campuses swarmed with returning servicemen, many of them mature veterans who had fought in combat, some of whom had played service football with the professionals. Blaik assembled another good team without much depth. In the first game, against Villanova, Blanchard was injured. Several ligaments in a leg were torn, and one of them pulled off a portion of bone. An ordinary man would have been through for the season, but Blanchard, thanks to his heavily muscled legs and exceptional willpower, missed only two games. However, Blaik claimed that, except for occasional flashes, he was not within 40 percent of his old form. Even with only 60 percent effectiveness, Doc was still the best fullback in the country.

Blaik called the team of 1946 "the Vindicators." It was determined to make a showing that would justify the superlatives lavished upon its two immediate and far stronger predecessors, and it succeeded. Villanova was disposed of 35–0. With Blanchard on the bench and the defense concentrating on stopping Davis, Arnold Tucker picked up the slack and his heroics helped the Cadets down powerful Oklahoma 21–7 and Cornell 46–21. Doc was back for the game with a great Michigan team at Ann Arbor. The Wolverines had much the same personnel that would win the national championship the next season. But for Army, they might have won it in 1946. Davis played probably the greatest game of his career. Because Tucker suffered a shoulder separation and a sprained elbow, much of the passing devolved upon Junior. On a trap play he slipped through the Michigan line and went 59 yards to a touchdown. He passed 41 yards to Blanchard, who made a "Hutson catch"; then Davis picked up a fumbled ball and fired it 31 yards to Bob Folsom in the end zone. His passes also set up the winning touchdown, which Blanchard scored on a line smash. The final count was 20–13, with Davis gaining 105 yards by running and 160 in seven completed passes out of eight attempted.

Columbia went down 48–14, Duke 19–0, and West Virginia 19–0. Against Columbia, Blanchard ran back a kickoff 92 yards to a score. Next on the schedule was Notre Dame. Long before the season started the buildup got under way. Both teams were undefeated when they met in Yankee Stadium in what was called the "Battle of the Century." Even sophisticated New York lost its nonchalance. Over a million requests for tickets were received. It was said that scalpers got as much as $200 for a single ticket. Notre Dame ruled a slight favorite, but the game developed into a bruising defensive battle, with neither side scoring. Army gained a total of 276 yards against Notre Dame's 271, but the Irish led in first downs, 10 to 9. Although Blanchard and Davis were unable to score, they emerged from the game with increased stature because of their phenomenal defensive work. Following the Irish came Pennsylvania, which was crushed 34–7.

With the war over, six top-notch players resigned from the Naval Academy. Deprived of such personnel, and playing a schedule tailored for the wartime powerhouses, the Midshipmen had won only one game, but they had an inspiring coach in Tom Hamilton and an Army game is something special. In the "big game" Army jumped into an early lead. After Tucker had passed to Davis for 30 yards, he then pitched out to Davis, who ran 14 yards to a touchdown. Blanchard scored after a 53-yard run and again after taking a 27-yard pass from Davis. Jack Ray converted after each touchdown.

The Middies were not idle. They scored a touchdown in the second quarter and two in the second half, but could not convert. Trailing 18–21, Navy launched another drive, and, with a minute and a half remaining had a first down on Army's three-yard line. The Cadets threw back three charges, and time ran out before the Middies could get off another play.

"You are the champions," Blaik used to tell his teams. "From you, people expect only perfect performances." Badly outplayed in the second half, the weary Cadets performed like champions in that goal-line stand when a three-year record hung in the balance. Blaik was voted Coach of the Year. The only major award that had eluded Davis in 1944 was the Heisman trophy. He won it in 1946. Tucker became the second football player to win the Sul-

livan Medal of the A.A.U. Blanchard, Davis, Tucker, Hank
Foldberg, end, and Joe Steffy, guard, were on first All-America
teams, while Barney Poole, end, and Arthur Gerometta, guard,
were second-team choices. Doc and Glenn were offered fabulous
salaries by the professional clubs, but neither could accept because of their obligation to serve three years on active military
duty. During their regular summer leave of absence, they were
featured in a movie, *The Spirit of West Point.* It was successful
and they were well reimbursed, but Davis, who had never been
seriously injured, severed a knee ligament while making the
movie. Both played with the College All-Stars in games with professional teams for charity.

That concludes the story of the college football careers of
that remarkable pair, but there is still something to be said about
Davis' baseball achievements. In that sport, also, he had to turn
down flattering offers from big-league clubs. He played center
field on the Army team for three seasons. In the spring of 1945,
the Cadets won all 15 college games played and, in addition, won
two out of three from both the Brooklyn Dodgers and Montreal
Royals. Davis captained the team in 1947, which won 17 college
games and lost one. In the three games with Navy, Glenn collected five hits in ten times at bat, scored six runs and stole five
bases.

Davis selected the infantry and was stationed in Korea. He
resigned in 1950, after serving the required three years, and
joined the Los Angeles Rams, with whom he had played several
exhibition games during the late summer of 1948 before he sailed
overseas. The layoff did not seem to affect him much although,
because of his bad knee, he was never able to cut as he had in
college. He made the team that won the Western Division title,
and he was in the running as "Rookie of the Year." In the championship playoff, lost to the Cleveland Browns 28–30, he took
part in an 82-yard pass play that established a league record. Bob
Waterfield passed 30 yards to him and he ran 52 to a touchdown.

The next season (1951), when the Rams won the world championship, he was not of much assistance because of a recurrence of the knee injury. That ended his fantastic athletic career. He became assistant promotion manager of the *Los Angeles Times*.

Blanchard was commissioned in the Air Force and became a jet pilot. He helped with the coaching at West Point in 1954, 1955, and 1956. On July 2, 1959, his plane caught on fire while approaching a thickly populated area near London. Instead of abandoning the plane, he remained at the controls and landed it in a field. For that brave act he was cited in orders. On May 24, 1960, he assumed command of the 77th Tactical Fighter Squadron based at Weathersfield Air Base, England. Doc is still with the Air Force, and has risen to the rank of lieutenant-colonel.

FRANK SEILER BUTTERWORTH

(5:11; 158)

Grantland Rice's fullbacks have all been discussed: Coy or Mahan (1928), Nevers (1939) and Nagurski since then. Walter Camp picked Butterworth at fullback on the All-Star team chosen in 1904, and rated him second only to Ted Coy for all-time honors in 1910. In 1927 George Trevor, himself a Yale man, created room for both Coy and Butterworth on his All-Time All-Yale team by moving the latter to a halfback position. Butterworth was the All-America fullback in 1893 and 1894, the years that the Elis were captained by Frank Hinkey, who was one of his closest friends.

Butterworth introduced a new style of line plunging. Instead of running low with his head down as was customary, he hit in a semierect position, taking the shock on his hips. That enabled him to keep his feet so that he could continue moving after breaking through a line. He had very strong legs, which gave him plenty of driving power. His plunges set up the winning touchdown against Harvard in 1892. He smashed his way to the sole touchdown in the Harvard game the following year, and scored three against Princeton in 1894. He was a good end runner who, on occasion, worked his way downfield for as much as 20 yards. He was strong on defense and ran interference well. His punting was definitely superior; he frequently kicked the ball 65 or 70 yards. In 1894 he enjoyed a time advantage in that respect, because that was the year that Walter Camp introduced the direct pass from center to the kicker instead of having the ball pass through the hands of the quarterback.

Butterworth followed other Yale men, McClung, Heffelfinger, and Charlie Gill, to California, where he coached in 1895 and 1896. His first team tied Stanford, but the next lost to the Cardinals. During 1898 and 1899 he assisted at Yale and then devoted himself to finance and politics. He served in the Connecticut State Legislature from 1907 to 1909 and was an unsuccessful candidate for governor in 1914. He became president of the New Haven Hotel Company, and died in 1950 at the age of seventy-seven.

JOHN ALEC KIMBROUGH

(6:02; 222)

Professor Lacy Lockert of Nashville, Tennessee, the most profound "footballogist" that I have ever known, believes that Kimbrough was the best of all college fullbacks. He bases his opinion in no small degree on Kimbrough's performance in the Sugar Bowl against Tulane after the 1939 season. Kimbrough dominated the later part of the game as neither Coy nor any other fullback, he maintains, ever dominated a game against a line as strong as the one Tulane possessed. Tulane had three All-America candidates in Tom O'Boyle at guard, Harley McCollum at tackle, and Ralph Wenzel at end. During that game he gained 152 yards on 26 runs from scrimmage. "Jarrin' Jawn" was a power runner, with a special emphasis on power. Wherever he played, critics declared that a harder-running back had never been seen in that region. The Associated Press labeled him "one of the most destructive fullbacks the game had known." He was also an excellent defensive back.

It was in 1939 that Coach Homer H. Norton led Texas A.&M. to the Southwest Conference championship, and Kimbrough, who played 455 minutes in ten games, led the circuit in scoring with ten touchdowns. In a critical game won from Southern Methodist 6–2, in which he played the full 60 minutes, John caught a pass to set up the lone touchdown of the game, which he scored himself on an end sweep after the Mustangs had dug in, expecting him to hit the line. The "Fighting Farmers" then went to the Sugar Bowl, where they defeated Tulane, the Southeastern Conference co-champions, 14–13. Kimbrough plunged to a touchdown. The Greenies went ahead, but he sparked a rally in which his runs of five and 18 yards put the ball on the 26-yard line. A forward pass ended in a lateral to Big John, who fought his way ten yards to a score. In his team's subsequent drive to keep possession of the ball till time ran out, on play after play he gained from seven to nine yards. In 1944, when Fred J. Digby picked an All-time Sugar Bowl team, Kimbrough was his fullback.

An upset loss, 0–7, to Texas forced Texas A.&M. into a tie with Southern Methodist for the 1940 conference title. In a regular-season game the Aggies had trounced the Mustangs 19–7, so they went to the Cotton Bowl, where Kimbrough put on another awesome exhibition. Fordham had a special defense rigged to hold him, but he smashed through it for 75 yards in 18 carries, and plunged to the winning touchdown. In odd moments he knocked down a Fordham pass that would have meant a touchdown and blocked a try for extra point. Texas A.&M. won, 13–12. During the season he gained 658 yards and seven touchdowns in

158 runs, caught nine forward passes and intercepted six to net his team 142 yards.

In both championship years, Kimbrough was virtually a unanimous choice for All-American. In those days the United Press picked an All-Bowl team from men who had distinguished themselves in the various bowl games throughout the country. Kimbrough was on the team both years. The champion Farmers of 1939 had other men of All-America caliber or close to it, such as Joe Boyd and Ernie Pannell, tackles; Marshall Foch Robnett, guard; Herb Smith and Jim Sterling, ends; and James Thomason, a blocking back. All except Boyd and Smith also played in 1940.

Kimbrough had hoped to go to West Point, but someone beat him to an appointment, and at Texas A.&M. he enrolled in the Reserve Officers Training Corps, which has furnished our country with many noted soldiers. He was commissioned in the Reserve and served on active duty with the Army throughout the war. In 1946, 1947, and 1948 he played professional football, under Dudley DeGroot, with the Los Angeles Dons of the All-America Football Conference. He quit playing to become associated in business with an oil firm at his hometown, Haskell, Texas.

It is said that, strangely enough, he did not really like football, but played in college from a sense of obligation to his school.

AWARD-WINNING FULLBACKS

Marshall Goldberg, *Pittsburgh*	CAMP (initial), 1937
Felix A. Blanchard, *Army*	HEISMAN, MAXWELL, CAMP, 1945
Emil M. Sitko, *Notre Dame*	CAMP, 1949
Alan D. Ameche, *Wisconsin*	HEISMAN, 1954
John Crow, *Texas*	HEISMAN, CAMP, 1957
Bob Ferguson, *Ohio State*	MAXWELL, 1961

8

GREAT PROS

	SPORTING NEWS, 1942	TREAT, 1952	OWEN, 1952	HELMS, TO DATE
ENDS:	Hutson	Hutson	Hutson	Hutson
	Hewitt	Hewitt	Chamberlin	Pihos
TACKLES:	Hubbard	Hubbard	Hubbard	Hubbard
	Edwards	Henry	Lyman	Stydahar
GUARDS:	Fortmann	Fortmann	Fortmann	Fortmann
	Michalske	Michalske	Michalske	Musso
CENTER:	Hein	Hein	Hein	Hein
QUARTERBACK:	Baugh	Baugh	Baugh	Baugh
HALFBACKS:	Clark	Clark	Grange	Grange
	Battles	Driscoll	Van Buren	Clark
FULLBACK:	Nagurski	Nagurski	Nagurski	Nagurski

NOTE: Hutson, Hubbard, Henry, Stydahar, Baugh, Clark, Grange, and Nagurski have been covered in previous chapters.

(BERLIN) GUY CHAMBERLIN

(6:02; 194 in college, 210 as a pro)

Steve Owen called Chamberlin "the winningest end" he ever saw, and believed that he made the difference in every close game in which he played. Guy played on the Nebraska varsity for three seasons, during which the Cornhuskers never lost. In 1914 he ran back a kickoff 95 yards against the Michigan Aggies, and scored against Kansas after a 70-yard run from scrimmage, to become one of the most prominent halfbacks in the Midwest and receive All-America honorable mention from Walter Camp. In his senior year (1915) he played end a large part of the time. Here is what he contributed in Nebraska's most spectacular victory, over Notre Dame 20–19. The Irish scored first. Chamberlin passed for a 37-yard gain, and a few plays later circled his own left end on a 20-yard touchdown run. Notre Dame scored again. Chamberlin took a 20-yard pass, passed for 24 more, and then scored on an amazing 10-yard run around end in which he dodged or ran over six men. For the clinching touchdown, Nebraska went 49 yards on two of Chamberlin's lefthanded passes. Jesse Harper, Notre Dame coach, said, "Chamberlin won the game for Nebraska," and the referee, Walter Eckersall, pronounced him "one of the greatest ends I have ever seen." Frank Menke, Parke H. Davis, and other noted authorities placed him on their first All-America teams, but Walter Camp left him off all three of his teams.

Failure to select Chamberlin, who was the outstanding player on the Nebraska team, indirectly caused Sir Walter to commit the biggest "boner" he ever perpetrated in his long and distinguished career as football's supreme arbiter. He named Vic Halligan, as a representative of the unbeaten Cornhuskers on the third team. Halligan was a splendid tackle—in his day. But he had been graduated the previous June and, naturally, did not play in 1915. A week or two after the selection appeared in *Collier's*, Camp published a letter in the same magazine, admitting his error and withdrawing Halligan's name, thus giving rise to an "on ag'in, off ag'in, Halligan" parody of a popular song of the time. Had Camp picked Chamberlin, he would have avoided considerable embarrassment. Although his corrected selection appeared in the *Spalding Guide,* the erroneous original has been faithfully copied by Dr. L. H. Baker, Frank Menke, Harford Powel, and other authorities. This writer remembers the incident very well because he was the tackle whom Camp named to the place vacated by Halligan.

In 1919 Chamberlin played with the Canton Bulldogs and then joined George Halas when the latter organized Staley's team at Decatur, Illinois. In 1921 Halas moved his team to Chicago, where it became the Bears. In the championship game of that year, won from the Buffalo All Americans, 10–7, Chamberlin intercepted a forward pass and ran 65 yards to a touchdown. He and Halas were the ends, and years later Halas called his teammate "the greatest two-way end of all time." The next two seasons saw Chamberlin back at Canton as player-coach, and the Bulldogs won the title each year without losing a game. When the franchise was sold to Cleveland, Chamberlin went along with the team and guided it to another championship. In 1925 he undertook a rehabilitation job at Frankford, a suburb of Philadelphia. In his second season with them, the Yellowjackets took the league title in a thriller with Chicago, 7–6, in which Chamberlin blocked the Bears' attempt at conversion.

This activity has given him an unusual record: coaching four champions in five years in three different cities or, if you prefer, playing on five championship teams in six years in four different cities! He closed his career with the Chicago Cardinals, as player in 1927 and coach the next year. Chamberlin was big and fast and was a deceptive runner and powerful on defense. Halas said it was almost impossible to cover him on a pass play, and Owen thought it uncanny the way he seemed to "smell out" opponents' plans. Chamberlin took up farming after football, and is now a state livestock superintendent in Nebraska.

WILLIAM ERNEST HEWITT

(5:11; 195)

Bill Hewitt might well have been the strongest defensive end in pro-league history. Like Armin Hary, Germany's Olympic sprint champion, his reflexes were so keen that he started faster than the other players, and frequently looked, from the stands, to be offside. Adept at outguessing opponents, a hard tackler and blocker, Hewitt had no equal at rushing the passer, and he was also an expert pass receiver. To add to his conspicuousness, he played without a headguard.

Bennie Oosterbaan, Hewitt's coach at college, called him "one of the very finest players ever at Michigan," and considered him to have been the best player on each of the three teams of which he was a member; but during his first two varsity years, he was rated by outsiders as just another good end. Even in 1930, when Michigan was unbeaten and tied for the conference championship, one looked in vain for Bill's name on any All-Western selection. Oosterbaan thinks he would have been All-American his last year (1931), when Michigan again tied for the title, had he not been shifted to fullback. The strange part of it is that his work in the backfield focused attention upon him, and by a strange process convinced the experts that he was really a first-class end. Against Minnesota, he ripped through tackle and ran 57 yards to the only score of the game, and throughout the season he did conspicuous work in backing up the line. Bob Zuppke was among those who chose him, as an end, on his All-Western team. Bill made quite an impression in the Shrine game in San Francisco at the close of the season and as late as 1943 was still listed as the best end to play on the East team since the inception of the series twenty years earlier.

It was odd that in 1931 the only All-America recognition Bill received was from the *New York Evening Post*, which placed him on its third team, yet the very next year, while playing with the Chicago Bears, he won a place on the second All-League team. He jumped to the first team in 1933 when he received 50 votes, more than any other player in any position. The Bears took the world championship game from the New York Giants, 23–21. In that game, Nagurski tossed a pass to Hewitt, who lateraled the ball to Bill Karr, who scored the winning touchdown. The next year the Bears had to be content with the division title. In 1935 it looked as though Bill were slipping. He failed to merit All-League rating, and early the next year was sold to the Philadelphia Eagles. With them he soared back to the first All-League team in 1936 and 1937, and held to a second-team berth in 1938. He retired at the end of the 1939 season, but in 1943, owing to the shortage of players because of the war, he returned to play that one season with the Philadelphia-Pittsburgh combination. After that, he resumed his work with a railroad. A few years later, on January 14, 1947, Bill was killed in an automobile accident.

PETER LOUIS PIHOS

(6:1; 210)

"Indestructible Pete" was of Hellenic descent, and like most famous athletes of such derivation, he was a "Glamorous Greek." It was not an empty title. For four seasons the big boy from Chicago played under Bo McMillin at Indiana. He wasted little time getting his name before the public. In 1942, his sophomore year, he took a 25-yard pass from Billy Hillenbrand and scored a touchdown that gave Indiana its second victory in history over Minnesota, 7–0. That year, *Liberty Magazine* conducted a poll of 1,706 players from 104 colleges, with each man voting only for men against whom he had played. Pete won an end berth on that All-America team by a good margin. The next year, Grantland Rice, the Christy Walsh Board, *Sporting News,* and others joined in making him a consensus All-America choice. During the season (1943) he caught 20 passes for 241 yards. On defense, he excelled in backing up the line. In a victory over Wisconsin, 34–0, he caught a touchdown pass and then moved into the backfield and plunged for two more touchdowns. Bob Hoern-schemeyer, back, and John Tavener, center, were other stars on that Hoosier team.

The season of 1944 found Pete playing a more deadly game. He was one of Uncle Sam's paratroopers. In Europe he won a commission, and he returned to the campus a war hero, in 1945, just five days before the game with Northwestern. Although still on terminal leave, he suited up. He caught a pass on the five-yard line and staggered to a touchdown with three Wildcats hanging on. The game ended in a 7–7 draw. Pete was moved to fullback and became the "crashing terror of the Midwest," according to Paul Hornung, a sportswriter. Colonel McMillin's "po' li'l' boys," as he called them, also included George Taliaferro, an eighteen-year old freshman halfback; Howard Brown, guard, another war veteran; John Cannady, center, a draft rejectee; and the ends Bob Ravensberg and Ted Kluszewski. With them and a strong supporting cast, Indiana won its first and only conference championship. Except for Northwestern, the Hoosiers defeated all other opponents: Michigan, Illinois, Nebraska, Iowa, Tulsa, Cornell College, Minnesota, Pittsburgh, and Purdue. Pete was placed second to Army's Doc Blanchard among the All-American fullbacks. In 1946 Indiana lost most of its top performers of the previous season, but still had Pete, and finished third in the conference.

From 1947 through 1955, Pihos played end for Philadelphia. Under "Greasy" Neale, the Eagles won the National League championship in 1948 and 1949, and Pete was an All-League end in both seasons. Then came two fairly lean years, but Pete bounced back to make the All-Pro team in 1952, 1953, 1954, and 1955. During three of those seasons, he led the league in pass receiving: 63 completions for 1,049 yards and 10 touchdowns in 1953;

60 for 872 yards and 10 touchdowns in 1954; and 62 for 864 yards and 7 touchdowns in 1955, his last year in competition. During his nine seasons in the big league he caught 373 passes for 5,169 yards and 63 touchdowns to set five club records. After his retirement from pro football, he became a salesman for a container company in Paoli, Pennsylvania, and during the seasons of 1959 and 1960, served under Andy Pilney as end coach at Tulane.

(WILLIAM) ROY LYMAN

(6:02; 210 in college; 240 as a pro)

"Link" Lyman, who is still considered by some football buffs as the greatest tackle ever to wear the uniform of the Chicago Bears, had no previous experience before attending the University of Nebraska. He learned the game as a freshman, and as a sophomore in 1918, started every game for the varsity. He again played in 1919, dropped out for a year, and returned, in 1921, to become an important cog in what was considered the most formidable football machine yet produced at that university. Fred T. Dawson coached the Cornhuskers, who ran up 283 points against 17 in eight games, only one of which was lost, to Notre Dame 0–7. That team won the Missouri Valley Conference championship with ease, and traveled east to halt Pittsburgh 10–0. Pop Warner's vaunted running attack was stopped cold by the big, rough Nebraska line, which was one of the strongest ever to come out of the West. The men Walter Camp singled out for special praise, in addition to Lyman, were Captain Clarence Swanson, end, and John Pucelik, guard.

Link signed to play pro football under his fellow Nebraskan, Guy Chamberlin, at Canton in 1922 and was teamed with Fats Henry. The Bulldogs were champions in 1922 and 1923 and, as representatives of Cleveland, in 1924. After Chamberlin left the organization, Lyman returned to Canton for the season of 1925. From 1926 through 1934, with 1929 and 1932 off years, Link played with the Chicago Bears and helped them win the world championship in 1933 and a division title in 1934. Those were the days of Nagurski and Hewitt. Link played regularly at left tackle in 1934, but he was not the terror of his earlier days, and quit at the end of the season to help coach at Nebraska. It is unfortunate, for the sake of the record, that honor teams were not selected when he was in his prime. As it was, Jack Reardon picked him for the All-League team in 1931 and for the second eleven in 1934.

Lyman was fast, and went downfield with the ends. At Nebraska he was a good ground-gainer on a tackle-around play, but he made his real reputation on defense. At that time, the defense was largely set, with each lineman having a fixed area of responsibility. Of course, thinking linemen have always shifted, but they did not have much latitude because of the tight lines. Link shifted more than anyone, especially after he became a pro. Sometimes he would play close to his guard and at other times be as far away as he could get. He could change position just as the ball was snapped and, with his weight and agility, was the most difficult to block of all tackles of his time. Steve Owen claimed that Link's shifting, sliding style was the inspiration for the modern complicated defense patterns. Lyman is still on the job, managing his own insurance business in Los Angeles, California.

ALBERT GLEN EDWARDS

(6:02½; 235 in college, 256 as a pro)

"Turk" Edwards was one of those big boys whom the opposition deemed wise to keep friendly and in good humor. Even so, he presented quite a problem, and there was no limit to what he might do if fully aroused. He was noted particularly as a power player, but his speed and agility could not be discounted, as was demonstrated in a game with Oregon State in 1930, while he was playing left tackle at Washington State. With three minutes of play remaining, and the score tied at 7–7, the Beavers were still pressing for a decisive score. A pass was partially blocked. Turk seized the ball before it could touch the ground and ran 26 yards to the winning touchdown—and to the conference championship. He always regarded that play as providing his greatest thrill in football. It was the usual thing for him to respond when the pressure was greatest.

Edwards, who came from Clarkston, Washington, played at Washington State in 1929, 1930, and 1931, when Orin "Babe" Hollingberry was coach. It was in 1930, when the Cougars took the conference title, that the line featured not only Edwards but also the center, Mel Hein. Authorities were not in accord as to which of those great players was most deserving of All-America rating. Many of the most influential selectors, such as the Associated Press, International News Service, *College Humor Magazine,* and George Trevor in the *New York Sun,* favored Edwards. Turk captained the team in 1931. With only two holdovers, the Cougars did not do too well, and as a result he did not receive the honors of the previous year, although he did appear on several All-America teams. He proved his ability in the Shrine game in San Francisco, and when an All-Time All-West eleven was selected in 1941, he was a member of it.

The season of 1932 found Edwards with the Boston Braves, who became the Boston Redskins the next year. In 1937 they moved to Washington, and Turk continued playing with them through the season of 1940. In 1937, in a game with the New York Giants for the Eastern Division title, he blocked a kick for the break of the game. The ball bounced into the end zone, where Wayne Millner fell on it for a touchdown and the Redskins went on to win 49–14. With Sammy Baugh passing beautifully, they took the world-championship game from the Chicago Bears, 28–21. The Redskins also were division champions in 1936 and 1940. Ray Flaherty was the coach. Edwards made the All-Pro team in his "freshman" year, 1932. He was also on the first team in 1933, 1936, and 1937 and on the second in 1934 and 1938. His character and leadership may be judged from the fact that he was named to coach the Redskins in 1946. He brought the team home in third place, and his contract was renewed for 1947 and 1948. In time he gave up football and became manager of a sporting-goods company in Seattle.

AUGUST MICHALSKE

(6:00; 210)

"Mike" Machalske is considered by some authorities as the finest guard that ever played pro football. Fast, smart, with keen competitive spirit, he was great at pulling out of the line, and his blocking was deadly. On defense he was seldom fooled. Generally he could outguess his opponents. Even if he did not, he had the ability and strength to fight his way through the interference to get at the man with the ball.

Like many of the men who developed rapidly in professional football, Mike had been thoroughly grounded in fundamentals while at Penn State, where he came under the coaching of Hugh Bezdek, one-time Chicago All-America fullback and a pupil of the great Stagg. In 1923, his sophomore year, Mike played at guard, and threw many key blocks to enable "Lighthorse Harry" Wilson to get away for spectacular runs. However, he was still largely an unsung hero, although Parke H. Davis had him on his honor roll in both 1923 and 1924. During the latter season, he came to the attention of Herbert Reed, one of the leading students and writers of the game. Reed placed him on his All-America team, but he was perhaps the only critic who recognized the wonderful talent of that hard-charging guard. Mike might have gone further the next year had not Bezdek moved him to fullback. His line plunging netted both touchdowns in a 13–6 victory over Michigan State, but in one season he did not become a great fullback.

In 1927, when professional football was just beginning to get on its feet, Mike joined the New York Yankees and did some notable blocking for Red Grange. He remained with that team the next season, and in 1929 transferred to the Green Bay Packers. That was the same year that Coach Curly Lambeau hired Cal Hubbard. Cal and Mike anchored the tremendous line that enabled the Packers to rule professional football in 1929, 1930, and 1931. Mike was among those honored on the initial selection of an All-Pro team in 1931. He made it again in 1935, his last full season with the Packers, although he came out of retirement to do some playing for them in 1937.

Mike then turned to line coaching, and was at Iowa State when, in mid-season, 1942, he was elevated to head coach. His 1944 team was his best. It placed second in the Missouri Valley Conference and lost only to the conference champion, Oklahoma 7–12. It. was no coincidence that Jack Fathauer and Charlie Wright, the All-Conference guards, were both from Iowa State. The Cyclones were third in the circuit in 1945. After they won only two games in 1946, Michalske resigned, although he was so well liked and respected that the college authorities urged him to remain. He continued coaching and has appeared on the staffs at Texas A.&M., Baylor, and Texas.

DANIEL JOHN FORTMANN

(6:00; 190 in college, 207 as a pro)

Danny Fortmann was an "infant prodigy." He was the youngest man ever to sign a National Football League contract.

At nineteen, an age when many boys are just starting their college careers, he already had completed three years on the Colgate varsity and in addition was a Phi Beta Kappa. Pop Warner's former righthand man, Andy Kerr, coached the Red Raiders in those days, and his razzle-dazzle, lateral-passing attack was something to see. Even the linemen joined in the fun and took passes and made touchdowns. The little Scotsman gave Colgate teams to remember. In Danny's last season (1935), Colgate defeated Syracuse for the eighth consecutive time and made it seven straight over Brown.

Danny was tried at halfback and end, but eventually found his niche at guard. No doubt it was because of his immaturity that he did not obtain a greater degree of prominence until his senior year, when Allison Danzig of the *New York Times* called him "one of the best linemen in the East," while Andy Kerr selected him on his All-Eastern eleven and invited him to play in the Shrine game with the East team of which Kerr was coach.

When George Halas signed Fortmann, the latter was thirtieth on the Bears' draft list. Danny seemed to mature overnight. In a game the College All-Stars played with the Detroit pro champions, in the fall of 1936, he went in as a substitute but won acclaim as "a bulwark of the line," and, significantly, when the Stars played an exhibition game with the New York Giants the next week, he drew a starting assignment. Fortmann played all his pro games with the Chicago Bears, who were world champions in 1940, 1941, and 1943, and division champions in 1937 and 1942. In his first two seasons, 1936 and 1937, he was on the second All-Pro team, but after that, for the remaining six years of his pro career he was not only on the first eleven but was also considered the Number One guard in the league.

Fortmann was very spirited, but he played clean and within the rules. In 1941, when he won an award as Lineman of the Year, he had been penalized only five yards during the entire season. He was remarkable at pulling out of the line to head the interference, and was a savage tackler and blocker. He played alert football, excelled in diagnosing opponents' plays, and was probably never trapped. While he was playing with the Bears, he studied medicine, and is now one of Los Angeles' better-known surgeons. In 1960 he was selected by *Sports Illustrated* for its Silver Anniversary All-America team.

GEORGE FRANCIS MUSSO

(6:02; 255)

If your knowledge of Millikin University is not very extensive, you will probably realize why so few ever heard of "Moose" Musso until he became a professional. After starring in all sports at the high school in his native town of Collinsville, Illinois, he moved on to James Millikin, as the university was then called, and made an outstanding record at football, basketball, baseball, and track. For four years he played left tackle for the Presbyterians, and each year his work received the highest praise from local authorities. Millikin captured the championship of the "Little Nineteen" of Illinois in 1929 and 1930, his first years in school. In his senior year, 1932, George captained the eleven. Leo T. Johnson was the coach.

George Halas, ever on the alert for unpublicized talent in the lesser-known colleges, gave Musso a chance with the Chicago Bears. That was in 1933 when Red Grange and Bronko Nagurski were wearing Chicago uniforms. At times Halas must have wondered if he had not been too generous. The big recruit was called a "man-mountain," but he was none too promising. Halas worked diligently with him, and Musso's response was truly extraordinary. Fiercely determined to make good, he slaved at the job. Of course, he had the ability, as Halas well realized. It took Musso a little time to become adjusted, but the coach's patience and labor were amply rewarded. Presently the devastating charge of the "Moose" was the talk of the league. At the end of the season, when the arbiters got around to making their All-Pro selections, they placed Musso on the second team.

Moose was still playing tackle, and he made the All-Pro team in 1935. He made it again in 1937, but by then he had been moved to guard and was publicly hailed by George Halas as "the greatest guard in professional football ranks." He was on the second honor eleven in 1938 and 1939. Musso was of even greater value to the team when he was appointed captain. He proved to be a courageous, fighting leader who inspired his mates. He played with the Bears from 1933 through 1944, and during those twelve years they won the world title four times (1933, 1940, 1941, and 1943) and the division title three times (1934, 1937, and 1942). He was with them in the famous 73–0 rout of the Washington Redskins in 1940.

After his retirement Musso went into the restaurant business in Edwardsville, Illinois. Local voters recognized his quality, and in November, 1958, he was elected Sheriff of Madison County by an overwhelming majority. He still holds the office.

MELVIN JOHN HEIN

(6:03; 210 in college, 230 as a pro)

There have been many wonderful centers in the pro game, but in almost everybody's book the greatest of them all was Mel Hein. He was an All-American in college, but it was not until he became a professional that he earned a place among the immortals of the game. Including schooldays, he played organized football for twenty-five years, and his sole injury was a broken nose, in 1941. Even in his last year in pro ranks, at the age of thirty-six, he still was turning in sixty-minute performances.

He was born in California, but his family moved to the State of Washington when he was a small boy. At high school he played a different position each year, in order: guard, center, halfback, tackle. As a tackle he made the All-League team at Burlington, Washington. He also participated in basketball, baseball, and track. At Washington State, he played center on the freshman team in 1927 and for the varsity the following three years. In his senior year (1930) he was described as an inspirational captain as he led his team to the Pacific Coast Conference championship and a trip to the Rose Bowl. For their appearance at Pasadena, Washington State dazzled the fans, but not the opposition, with completely red uniforms, including helmets and shoes, but after they lost to Alabama, the uniforms were burned and a decree issued banning the nickname "Red Devils."

Hein's versatility may be judged from the fact that in 1930 Grantland Rice picked him for his All-America team as a utility lineman, the Christy Walsh Board as a tackle, Lawrence Perry as a guard, and Lou Little and others as a center. The college has retired Mel's number 7, and his jersey is enshrined in the trophy room at Pullman. While in college, he also engaged in basketball and track and was a member of the Student Board of Control and the Crimson Circle, the latter a senior men's honorary society based on service and scholarship.

Mel played with the New York Giants from 1931 through 1945, fifteen years. Only Sammy Baugh, with one year more, had longer service in the big league. In 1931 and 1932, Mel made the second All-Pro team, and for the following eight years was a first-team choice. He was again on the second team in 1941. In the 1935 balloting, he received more votes than any other player, regardless of position, and in 1938 he was the first recipient of the Most Valuable Player award. As that award is no longer in competition, he will remain the only lineman (exclusive of ends) ever to attain it.

To reach and hold such a position of preeminence, Hein had to possess to a superlative degree all the requirements of a center and a linebacker. He was alert mentally and physically, and was cool under pressure. Steve Owen said that Mel required very little coaching, and was a clean player who, to the best of his recollection, lost his temper only once during the many years he played with the Giants. An opponent played him "dirty," and Mel blocked him in a perfectly legitimate manner, but so savagely that the unfortunate fellow had to be carried off the field. Comparatively speaking, the Giants were able to contain Don Hutson better than the other teams because Hein had the ability to force him toward the sideline, where his freedom of maneuver was restricted. In 1938 Mel intercepted a Green Bay pass intended for Hutson, and raced 50 yards to a touchdown. The Giants had a play in which Hein was on the end of the line, and hence eligible to receive a forward pass. He would snap the ball to Quarterback Harry Newman, who passed it back to him. While Newman feinted passes to the backs, Hein would jog down the field—10, 20, sometimes 30 yards before it was discovered that he had the ball.

After serving as head coach at Union College, Schenectady, New York, in 1946, Hein specialized in line-coaching: with the Los Angeles Dons in 1947 and 1948, New York Yankees in 1949, Los Angeles Rams in 1950, and the University of Southern California from 1951 to date. He has the reputation of being a gentleman on and off the field.

JOHN LEO DRISCOLL

(5:11; 150 in college, 170 as a pro)

Northwestern had lost 17 straight conference games over a period of three years when, in 1916, a junior named "Paddy" Driscoll, captained the team. Paddy was a local boy, not very large, but smart, well coordinated, and a good leader. He was a fast, deceptive runner whose pivoting and change of pace made him doubly dangerous; he could pass, punt, and drop-kick with the best in the game, and was a flawless defensive player. In 1915, when he ran back a kickoff 85 yards against Iowa, Camp had given him All-America honorable mention. Northwestern had not beaten Chicago since 1901, but in 1916 Captain Paddy took care of the Maroon. He scored a touchdown and kicked a field goal from the 43-yard line for nine points in a 10–0 victory. The Wildcats, coached by Fred J. Murphy from Yale, also downed Indiana, Iowa, and Purdue, as well as nonconference Drake and Lake Forest. At the season's end Northwestern, the perennial tail-enders, fought Ohio State for the conference championship. The Wildcats could not hold Chic Harley, and suffered their only defeat of the season. Camp placed Driscoll on his third All-America eleven, and gave honorable mention to Richard Koehler, fullback. Paddy was reelected captain for 1917, but the war was on and he moved to other fields.

In 1918 Driscoll was on duty at the Great Lakes Naval Training Station. Coached by Lieutenant Clarence L. McReavey, former Naval Academy halfback, the Bluejackets got together quite a football team. It was undefeated, tied Notre Dame and Northwestern, downed Navy, Rutgers, Illinois, Iowa, and Purdue, and was invited to oppose the Mare Island Marines in the Tournament of Roses game on New Year's Day, 1919. The thermometer read twenty-five degrees on the day of the game, one of the coldest days in Pasadena history, but Paddy Driscoll, who played quarterback, was quite warm. In running from scrimmage and in returning kicks and in passing (he completed four of eight), he gained 236 yards. George Halas, former Illinois end, also enjoyed a good day. He took a 22-yard pass from Driscoll and ran ten yards to a touchdown, and also got away for a 77-yard run after intercepting a pass. Great Lakes won, 17–0. Camp selected an All-America Service team, and from the Blue-jackets he named Driscoll, Hugh Blacklock, Michigan State, tackle, and Charles Bachman, Notre Dame, center, on the first team; Halas and Captain Emmett Keefe, Notre Dame, guard, on the second, and Dick Reichle, Illinois, end, on the third. For his All-Western Service team Walter Eckersall selected Driscoll, Blacklock, Keefe, and another guard from Notre Dame, Keith Jones.

George Halas organized his Staley team in 1920, and Driscoll signed with his good friend. But he had previously agreed to play with the Chicago Cardinals, and the league officials would not permit him to change his affiliation. He continued with the Cardinals through 1925, serving as player-coach in 1921 and 1922. In 1923 he scored 27 points (four touchdowns and three conversions) in a game against Rochester, and during the season of 1925, when the Cardinals won the championship, he kicked 11 field goals, setting a league record by getting four against Columbus, one from the 50-yard line. He had also drop-kicked successfully 50 yards against Milwaukee in 1924, to tie Fats Henry's record for distance. During his entire professional career, he kicked 49 field goals, which then constituted a record. In 1926 he finally joined Halas and the Bears, and by way of celebration scored all points in a 16–0 victory over the Cardinals. He retired as a player at the end of the 1928 season but continued in the Bear organization as a coach. After some high-school coaching, he headed the staff at Marquette from 1937 through 1940. He was none too successful with the Warriors, but produced, in Ray Apolskis, a center of All-America caliber. He then returned to the Bears, and is still part of their "brain trust." He served as head coach in 1956 and 1957.

CLIFFORD FRANKLIN BATTLES

(6:01; 195)

Cliff Battles played at West Virginia Wesleyan in 1929, 1930, and 1931. Had he performed for one of the larger institutions, he would undoubtedly have been rated as high among college players as he later was among the pros. He was a remarkable all-around man. In addition to football, he excelled at baseball, basketball, track, tennis, and swimming, and was a Phi Beta Kappa student.

In 1930, when Navy selected him for its All-Opponent team over Marchmont Schwartz, the Notre Dame All-American, he ran away from Wesleyan's old rival, Waynesburg, with dashes of 98, 96, 82, and lesser distances. He also did well against the big teams, of which a number appeared on the schedule. After leading a 68-yard march, he plunged to a touchdown against New York University, caught a 15-yard pass in the end zone against Navy, ran 90 and 70 yards to scores against Georgetown, and 74 yards to one against Duquesne. Wesleyan lacked suitable material with which to support him, and compiled a record of four victories, five defeats, and two ties. In Cliff's senior year, 1931, the record was somewhat better, six victories and a surprising tie with Navy against three losses. That year, Battles scored 15 touchdowns and was credited with runs of 86, 62, 57, and 54 yards.

Cliff joined the Boston Braves in 1932 and received All-League honorable mention. The next year, when the Braves became the Redskins, he was on the first All-League eleven. That season he experienced a particularly pleasant day against the New York Giants, gaining 215 yards in 16 attempts. He was again a member of the All-League team in 1936 when the Redskins won the Eastern Division title but lost the world championship play-off to the Green Bay Packers. Battles' valedictory year as a professional player, 1937, was probably his best. He repeated as All-League halfback and he led the league in ground gaining, with 874 yards in 216 attempts.

The Redskins had been transferred to Washington that season, and with stars such as Sammy Baugh, Turk Edwards, Wayne Millner, and others to support Battles, they ruled the football world. The game with the New York Giants for the divisional title was reminiscent of Cliff's college days. He scored two touch-downs on line smashes. He set up the first by catching a pass from Baugh and the second on a 75-yard run on a reverse play. His 76-yard run after intercepting a Giant pass placed the ball in position for another touchdown. The Redskins won 49–14. John Kieran termed the game "The Massacre of Coogan's Bluff" while the *New York Times* informed its readers that no greater back than Battles had ever appeared on the Polo Grounds. The next week the Redskins took the championship play-off from the Chicago Bears, 28–21. One of their touchdowns came after Baugh threw 42 yards to Battles on the seven-yard line, and the latter then scored on a sweeping reverse.

From 1938 to 1942, Cliff assisted Lou Little as backfield coach at Columbia. Sid Luckman and Paul Governali were two of the several outstanding backs he helped develop. He was in the United States Marines during World War II, and in 1944 coached the El Toro Marines in California, one of the strongest service teams in the West. During the two years that he coached in Brooklyn (1946 and 1947), the material was not of the type and depth to place the Dodgers in the championship class. He became a manufacturer's representative for heavy machinery and made his home in Bethesda, Maryland.

STEVE W. VAN BUREN

(6:01; 205)

"Moving Van," as facetious sportswriters were to call Van Buren, could punt and pass and was good on defense, but what made him famous, particularly after he became a professional, was his ferocious drive off his own right tackle. When he broke through he was nimble enough to sidestep the secondary, and once in the clear he was a fast, elusive runner. But it was his ability to break through that was truly remarkable when one considers that the opposition knew where he was going to strike, and even famous pros could not stop him consistently.

The big redhead was born in Tela, Honduras, but later made his home in New Orleans, where he played football for Warren Easton High School. At Louisiana State University he took an engineering course. Coach Bernie Moore started him as a blocking back, but by 1943 Steve was the Bayou Bengals' chief offensive weapon. That year, Louisiana State with an all-civilian team finished second in the Southeastern Conference behind Georgia Tech's Navy V-12 outfit. Louisiana State was invited to the Orange Bowl to play Texas A.&M., a team that had beaten it 28–13 during the regular seasons. In the bowl clash Steve was the whole show. In a 60-yard drive he passed for 23 yards, ran for 28, and scored the touchdown. A quick kick by him put the Aggies on the defensive, and he later passed 35 yards into the end zone for another score. Then, as a climax, with Texas A.&M. ahead, he broke through right tackle and ran 63 yards to the winning touchdown. The Tigers took the game 19–14. In an earlier game he had run back a punt 81 yards to score against Georgia. For the season he was second in the nation in scoring with 110 points—16 touchdowns and 14 conversions; and second in ground gained by rushing with 847 yards in 150 attempts. In total offense he gained 1,007 yards in 186 plays.

Steve played with the Philadelphia Eagles from 1944 through 1951. He was named to the All-League team in 1944, 1945, 1947, 1948, and 1949. In 1945 he led the league in scoring, with 110 points; most touchdowns, 18; and ground gained by rushing, 832 yards in 143 attempts. He continued to show the way in rushing with 1,008 yards in 217 tries in 1947; 945 in 201 in 1948; and 1,146 in 263 in 1949.

In 1947 Van led the Eagles to a divisional title, but they lost the championship play-off to the Chicago Cardinals 21–28. They captured top honors the next two seasons, defeating the Cardinals, 7–0, in a driving snowstorm in Philadelphia in 1948 and the Los Angeles Rams, 14–0, in mud and rain at Los Angeles in 1949. Big Steve seemed to thrive on bad footing. He was seldom stopped and was the hero of each game. In the 1948 play-off game, after a run of 26 yards, he powered the ball over for the only touchdown of the contest. Against the Rams in 1949 he scored no touchdowns, but gained 196 yards in 31 tries. In both 1948 and 1949, he received the Washington Touchdown Club award as the outstanding player in the National League.

A foot injury handicapped Steve in 1950 and 1951 and, after he shattered a knee in 1952, he quit playing. He worked for the Eagles as a talent scout and speechmaker until 1955, when he went into the automobile business; but he returned to the Eagles fold in 1962. Earle "Greasy" Neale, who coached the Eagles to their championships and who had played with Jim Thorpe, called Van "the best offensive halfback who ever lived."

PRO HALL OF FAME
Helms Athletic Foundation

Benjamin Agajanian, g.
Frank Albert, q.b.
Clifford Battles, b.
Samuel Baugh, q.b.
Charles Bednarik, c.
James Benton, e.
Raymond Bray, g.
Anthony Canadeo, b.
Earl "Dutch" Clark, b.
Charles Conerly, q.b.
John "Paddy" Driscoll, b.
William Dudley, b.
Albert "Turk" Edwards, t.
Thomas Fears, e.
Ray Flaherty, e.
Daniel Fortmann, g.
Otto Graham, q.b.
Harold "Red" Grange, b.
Louis Groza, t.
Melvin Hein, c.
Wilbur "Fats" Henry, t.
Arnold Herber, b.
William Hewitt, e.
Clarke Hinkle, b.
Elroy Hirsch, e.
Robert "Cal" Hubbard, t.

Donald Hutson, e.
Frank Kilroy, t.
Alphonse "Tuffy" Leemans, b.
Sidney Luckman, q.b.
Roy Lyman, t.
George McAfee, b.
John Blood McNally, b.
George Musso, g.
Bronko Nagurski, b.
Al Nesser, e.
Ernest Nevers, b.
Joseph Perry, b.
Peter Pihos, e.
Edward Sprinkle, e.
Kenneth Strong, b.
Joseph Stydahar, t.
James Thorpe, b.
Yelberton Tittle, q.b.
George Trafton, c.
Emlen Tunnell, b.
Clyde "Bulldog" Turner, c.
Norman Van Brocklin, q.b.
Steve Van Buren, b.
E. Doak Walker, b.
Robert Waterfield, q.b.
Alex Wojciechowicz, c.

MOST VOTES FOR ALL-NATIONAL LEAGUE TEAM

1933 William Hewitt (50), Bears
1934 Bronko Nagurski (48), Bears
1935 Melvin Hein (43) New York

1936 Cliff Battles (43), Washington
Dutch Clark (43), Detroit
Don Hutson (43), Green Bay

1937 Joe Stydahar (43) Bears

JOE E. CARR TROPHY

Most Valuable Player—National League

1938 Melvin Hein, New York	**1943** Sidney Luckman, Bears
1939 Parker Hall, Cleveland	**1944** Frank Sinkwich, Detroit
1940 Ace Parker, Brooklyn	**1945** Bob Waterfield, Los Angeles
1941 Don Hutson, Green Bay	**1946** William Dudley, Pittsburgh
1942 Don Hutson, Green Bay	**1947** discontinued

MOST VALUABLE PLAYER AWARD

All-America Football Conference

1946 Glenn Dobbs, Brooklyn	**1948** Otto Graham, Cleveland
1947 Otto Graham, Cleveland	Frank Albert, San Francisco

1949 discontinued

WASHINGTON TOUCHDOWN CLUB AWARD

Professional Player of the Year

1943 Sammy Baugh, Washington	**1952** Lynn Chandois, Pittsburgh
1944 Leroy Zimmerman, Philadelphia	**1953** Louis Groza, Cleveland
1945 Bob Waterfield, Los Angeles	**1954** Norm Van Brocklin, Los Angeles
1946 William Dudley, Pittsburgh	**1955** Gene Brito, Washintgon
1947 Sammy Baugh, Washington	**1956** Frank Gifford, New York
1948 Steve Van Buren, Philadelphia	**1957** John Unitas, Baltimore
Otto Graham, Cleveland	**1958** John Unitas, Baltimore
1949 Steve Van Buren, Philadelphia	Jimmy Brown, Cleveland
Otto Graham, Cleveland	**1959** Charles Conerly, New York
1950 Bob Waterfield, Los Angeles	**1960** Norm Van Brocklin, Philadelphia
1951 Otto Graham, Cleveland	**1961** Paul Hornung, Green Bay

◆ ◆ ◆

UNITED PRESS INTERNATIONAL

Player of the Year—National League

1953 Otto Graham, *Cleveland*

1954 Joe Perry, *San Francisco*

1955 Otto Graham, *Cleveland*

1956 Frank Gifford, *New York*

1957 Yelberton Tittle, San Francisco

1958 Jimmy Brown, *Cleveland*

1959 John Unitas, *Baltimore*

1960 Norm Van Brocklin, *Philadelphia*

1961 Paul Hornung, *Green Bay*

Player of the Year—American League

1960 Abner Haynes, *Dallas*

1961 George Blanda, *Houston*

PERSONNEL INDEX

796.332
W546f   16651

Weyand, Alexander
    Football immortals.